Practical

Psychotherapy

Practical Psychotherapy

By

Myron F. Weiner, M.D.

Vice-Chairman, Department of Psychiatry,
The University of Texas Health Science Center,
Dallas, Texas

BRUNNER/MAZEL, *Publishers* • New York

Library of Congress Cataloging-in-Publication Data

Weiner, Myron F., 1934–
  Practical psychotherapy.

  Bibliography: p. 303.
  Includes index.
  1. Psychotherapy.   I. Title.   [DNLM: 1. Psycho-
therapy. WM 420 W4234p]
  RC480.W376   1986   616.89′14   85-24298
  ISBN 0-87630-408-0

Copyright © 1986 by Myron F. Weiner

Published by
BRUNNER/MAZEL, INC.
19 Union Square
New York, New York 10003

MANUFACTURED IN THE UNITED STATES OF AMERICA

To Jack,
with admiration
from your son

Contents

Foreword

In this new book Dr. Myron Weiner consolidates his exhaustive knowledge about psychotherapy – in all its forms – into a marvelously cohesive exposition. Firmly grounded in psychodynamic theory the author moves easily among the cognitive, emotional and behavioral methods of psychotherapy and presents a comprehensive survey of psychological development through all of the life stages. We are fortunate that he has culled from the overwhelming number of different systems and techniques of psychotherapy that which has proved to be most effective. For beginning therapists there is the opportunity to learn basic theory and technique and for experienced clinicians there is the opportunity to compare their approach to Dr. Weiner's high standard of practice.

At the beginning of this exceptional book the author tells us that his thinking has been influenced by two psychiatrists, Adolph Meyer and Jules Masserman. For the occasional reader who may not be familiar with one or both of these men I should like to briefly mention something about each.

Adolph Meyer (1866–1950) was a Swiss psychiatrist who emigrated to the United States to eventually become director of the famous Phipps Clinic at Johns Hopkins Medical School. His concept of psychobiology holds that in order to understand the whole person, the life history of the individual must be studied carefully and in great depth. As a result, the path toward healthier behavior becomes clear, and a wholesome integration of the personality eventually occurs. Meyer believed that people were capable of restoring themselves to high levels of functioning when guided by a trained therapist who enlisted the patient's cooperation in the therapeutic process. The therapist must have a combination of attributes, among which are those of investigator, biographer, artist, educator, and experienced guide. Meyer was to become a commanding figure in American psychiatry.

Jules Masserman (b. 1905) studied psychobiology under Adolph Meyer and is Professor of Psychiatry at Northwestern University Medical School. His concept of the biodynamic approach holds that all behavior originates from the combination of genetic potentialities, developmental phases, and individual environmental experiences. Therapy aims to relieve each patient's physical, social, and psychological distress. He proposes a flexible approach to psychotherapy that advocates using a variety of methods to alleviate biopsychosocial anxiety, provided that the methods used are carried out judiciously, competently, and with the utmost regard for the patient's welfare.

Both Meyer and Masserman convey a sense of the person's capacity for continued growth throughout the life cycle, both are imbued with an optimistic world view, and both show a profound respect for individual worth. I am pleased to write that Dr. Weiner carries on the tradition of those two outstanding psychiatrists.

Psychotherapy is the art and science of making troubled people feel better. It is a method of healing that goes back to antiquity and it is the only health science to use words and speech as its instruments. It depends also on the unique relationship between the therapist and the patient, built upon mutual trust and the empathic capacity of the doctor to place himself or herself in the patient's place.

Psychotherapy is very much criticized, however. Some attack it for what they believe to be its metaphysical, semi-illogical constructs, others for the absence of rigorously defined criteria for cure. Dr. Weiner disarms both sets of critics. Those who are suspect of the metaphysical will be reassured by the use of the word practical in the title. Indeed, Dr. Weiner's approach to psychotherapy is pragmatic, full of common sense (Meyer's term) and thoroughly understandable. Those critics who demand to know who is cured and how or why cure occurs will also be comforted as they read the many case reports scattered throughout this book which deal with just these issues. With the integrity of the true scientist the author does not hold back cases in which therapy was not successful, and he suggests why cure was not accomplished.

Dr. Weiner is a knowledgeable practitioner in the art and science of psychotherapy, and this book allows us to share his long experience in what has been called the loneliest profession. It is a profession that requires great skill and great sacrifice. Dr. Weiner has demonstrated both of these capacities not only in his work with patients, but also in the arduous task of writing this book. He has rendered a great service to all of us who practice psychotherapy.

Benjamin J. Sadock, M.D.
Professor of Psychiatry
New York University School
of Medicine

Acknowledgments

It has taken more than 20 years to write this book. It evolved bit by bit from interest in specific issues such as therapist disclosure and therapeutic impasses. The basic framework was established while teaching courses in group psychotherapy, and the material crystallized during three years of teaching an individual therapy course.

The material presented is a distillate of experiences with patients, supervisees, colleagues, and supervisors, as well as my own analysis with Dr. Fred Davis. I have incorporated some of the wisdom of Bill Moore, Bob Beavers, David Fuller, Larry Martin, Claude Nichols, George Nicolaou, Bob Webb, Bob Long, Merlan DeBolt, and Bernard Goldstein. Allan Shirks collaborated with me as student and colleague. Jaye Crowder helped expand my thinking about unconscious learning. My ideas on transference management were widened by Leston Havens and Roy Aruffo.

I have enjoyed the capable assistance of Lisa Jackson, with whose help I completed this manuscript while in New York for a year learning about aging. I appreciate the loving tolerance of my boss, Ken Altshuler, and the patient listening of my wife Jeanette as we proofread aloud the last draft.

Thank you, everyone.

New York City
January, 1985   *Myron F. Weiner, M.D.*

Preface

This book is a guide for therapists who, while recognizing the unconscious dynamics of their patients' emotional lives, need for varied reasons to produce symptomatic relief quickly. The author, who is not an advocate of short-term therapy, finds that treatment can be occasionally completed in one interview, but there are many instances in which the quickest treatment requires years. The author believes that treatment should be as short or long as it needs to be, although the actual length of treatment may be governed by such factors as insurance coverage or the length of a college semester.

The clinical situations described in this book are largely drawn from the author's own work with patients, many of whom were unsuitable for a therapeutic technique that uncovered and dealt with unconscious conflict through the development and resolution of a transference neurosis.

The author, while not a psychoanalyst, was trained in the psychoanalytic tradition and holds to the idea of a dynamic unconscious. In addition, the author's experiences treating groups, couples, and persons with psychotic illnesses and other severe ego defects have acquainted him with the potency of many nonanalytic techniques.

The techniques described in this book are an extension of the psychobiological approach of Adolf Meyer (Muncie, 1959) and direct descendants of Jules Masserman's biodynamic approach (Masserman, 1980; Weiner, 1985); they take into account the biological and social contributions to emotional disorders and deal with them directly when indicated.

This book is not a critique of psychoanalytically oriented therapies. Such therapies can be effective when judiciously applied. The fundamental difficulties with approaches that attempt to resolve unconscious conflict have been their overuse and the fact that therapists tend to blame their treatment failures on patients' lack of basic trust, motivation, cooperation, or ego strength. Placed in the appropriate context, analytic techniques are useful, but they have a narrow range of indications and many contraindications.

The author agrees with the current trend of applying a specific treatment for a specific symptom diagnosis, but he has found it more useful in practice to vary treatment techniques in relation to ego strength, ego structure, type of crisis, and patients' motivation for treatment or aptitude for self-understanding. In most cases, these factors and not the syndrome diagnosis determine how patients can be dealt with psychologically. In clinical practice, outpatients often fall into more than one diagnostic category. The same person who is diagnosed as phobic may also fit the descriptive criteria for dysthymic disorder and histrionic personality.

For didactic purposes, the author compares and contrasts three levels of psychotherapy: repressive, ego-supportive, and evocative, but the reader is urged to bear in mind that the distinction between levels of therapy is not sharp, and that the differences between the three types of therapy presented are more quantitative than qualitative. The main differences are in emphasis on certain interventions or in dealing selectively with the intrapsychic structures of ego, id, and superego.

While individual chapters are devoted to repressive and ego-supportive therapies, the author has elected not to discuss evocative therapies in depth. Too little has been written on the conduct of repressive and ego-supportive therapies, and there is so much material on evocative therapy, including the works of Greenson (1967), Langs (1973), and Wallace (1983), that an additional chapter would only repeat what has already been said well.

The author aims to present a balanced approach in which intrapsychic, biological, and social factors are adequately considered and dealt with, and in which no single therapeutic approach is valued more highly than any other or held forth as truly curative, while other approaches are held to be merely palliative. There is no ultimate cure for the problems of living, and all forms of therapy have their limitations. Our aim as therapists is to find the best means to deal with our patients at the point in their life when they seek help. At another point, an entirely different approach may be indicated. It is the author's hope to give psychotherapists the necessary flexibility to respond to those different needs.

CHAPTER 1

Introduction

For many years, psychotherapy has been practiced as a cheapened form of psychoanalysis: an attempt to stimulate insight into unconscious dynamics and resolve unconscious conflicts through making transference interpretations (Langs, 1973), frequently with patients who cannot afford, do not wish, or are otherwise unsuitable for psychoanalysis. Many therapists pursue the goals of psychoanalysis without the technical means or appropriate patient material, or with patients who lack motivation for that kind of treatment.

There are now many effective techniques for treating psychologically based symptoms, that do not require the development of insight into unconscious mental forces (Karasu, 1977). Performance anxiety, phobias, and compulsive behaviors can be altered by behavioral means; impotence and premature ejaculation through education and alteration of sexual practices. In spite of those discoveries, it is often held that although insight may not be necessary to cure certain symptoms, it is the *best* way, and that without developing insight into the origin of symptoms, susceptibility to their redevelopment remains unchanged.

Indeed, there is more to behavior than behavior, but it must be addressed directly at times, with or without reference to underlying causes.

Practical psychotherapy differs from diluted psychoanalysis. It incorporates nonanalytic interventions in a balanced fashion, making no assertion that any one intervention is intrinsically more worthwhile or more curative than any other.

A practical approach acknowledges that thoughts, feelings, and behavior are influenced by unconscious motivation and conflict, but does not hold that resolving conflicts through developing insight is usually or even frequently the best means of dealing with symptoms stemming from those motivations or conflicts. The psychoanalytic concepts of psychosexual development, fixation, and regression are also important in treating patients, but regression need not always be reversed or fixations overcome, and fixations and regression are overcome more often by other measures than by interpretation.

Being practical demands that clinicians make judgments about their patients that facilitate focused therapeutic activity. Therapists direct the therapy in conjunction with their patients, sometimes following the patients' lead, but therapists often take the lead in focusing patients' attention on their thoughts, feelings, behavior, or their real external world. While recognizing that every person partially creates his own reality through his behavior or perceptions, practical therapists take into account the need to adapt to certain life situations that are temporarily or permanently unchangeable.

Although their focus is on a designated patient, therapists need not confine themselves to dealing with the designated patient. They may involve the patient's larger social network when the designated patient cannot alter his environment or himself so as to permit growth or successful adaptation. Therapists need an attitude of openness toward patients and an awareness that people are in a constant state of flux. They also need to recognize that the same types of problems may need to be treated in different ways in different contexts. A practical approach acknowledges that striving toward health is present in many people, but relies more heavily on the technical expertise of therapists than therapist-offered conditions such as empathy. positive regard, or genuineness as the principal means of treatment.

Above all, a practical approach recognizes the paradox inherent in the need to recognize people as individuals and the concomitant need to define syndromes that respond to specific treatments. While agreeing with the need for syndrome diagnosis, therapists also focus on the dynamic elements that contribute to the formation of those symptom complexes. Thus, therapists understand that a particular cluster of symptoms can develop new facets and ramifications and change into another symptom cluster under their very eyes. Therapists therefore need not always make a definitive diagnosis to do effective therapy. Therapists do need a working diagnosis that fits the presenting signs and symptoms and leads to a productive therapeutic interaction.

Being practical means that the therapist acknowledges the biological, social, and psychological variables that affect the mind; the approach of the practical therapist incorporates medications, milieu therapies, and work with patients' intrapsychic life and interpersonal network, as the following case illustrates.

Mrs. A. R. was first seen in a general hospital following a suicide attempt with antidepressant medication. She was a widow who had remarried less than a year previously. Her symptoms began with the sudden onset of insomnia six weeks earlier. Her appetite waned and she lost 10 to 12 pounds over a period of weeks. Her symptoms were diagnosed by her internist as depression, and he prescribed the antidepressant medication with which she overdosed.

When first seen by the therapist, she was severely depressed and self-recriminating, but appeared to be developing insight into her difficulties. She attributed her upset to events that followed her second marriage. She had moved to a larger city and had left the social circle and the work that had sustained her over the many years since her first husband's death. She had moved into a house that she had not selected and did not like, and found that she and her new husband did not communicate as openly as she had communicated with her first husband. She also felt unable to live up to the standards set by her husband's deceased wife, who was described by him and others as having been a saintly woman.

Because she had many strengths and had no previous history of emotional difficulties aside from a period of mild depression after the death of her first husband, she was treated as an outpatient with a tricyclic antidepressant and hypnotic drugs and was seen in twice-a-week psychotherapy.

She discussed areas of conflict between herself and her husband, and some of the other stresses related to her new marriage. Her mood improved, and after six weeks, she reduced her visits to once a week. Six months after beginning treatment, her mood became less stable, and attempts at working toward further insight seemed to dangerously exacerbate her self-criticism. After nearly a year of therapy, and in anticipation of a strong negative response to the impending anniversary of her suicide attempt, she was changed from her tricyclic antidepressant medication to a monoamine-oxidase-inhibiting drug. Within two weeks, her symptoms abated and her mood stabilized. She was seen infrequently until she discontinued her visits after a total of 16 months of treatment.

Mrs. A. R. was next seen nearly a year and a half after her last visit. She had been panicky, depressed, had been having difficulty sleeping, and had felt suicidal for a week. After two weeks of psychotherapy and antidepressant medication, she continued to be suicidal. She was hospitalized so that she could be observed closely, could participate in milieu therapy, and could be safely given larger doses of antidepressant medication. She failed to improve after five weeks of inpatient care, during which her antidepressant had been pushed to maximum dosage and she had been encouraged to deal with her feelings about herself, her children, and her marital situation. She was transferred to another hospital for three weeks and received a series of six electroconvulsive treatments. Her symptoms cleared completely for two weeks, after which she reported a return of uneasy feelings. At that time, instead of restarting her electroconvulsive treatment or her antidepressant medication, she was encouraged to ventilate the negative feelings toward her husband that had been accumulating during her two weeks at home. She did so, and experienced considerable relief. In the weeks that followed, she and her husband discussed seriously their likes and dislikes concerning each other. She especially confronted him with his tendency to hold his anger in. She felt the need for continued psychotherapy for only a short time afterward and discontinued her second period of treatment after about five months.

Mrs. A. R.'s treatment illustrates the flexible use of supportive psychotherapy and other types of treatment measures, with the therapist making as much use of psychotherapy as the patient's ego could allow. When her ego was too overwhelmed to accept suggestions or to use self-observation and self-exploration constructively, other measures were employed. In the process, she dealt with her guilt over her anger toward her new husband, grieved for her deceased husband and her former life, and dealt vigorously with those aspects of her new spouse and new life that she found frustrating and nonsupportive.

BASIC TREATMENTS

The therapist's work with Mrs. A. R. illustrates (1) modifying the environment to fit patients' needs and limitations (in this case, hospitalization); (2) helping patients face their present real-life situation (encouraging Mrs. A. R. to deal with the reality of her new marital relationship); and (3) altering patients' mode of adaptation or their ability to alter their new environment (reducing her guilt over her anger toward her husband so that she could deal with him more effectively).

Stated in a different way, patients' environments can be shaped to accommodate a psychological limitation; patients can use skills that enable them to function in spite of that limitation, or they can be cured of it. Those three treatment types are the basis of all psychotherapies.

Let us illustrate these three basic types of treatment in more detail.

Environmental Modification

Our consideration of modifying patients' environment to meet their needs begins with two illustrations; temporarily siding with neurotic needs, and manipulating the environment to better meet maturational needs. Both examples demonstrate the principle of beginning therapy by dealing with patients at their present level of function.

> At the beginning of her therapy, Mrs. A. J. was encouraged to give in to her fear of driving, to avoid unnecessarily chauffering her children, and to avoid trips to unfamiliar parts of town. Temporary siding with the patient's neurotic compromise of her ego function helped diminish her daily pressures enough that her therapy could focus on some of the factors contributing to her symptomatology; her angry dependence on her husband, her wish for a life of her own, and her fear of losing control of herself. As her anxiety diminished, the therapist encouraged her to drive distances that had formerly been frightening. Each new level of function she reached was, of course, followed by a transient wave of anxiety. The therapist's permission to give in to her phobic symptoms at the beginning of treatment added healthy regression to her limited repertoire of coping mechanisms, and thereby facilitated her dealing with subsequent upswings of anxiety.

Acceding to neurotic needs to unburden a conflict-compromised ego frequently has the salutary side effect of modifying the relationship of patients' superego to their ego through identification with the therapist's nonjudgmental permissiveness.

The environment can also be modified to meet developmental needs. For example, parents of overly aggressive children often do not set adequate limits because they fear stimulating more aggression, and because of guilt stimulated by their own aggression. Parents of diabetic children often feel guilty because their child has diabetes, and hesitate to frustrate a child whom they feel life has already dealt a cruel blow (Weiner, 1976a). As parents begin to set appropriate limits on children's behavior, they find to their amazement that children are more manageable. In supplying external limits for children's aggression, they shore up the functioning of the children's immature egos, which cannot yet contain their aggression. Failing to augment children's ego function forces their immature ego to cope through undirected aggression, which is often their primary nonregressive coping mechanism.

The foregoing examples deal with modifiable inadequacies in ego function, but therapists employ the same basic principle in dealing with irreversibly impaired ego function. They encourage function at the level at which patients can cope best; not at the level at which impaired persons feel they *ought* to cope or unrealistically aspire to cope. However, the principle is applied differently in the two situations. Therapists do not push permanently damaged persons toward more complex levels of integration unless their impairment stems partly from their emotional reaction to their deficit. The following example illustrates modifying reality to fit the needs of a permanently impaired person.

The parents of Mr. L., a 22-year-old man, sought advice in dealing with him. He had been unable to cope with the demands of college life, and during his last semester had pretended to attend classes, but actually spent his time in his room playing his guitar. His parents said that he had become strongly preoccupied with his appearance, fancied himself disfigured by acne, and used that excuse to avoid personal relationships.

When interviewed, Mr. L. said he had dropped out of college because it was irrelevant to his life's work of composing music. He was going to become a famous popular music writer, although he could neither read nor write musical notations. He talked at length about the severe disfigurement caused by his acne, and the various medications and dietary remedies he had employed. Each had helped, but none had completely cured him. He said that when cured, he would begin to socialize again. He was euphoric. He saw no difficulties in his life. He felt his parents were obliged to support him until he became self-sufficient through his music.

It seemed to the therapist that Mr. L. had been unable to cope with the social and intellectual demands of college life, and had retreated defensively into daydreaming about the recognition that would come when his genius was finally appreciated. His concern about his skin was of delusional proportions, and the remedies he proposed reflected gross distortions of his thought processes. On the other hand, he suffered little discomfort when allowed to be isolated, and had become firmly entrenched in fantasy over the preceding four years.

After a number of sessions with Mr. L. over a period of months, the therapist told his parents there was little hope that Mr. L. would begin to face reality without an extended period of hospitalization, and that the prognosis for improvement was dim because of the young man's acceptance of his retreat from reality. The parents considered the situation carefully, evaluating their own financial and emotional assets. Because of the expense of prolonged hospitalization, the questionable prognosis, the fact that their son was emotionally comfortable, and the absence of danger to himself or others, they structured reality to accommodate his needs. They gave him a small allowance that enabled him to rent a garage apartment, to buy food and clothing, and to live on his own.

He was lost to follow-up, but several years later he was featured in a newspaper article that described him as a budding composer, although none of his work had ever been sold or performed publicly. No change had occurred in the relationship of his superego to his ego as the result of his visits with the therapist. None was necessary. His delusions about his skin and the expectation of future fame allayed any disappointment with himself for failing to enter the mainstream of adult life.

Other irreversible situations can be dealt with similarly. Irreversibly phobic people can be helped to avoid anxiety-stimulating situations. Often, they lack the ability to manage complex social situations, or their family relationships would be endangered if they became more mobile. In these cases, it may be wise to encourage them to be less hard on themselves; to relax and enjoy television instead of pushing themselves into uncomfortable situations. Here, as before, therapists help defend patients' egos against their superegos and they are encouraged to use avoidance, regression, and passivity to shield against the anxiety that would be generated by struggling against their neurotic fears.

Facing Reality

Forcing a person to accept reality is well exemplified by milieu treatment of a conversion disorder. After having been told that he has no serious physical disorder, a man who feels unable to move one leg may be told that his strength will return only if he uses the leg, and that he therefore will be obliged to walk from his bed to a dining area if he wishes to eat. Positive (not punitive) encouragement to function in the face of the felt disability has a number of positive effects. It assures patients that they are physically intact, and that they can overcome their difficulty through effort. It undercuts the use of regression, passivity, and physical complaints. The "paralyzed" person is encouraged to acknowledge that he can use his leg. Having accomplished that, he may have little motivation to deal with the emotional significance of the symptom.

Persons who develop conversion disorders have found a convenient loophole in their superego's rules. Avoiding personal responsibility is acceptable if based on physical disability (Sullivan, 1956). That, of course, is a perfectly reasonable exception. It is the therapist's job to demonstrate convincingly that no physical disability exists, and words alone are frequently insufficient.

Forcing an acceptance of reality often involves more than the designated patient. One must often address patients' environment before there can be any hope of successfully addressing their symptoms, as illustrated below.

> The parents of an unmarried 25-year-old woman sought to help their daughter face the demands of everyday life, including the care of her 5-year-old son. Her child, born out of wedlock, had been raised by his grandparents, who thoroughly enjoyed his company. In discussing the situation with the distressed couple, it became evident that they provided little incentive for their daughter to face reality. The mother, for example, reported anxiously that her daughter took drugs, but the daughter denied drug-taking when confronted. The daughter regularly medicated herself with a prescription analgesic her mother gave her from her own supply because of the daughter's threat that "something awful" would happen if she were refused the drug. In short, the parents actively colluded with their daughter. For the daughter's treatment to be successful, the parents needed to acknowledge and then discontinue their helping her avoid anxiety and responsibility.
>
> That recommendation was made to the couple, who did not return for further advice.

Part of the initial work toward facing the real issues in a patient's life may include medication to augment ego function. Id drives can be dampened by antipsychotic drugs when they threaten or impair reality testing. Superego demands can be diminished in some cases by antidepressant drugs. Crippling anxiety resulting from the ego's reaction to unconscious conflict can be reduced by minor tranquilizers. Judicious use of medications can free enough ego energy from warding off threatening stimuli from within to enable adequate coping with external reality.

Where biological vulnerability plays a large role in the development of patients' symptoms, as in schizophrenia (Kety, 1978) and in bipolar affective disorders (Klerman, 1978), facing reality may entail accepting long-term use of medication to cushion against emotions that can precipitate a severe symptomatic relapse.

Cure

Curing a symptomatic process demands not only that the presenting symptoms be alleviated, but that the primary pathologic processes be altered or arrested. To speak of a permanent cure, one must show that the tendency toward mobilizing the pathological mechanisms is eliminated or greatly reduced.

The treatment of mild obsessional symptoms in a healthy personality will serve as an example. Emotional decompensations begin with a relative weakening of the ego in relation to the id, the superego, or external reality. In a mild obsessive disorder, weakening of the ego in relation to the id allows certain unwanted thoughts to intrude into consciousness. Ego weakening may result from a single severe trauma, such as the threatened loss of a loved person or a cherished goal. More often, the psychological trauma aggravates a preexisting imbalance resulting from a relative weakness of the ego in relation to the id or superego. That weakening may be due to an intensification of id drives or a drain of the energy available to the ego for adaptation and for its own defense (Brenner, 1973).

In this situation, the ego can be strengthened so that it is better able to contain (by repression) the contents of the id. The means used to strengthen the ego depends on the cause of the ego's energy depletion. A real or symbolic loss can be dealt with by allowing grief to occur, by surfacing the positive and negative feelings toward the person who is gone or by encouraging the person to grieve for the goal that is unattainable, and by encouraging the individual to form new attachments and new goals.

To repair the predisposition to a symptom such as unwanted intrusive thoughts, therapists help patients to bolster or reorganize their means of psychological defense and adaptation. Patients can be taught directly or through self-reflection to become aware of, and to accept, threatening feelings instead of defending themselves by repression and isolation (stripping the affect from a thought). As feelings are exposed and become less threatening, patients' use of repression and isolation diminishes. As patients become able to substitute mature self-acceptance for repression and isolation, they become less vulnerable to the formation of obsessive symptomatology.

Cure occurs at an interpersonal level as well as an intrapsychic level. At an interpersonal level, cure is achieved when indirect communication (I'm trying to cleanse myself of unwanted thoughts) is replaced by open expression of feelings such as anger (Haley, 1971). Patients can more effectively voice legitimate complaints or make demands to which others can respond, and symptoms are no longer needed as a means to avoid thoughts, feelings, or responsibilities.

AIMING THE INTERVENTION

Therapeutic interventions can be directed toward the ego, the superego, or the id, singly or in combination. All psychotherapeutic interventions involve the ego, which is the part of the psychic apparatus that receives information from the outside world and through which the id and superego act on the outside world. Interpersonal or environmental factors may also have to be addressed simultaneously because of their reinforcement of symptomatic behavior.

Id-Directed Intervention

The id is the part of the self that is unacceptable to the ego. It contains the portions and derivatives of the sexual and aggressive drives that are repressed by the ego (Freud, 1932/1964). While the strength of each person's sexual and aggressive drives is biologically determined, the ego can enhance, block, or alter their aim, object, or means of expression. The ego blocks drives by repression or suppression, which use psychological energy and decrease the energy available for other tasks or for pleasurable activities. When ego energy is in short supply, the ego conserves energy by allowing partial discharge of id impulses in ways that the superego finds acceptable, and that are also acceptable in reality. Both real and symbolic discharge serve to reduce pressure on the ego. For example, sexual activity involving real physical intimacy is allowed by the ego under certain circumstances. Under other circumstances, it allows only a smile or a wink.

The aim or object of an id impulse or drive can be changed as a means to allow discharge. A change in aim is exemplified by the voyeur's conversion of the impulse to sexually penetrate to the urge to visually penetrate. A change of object is illustrated by the displacement of repressed anger from a feared parent onto a parent surrogate, such as an employer. Aggression may be expressed by inappropriate passivity and may manifest as passive obstructionism. The pressure of repressed drives on the ego can be relieved by altering the drives, as well as by real or symbolic discharge. Reducing the intensity of the drives themselves can be accomplished only by physical or chemical means, and may be necessary when the ego is overwhelmed by drives that result in inappropriate aggressive or sexual behavior, or against which it can only defend through use of psychotic mechanisms.

Superego-Directed Intervention

The superego is the agency of the mind that makes id impulses seem forbidden to the ego (Greenson, 1967), and punishes the ego through guilt. Superego changes can be brought about through insight, new learning, imitation, or identification. Insight and new learning go together. As patients become aware of their self-defeating standards, they become amenable to learning alternative attitudes that will serve them better. They reinforce that learning through experimenting with their tentative new values. Imitation and identification assume greater prominence in group therapy than individual therapy, although the overall mechanisms of change are the same in both types of psychotherapy (Weiner, 1982a). In both kinds of treatment, patients project aspects of their superego onto the therapist and/or the group. Individual therapy patients come to understand their projections and reassess their values in the light of their adaptiveness in their current life situation. The acceptance by peers in group therapy prevents the superego from interfering with learning by its assertion that "nobody would like you if he knew the real you" (Yalom, 1975).

A superego that allows the ego to discharge dangerous id impulses can be augmented through institutionalization in which real limits or punishments regulate behavior until the patient's ego becomes able to. This process is frequently the treatment of choice for delinquent adolescents whose peer group and parents reinforce pathological behavior. In residential treatment, peer pressure ("I *am* my brother's keeper") added to close supervision serves as a nidus for superego formation.

Persons whose superego cannot help their ego control destructive sexual or aggressive behavior may require permanent superego augmentation in the form of institutional walls. Even under those circumstances, severely disturbed individuals can be so unpleasant that not even a psychiatric facility will tolerate their behavior, as seen in the following case.

A 20-year-old diabetic woman was unable to obtain readmission to a state psychiatric facility, although she self-injected potentially lethal overdoses of insulin at least once a month. She had created the same conditions in her adult life that had existed in her abused, neglected childhood. Because she abused the hospital staff during numerous admissions, she was rejected and abandoned as an adult. The hospital staff eventually took the stand that she was not mentally ill; merely a person with a trouble-making personality disorder who disrupted hospital routines and upset interstaff relationships. By self-destructive use of her insulin, she required medical invasions as traumatic as the sexual abuse she had experienced as a child. She died of suffocation in a general hospital when an intravenous tube was accidentally pushed through a major vein in her neck and the intravenous infusion flooded her chest cavity.

Ego-Directed Interventions

The ego can be modified by chemical or psychological means. The ego can be modified chemically by minor tranquilizers that reduce crippling levels of anxiety to levels that do not greatly impair coping with reality. For patients whose chief complaint is anxiety, such medications often supply enough relief that there is no felt need or therapeutic indication for further intervention.

Persons who seek help from mental health professionals usually suffer from chronic anxiety that has not responded well to ordinary suppressive measures or to the passage of time. Mild to moderate levels of anxiety motivate involvement in psychotherapy. Severe anxiety hampers self-observation and focuses the ego's attention on directly relieving its own suffering instead of the dynamic interplay of forces that produce or contribute to the ego's discomfort. Use of tranquilizers may facilitate psychotherapy by reducing anxiety enough so that the ego can engage in self-observation and observation of its interpersonal field.

SUMMARY

Almost every type of psychological treatment involves helping patients to modify their environment to better fit their needs and limitations, helping patients face their present life situations, and altering the way patients think, feel, and behave. Helping patients change within themselves is also accomplished by id-directed interventions, superego-directed interventions, and ego-directed interventions. Ego-directed interventions will constitute the bulk of the material presented under the headings of repressive, ego-supportive, and evocative therapies.

Choosing a therapeutic technique and employing various therapeutic interventions in the context of that technique requires the therapist to understand coping and defense mechanisms and psychopathology. Chapters 2 and 3 will deal with those subjects from slightly different but complementary points of view. It must be emphasized that all human behavior requires examination of its developmental, psychological, and social context before one labels it or treats it as pathological or maladaptive.

CHAPTER 2

Maturation, Coping, and Defense Mechanisms

Therapists need to understand patients' means of coping with the world and dealing with their own thoughts and feelings. In addition, it is important that they have sufficient awareness of psychosexual development to understand the ontogeny of patients' behavior and enough awareness of the specific life tasks faced by their patients to place their therapeutic endeavors in context.

I will briefly review the process of psychosexual maturation from birth through adolescence, will then discuss the tasks of the different stages of adult life, and will conclude with a discussion of coping and defense mechanisms. This information will help therapists to understand their patients' behavior within the therapeutic hour and in their life setting. In addition, it will help determine the focus, type, and duration of therapy.

MATURATION

The problems brought to psychotherapists are frequently failures of maturation. Therapy in these patients may consist of attempts to restimulate the healthy maturational process of working through or abandoning wishes, conflicts, and identifications responsible for fixation at or regression to immature levels of psychological function.

The development schemas that will be employed are those of Piaget (1954), Freud (1905/1960, 1923/1961, 1932/1964, 1940/1964), Erikson, (1959, 1963), and Levinson (1978), which are summarized in Table 1.

The first important postnatal step in psychological development is the bonding of children to their mothers. Bonding seems to be an innate process that requires little reinforcement. During the first stage of life, infants come to trust that their needs will be satisfied by the outside world and begin to distinguish what is inside from what is outside them.

The distinction between inside-me and outside-me marks the beginning of ego boundaries and reality testing; the ability to determine what is going on in one's self and one's environment and to know the difference between the two (see Figure 1).

It is held by many therapists that without the provision of a holding environment by the therapist (Winnicott, 1965) which is comparable to an adequate mother's uncritical acceptance of her child's needs (without always satisfying them), patients cannot form enough basic trust of the therapist to do psychological work.

Freud (1904/1953) spoke of the first year of life as the *oral stage* of development, based on his assumption that a person's *psychic energy* or *libido* is first concentrated in the vicinity of the mouth, the organ with which infants explore their environment before their eyes and ears begin to give reliable, understandable information. Excessive frustration or overindulgence at any stage of development can cause a fixation of the individual's emotional development at that point, or a tendency for the person to regress to that emotional level when he or she is faced with frustration at a higher level of function.

The concepts of *regression* and *fixation* help to explain much of patients' life-styles and interactions during the therapeutic hour, and are most readily understood as they occur in early childhood (Brenner, 1973). Babies who are beginning to walk become frustrated by their inability to stand independently, plop to the floor dejectedly, and start to cry, but then pop their thumb in their mouth and suck furiously until their tension level is reduced enough to make another try at walking. Such a child has temporarily regressed to an earlier level of satisfaction (sucking) before attempting to master a more complicated type of motor satisfaction (walking). Another baby, who readily masters walking, walks with thumb in mouth, blanket dragging behind, and rubbing it against one cheek. This child has maintained a fixation from an earlier stage. A higher level of adaptation has been mastered, but the child is not willing to give up earlier modes of satisfaction. However, even this type of fixation has adaptive value because the blanket serves as a *transitional object*, a bridge between bonding to mother and bonding to other things, then other people.

In the therapeutic hour, a patient who begins to muster her strength and face previously avoided situations temporarily regresses psycho-

TABLE 1
Comparative Schemes of Development
Childhood and Adolescence

Age	INTELLECTUAL DEVELOPMENT — Piaget	PSYCHOSEXUAL DEVELOPMENT — Freud	PSYCHOSOCIAL ERA — Erikson	OUTCOME
1	Sensory Motor	Oral	Basic Trust vs. Basic Mistrust	Self-Other Distinction / Recognize Stranger
2	Sensory Motor	Anal	Autonomy vs. Shame, Doubt	Locomotion, Speech
3		Phallic		Gender Identity
4	Preoperational			
5	Preoperational	Oedipal	Initiative vs. Guilt	Peer Play
6	Preoperational			
7	Preoperational			
8				
9	Concrete Operations	Latency		Formal Learning
10	Concrete Operations		Industry vs. Inferiority	
11	Concrete Operations			
12		Preadolescence		
13		Preadolescence		Intimacy with Peers
14				
15	Formal Operations			Adult Sexual Identity
16	Formal Operations	Adolescence	Identity vs. Role Confusion	Part-time Work
17				
18				
19				
20				Higher Education/Work

Comparative Schemes of Development
Adulthood

Age	PSYCHOSOCIAL ERA (Erikson)	TASK (Levinson)	OUTCOME
18		Pulling Up Roots	Leave Family of Origin
20			
24		Provisional Adulthood	Establish Intimacy, Job Identity
28	Intimacy vs. Isolation	Early Adult Transition	Commit to Job, Family
32		Early Adult Transition	
36		Early Adulthood	Productive Work and Family Relations; Child Rearing
40			
44		Middle Adult Transition	Evaluate Accomplishments Against Aspirations / Women Re-Establish in Working World
48	Generativity vs. Stagnation	Middle Adulthood	Deal with Loss of Youth
52			Deal with Senior Job Status
56		Middle Adulthood	Involvement with Grandchildren
60			
64	Ego Integrity vs. Despair	Late Adult Transition	Deal with Retirement, Reduced Physical Capacities
68			
72		Late Adulthood	Deal with Loss of Function, Friends, Family

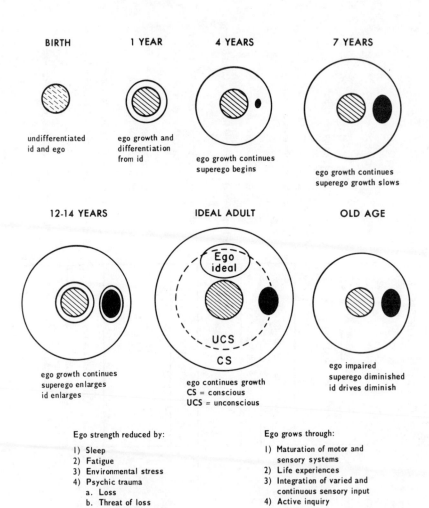

BIRTH

undifferentiated
id and ego

1 YEAR

ego growth and
differentiation
from id

4 YEARS

ego growth continues
superego begins

7 YEARS

ego growth continues
superego growth slows

12-14 YEARS

ego growth continues
superego enlarges
id enlarges

IDEAL ADULT

Ego
ideal

UCS

CS

ego continues growth
CS = conscious
UCS = unconscious

OLD AGE

ego impaired
superego diminished
id drives diminish

Ego strength reduced by:

1) Sleep
2) Fatigue
3) Environmental stress
4) Psychic trauma
   a. Loss
   b. Threat of loss
   c. Reactivation of old
      conflict
5) Impaired perception and
   integration of stimuli

Ego grows through:

1) Maturation of motor and
   sensory systems
2) Life experiences
3) Integration of varied and
   continuous sensory input
4) Active inquiry

Figure 1. The Psychic Apparatus Through Life

EXPLANATION
Figure 1

The Freudian view of psychological development is depicted in Figure 1. The family forces that shape each person are omitted from these diagrams for the sake of simplicity. The circle diagrams help to concretize individual psychosexual development and form the basis for Chapter 3 of this book, which deals with psychopathology.

The child's mind at birth is shown as a mass of undifferentiated psychic energy from which id and ego develop. The ego is the part of the psychic apparatus in contact with reality, mediating between our drives, our wishes, and the outer world. The id is the thoughts and feelings that are actively repressed by the ego because they are experienced as dangerous to the ego. Ego growth continues until middle or late adulthood. The superego begins its development in the late oral period and continues during the phallic and oedipal periods. It is the child's incorporation of parental values. By age seven, there is usually sufficient repression of the id by the ego and sufficient control of the ego by the superego that children can work together in groups.

At puberty, the maturation of the sexual apparatus and the musculoskeletal system intensifies id drives. The superego enlarges to compensate for the increasing id drives and is modified so that its values are no longer absolute. The ego continues its growth. The diagram representing the ideal adult shows that most of the ego is unconscious. The id has been totally repressed into the unconscious. The largest portion of the superego is unconscious, with the conscious portion being those standards of conduct and behavior we call conscience. The *ego-ideal* is our partly conscious, partly unconscious notions of what we *ought* to be; our ideals and aspirations for ourselves.

The diagram of the individual in old age shows shrinkage of the ego due to reduced physical vitality, a reduction in the number of brain cells, and a reduction in the acuity of the sense organs. The lessening of sexual vigor and the aggressive drive serves to reduce the pressure of the id on the ego, and maturation plays a role in reducing the irrational demands made by the superego.

logically and sees the therapist as a cruel taskmaster who dominates her life. She may also see the therapist as a source of nurturance and may delay leaving at the end of the hour. More malignant forms of regression can also occur. A teenaged boy, for example, stopped taking his immunosuppressants and rejected his transplanted kidney because he was pressured to function at a higher level than he could emotionally tolerate. He had lived at home all of his life. His parents had pushed him to move out and be self-sufficient, assuming that because he no longer needed dialysis, he no longer needed them on a day-to-day basis (Armstrong & Weiner, 1981).

Psychologically fixated patients may cling from the very beginning of therapy, insisting that therapists must be available to them 24 hours a day, thus in fact replicating a real mother–infant relationship. Of course, therapists do serve as transitional objects or bridges to the real world of interpersonal relationships (Slipp, 1982).

The process of *separation-individuation* (Mahler, 1979) also begins during infancy. As infants begin to distinguish themselves from their mothers, they also attempt to separate from them. At six months of age, infants scuttle away from their mothers, but rush back quickly if startled. At that stage, and for the first two years of life, children are in Piaget's *sensory motor stage* of development. In the sensory motor stage, what cannot be seen, felt, or heard no longer exists for children. As children become better able to retain a mental image of mother, they can go farther away from her and maintain a sense that she is still there. The ordinary child is three years old before reaching that stage, which Piaget terms *object constancy* (Piaget, 1954).

The id is increasingly kept in check by the developing ego. As the ego grows, it assumes control of the discharge of id impulses. The two basic mechanisms by which the ego keeps the id in check are suppression and repression. *Suppression* is conscious restraint or self-denial. *Repression* is an unconscious mechanism by which the ego submerges impulses into the unconscious part of the mind. The infantile forces that have been relegated to the unconscious portion of the mind constantly press for discharge, and are particularly evident in dreams. When repression becomes inefficient or inadequate, other defense mechanisms are brought into play, as we will see in the discussion of coping and defense mechanisms (see p. 34).

By age two, having progressed further in the process of separation-individuation, children assert their individuality and their capacity for self-regulation. This stage of life corresponds to Erikson's stage of *autonomy versus shame and doubt*, and its successful outcome leads to the development of self-control and willpower. The equivalent term in Freud's scheme is the *anal stage* of psychosexual development.

By the second year of life, children's intellectual development has passed from the sensory motor stage of intellectual development to the *preoperational stage* of Piaget, from a stage in which things exist only if they can be seen or touched to a stage in which objects and acts are remembered. Children in the sensory motor stage will cry over an object that is lost from view. To children at that stage, what is gone from view no longer exists. In the preoperational stage, they believe that it still may exist and will search for it. Children learn in their own way the law of conservation of matter; that material things do not ordinarily cease to exist.

Between 18 months and three years of age, a child's sense of himself or herself as a boy or girl has developed firmly. The children's *gender identity* is more strongly related to the role assigned by their family than their anatomy (Stoller, 1968). At this age, children discover their genitals and enter the Freudian *phallic phase* of psychosexual development. Concern about the intactness of one's genitals if one is a boy, and the wish for a penis, if a girl, can be the basis for significant fixations in psychosexual development. Exhibitionists and sexual athletes compulsively attempt to prove the intactness of their genitals. Females who assume the dominant role in lesbian relationships and don an artificial phallus during sexual intimacy with their partners fulfill their own wish for a penis.

Conscience formation begins with the child's incorporation of the parents' "no." Children of this age can be seen spanking their own hands and can be heard saying "no" to themselves. The conscience or *superego* comes to the aid of the ego in helping to repress unacceptable drives and wishes into the unconscious. It is formed by incorporating the parents' attitudes as the child sees them, and punishes the ego with guilt if they are transgressed. Because of the child's primitive thinking processes, the conscience of the very young child is primitive. Actions are either right or wrong. They warrant punishment or they don't, and there are no modifying circumstances or exceptions.

By the ages of four to six, children undergo considerable *decentering* (Piaget, 1954); children are able to involve themselves with other people and things (object-relatedness) in their environment in addition to being involved with themselves and their own needs. The same process is described in Freudian terms as the children's relinquishing of *primary narcissism* (the child's total self-involvement and self-love), and developing the ability to regard others and deal with them as people with their own individual needs as well as means to one's own satisfaction (Brenner, 1973). The transition from primary narcissism to object-relatedness is painful, and in the process growing children learn to experience and tolerate *ambivalence*, the presence of opposite feelings toward the same person when he or she both gratifies and frustrates. It is difficult for children at the preoperational intellectual level to understand that the same person can cuddle and spank. There is at first a mental separation into bad mother and good mother, or bad father and good father. Those separate mental images unite as children become mature enough to tolerate ambivalence and to recognize that one person may have many qualities.

Children may become fixated at the preambivalent stage in relation to one or both parents because of factors within the family relationship. A child may hold a negative view of its mother because of greater experience with the mother as a disciplinarian, while viewing a more distant father positively because he is less involved with day-long control and discipline. In that situation, the mother may be seen as all bad and the father as all good. This view of the parents may also be perpetuated by them for their own gain in an unsatisfactory marital relationship. In most circumstances, we see the development of the *Oedipus complex* between ages four and six; the attraction of the child to the opposite-sexed parent and the child's wish to exclude the same-sexed parent from their relationship. Children identify with the same-sexed parent and begin rehearsing an adult role.

As children acquire more motor skills and develop language and communicational skills, they also begin to develop the capacity to delay gratification. The ability to tolerate the tension of waiting until one's needs can be better met is called the *reality principle*: tolerating the tension of delay in order to attain later pleasure or gratification. By contrast, infants only know that they are enjoying the moment or are uncomfortable. If the pleasant sensation stops, or if discomfort begins, infants demand that something be done about it right now. That is known as the *pleasure principle*: the immediate seeking of pleasure and the avoidance of pain. Partial abandonment of the pleasure principle (we never give it up entirely), increased ego growth, the ability to tolerate frustration and to focus attention enable children to begin formal schooling. The development of the superego helps, too. Having internalized rules of conduct, seven-year-old children do not require constant supervision to be certain that they do not injure or steal from others. The parental supervisory role has been introjected as the superego, and the superego uses guilt to help children regulate their own behavior.

The period of psychosexual development that coincides with beginning school is known in Freudian terms as latency. The Oedipus complex has been repressed, in boys supposedly because they fear losing their penis, and in girls for fear of losing their mothers' love. Erikson describes the basic conflict of this stage as *industry versus inferiority*. Children learn to work for what they get and to gain recognition by producing things or by accomplishments outside the family. Their intellectual equipment is also functioning better, they continue decentering, and they enter Piaget's *concrete operational stage* of intellectual development.

In this stage, they become able to change their thinking when given evidence that their views are incorrect, and become aware of the interchangeability of dimensions such as height and width. Preoperational children cannot understand that a tall, narrow glass can hold as much water as a short, wide one. The decentering process of the child in the concrete operational stage has progressed to the point that the child can be asked to imagine something from another physical point of view or from another person's point of view. In addition, they become aware that matter remains constant; it is neither gained nor lost. When younger children watch a full container of water being emptied into a larger container, they see that the larger container is less full. When asked why, they say there is less water in the larger container, but cannot say where the lost water has gone. Children at the concrete operational stage say that there is an equal amount of water in both containers, but that the larger one is less full because it is larger and can hold more.

Elementary school children learn to function autonomously outside the family circle and begin learning the values of the larger society. They learn how to compete with peers and how to deal with authority. Children of both sexes engage in preliminary sexual exploration, but are less interested in how the genitals work than what they look like.

Around the age of 11 or 12, children enter the final stage of intellectual development described by Piaget; the stage of *formal operations*. We must bear in mind that perhaps no more than 30 percent of all adults reach this level of intellectual development. It is the ability to imagine what *could* be; imagining what is possible beyond what children know to exist. Other worlds can be imagined, as well as other ways of performing ordinary tasks. Indeed, other parents can be imagined, and one's own parents are often severely criticized for failing to come up to the standards of the ideal parents whom children imagine their friends to have. In addition to enabling criticism of parents, the stage of formal operations also enables scientific thinking; it allows the development of hypotheses testable by observation or experimentation.

In preadolescence, hormonal changes begin that culminate in biological puberty. The ability to sublimate aggressive and sexual drives into schoolwork and team play begins to break down and preadolescents become irritable, dissatisfied, and difficult to control. Children justify their irritability by finding their teachers too strict and assignments too difficult. They project their aggression onto others and feel that the school is out to get them. Groups of children unite and act against their supposed adult persecutors.

Adolescence is when physical maturity becomes complete. Often, intellectual and emotional development lag behind. Blos (1962) suggests that adolescents deal with three basic psychological tasks: separating from the parents, integrating tender feelings with sexual feelings, and developing a stable identity. Identity formation is seen as the heart of adolescence by Erikson, who describes the success of this stage as establishing a *personal identity* and its failure, *role confusion*.

The completion of biological adolescence is not equivalent to emotional maturity. Emotional maturation can continue throughout life, and adolescence is a very early stage in that process (Vaillant, 1977).

There is usually a marked psychological regression in early adolescence. The child, biologically propelled forward, clings to the vestiges of early attachments. The jokes about excretory processes that are so commonly told and giggled over by early adolescents may be seen as a partial ego regression. Early adolescent boys and girls get cuddly with the parent of the opposite sex and have the opportunity to rework the outcome of their earlier oedipal struggle. There is also an important reworking of the superego from a rigid eye-for-an-eye system to a more flexible, reasonable set of standards.

Adolescents who have moved into the stage of formal operations can see the conditional aspects of right and wrong; that under some circumstances there is justification for doing what was formerly held to be wrong. Hence, it is all right to steal or to cheat if one does so for the right reason; the end can justify the means.

Although many teenagers have entered the formal stage of intellectual operations, are able to see the world from many points of view, and are able to anticipate consequences, their psychological regression makes it difficult for them to believe that adverse consequences will occur.

The fickleness of teenagers in their personal relationships seems to be based on transient identifications that pave the way for more enduring identifications. Children tentatively try on an identification with one person by becoming a friend and reject or abandon the friend when the identification does not seem to fit. Overidealization of friends appears to be based on the same mechanism. Falling in love and romantic crushes set the stage for girls and boys to differentiate as men and women by loving in a person of the opposite sex the qualities in themselves that they deem inappropriate to their own sex (see Figure 2). The "bisexuality" referred to in Figure 2 concerns culturally ascribed masculine and feminine traits, not sexual preference. A girl loves her boyfriend's robust activity; he loves her tenderness. Having made the transition to more adult maleness and femaleness, boy and girl fall "out of love" and eventually select partners on the basis of attributes other than their stereotyped maleness or femaleness.

There are, of course, many miscarried love relationships in adolescence. They are frequently based on Oedipal themes. A girl falls in love with a boy primarily because he is misunderstood, as dad was by mom. In adulthood, she becomes a woman who is attracted to degraded men; for example, a woman who repeatedly marries alcoholic men. A man, on the other hand, may select a woman for the ideal qualities she shares in common with his mother, but may have to seek sexual satisfaction with a degraded woman, such as a prostitute, because of the incest barrier and fear of retaliation by the father, now incorporated into his superego. Degradation of the loved one is often the price exacted by the superego for choosing a person who in some way symbolizes an unattainable parent (Weiner, 1980).

In our culture, physical separation from parents is usually achieved by the end of adolescence, when young adults go to work, to college, or join the military. By this time, the individual's identification as a sexually adult man or woman is fairly stable, but there is considerable autoeroticism during adolescence, which serves as a retreat from the opposite sex and a rehearsal for sexuality, and frequent sexual experimentation with members of the same sex. Career identity frequently is not established until young adulthood, during or following completion of college, or at times even later in life. In recent years, there has been a tendency to delay career decisions until the late twenties with a substantial moratorium period between completion of biological adolescence and active pursuit of a career. This may be good because it allows late adolescents to form a personal identity before forming a work identity, and thereby gives them broader coping skills. Erikson (1963) defines the basic conflict of young adulthood as *intimacy versus isolation*, and suggests that the capacity for affiliation and love develops at that stage.

Young adults usually work at a paid job or work toward implement-

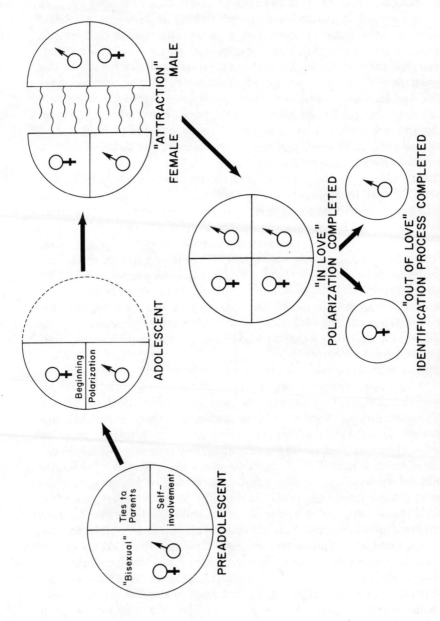

Figure 2. "Falling in Love" and Sexual Differentiation

ing a career choice through continued education. It is likely that protracted dependence on parents and educational institutions slows the process of psychological maturation. Those who work at paid jobs seem to mature more quickly than those who go to school, but the continued psychological openness of those who pursue advanced educations opens them to a variety of maturational changes that are less possible for those who assume a great deal of personal responsibility early in life.

Marriage is a sign of the person's willingness to be treated as an adult and to assume adult responsibilities. Marriage signifies that the individual is willing to take a step beyond romantic love and to move into a legal commitment to work on a relationship. Marriage is used by many young adults to escape parental domination; these young people feel that a marital relationship confers independence. Such marriages often fail because marital relationships demand cooperative work with another person and putting his or her needs on a par with one's own.

Parenthood, too, is a step toward adult responsibility. Parenting requires more than does the marital partnership. Parenting young children requires that their needs be placed above the parents'. Parents gradually shift their relationship with maturing children so that by the time the children leave home to enter the world as adults, they are assuming most of the responsibility for themselves.

Ideally, men and women come to grips with their own sexuality before marriage and parenthood. This is probably not true of people who marry in their late teens or early twenties. Learning the distinction between sexual penetration and pleasuring another person is difficult for the male, who often equates sexual satisfaction with orgasm, and for whom giving subtle sensual pleasuring may have the regressive connotation of petting as a small child. Women, on the other hand, learn to experience the vagina as a source of sexual pleasure in addition to clitoral stimulation. Men and women have different arousal patterns. Woman arouse more slowly but sustain arousal longer and are able to reach multiple orgasms, while men arouse quickly and experience a refractory period following orgasm (Sadock, 1980). Integrating the subtleties of these patterns of arousal and release requires sensitivity to one's own and one's partner's needs and the ability to communicate one's own needs to the other. Adult sexuality is clearly a complicated interpersonal issue.

The stage of early adulthood, according to Levinson (1978), encompasses the years from the late teens into the forties, and encompasses many biological, psychological, and social changes. At the beginning of early adulthood, men and women are fully physically mature and are at the height of their physical powers. In passing from the twenties into the thirties and forties, physical endurance declines and other signs of aging appear. Disorders related to stress and to stressful ways of living begin to appear, such as peptic ulcer and coronary artery disease. At the end of the early adult years, women begin to lose their reproductive capacity. A man's lessening physical abilities as he reaches the end of early adulthood remind him that his ability to undertake new physical pursuits is limited and that more sedentary activities will need to become sources of enjoyment.

Numerous psychological changes occur during early adulthood. The first is the initiation into the world of adults, in which the rules learned in childhood games or in living at home with mom and dad no longer apply. People in early adulthood learn to devise rules that work for them while paying lip service to generally accepted rules of conduct. They learn to lie when necessary and to tell the truth when it is the most useful, to present the best side of themselves to a new employer, and to relax only when the job has been mastered. They develop the ability to cultivate adult friends, but remain sufficiently separated from them so that they do not blindly follow wherever they are led.

Those who choose to raise children reexperience their own growing up, and have the opportunity to vicariously rework their own childhood conflicts and to confer upon their children what they would have liked for themselves as children. Usually, the early adult stage of life encompasses the entire growing up period of one's children. One of the endpoints of early adulthood for women, in addition to menopause, is the departure of their children. They may then (if not before) choose to define themselves as a person apart from their mates and children, and reenter the working world that they may have left to raise their children.

Dramatic changes in social roles occur during early adulthood. Early adults are apprentices in the adult world; they are junior members of society. Early adults in their forties are often at the height of their social and professional powers, have achieved their maximum work and social accomplishment, and are well-entrenched members of the working world. Changes in social role for women during this period of time are more complex than the social changes for men. Childbearing women frequently suspend their work careers and spend much of their early adulthood in child-rearing, thus placing their career development considerably behind that of those women who have not interrupted their careers. While men usually identify with their job or profession, women tend to be caught between their work or professional identities and their identities as wives and mothers. Some women establish lifelong identities as mothers. Others must seek new identities once they are past child-rearing (Mogul, 1979).

As increasing numbers of women enter the working world (nearly 40 percent of today's work force is female), there are fewer women left in neighborhoods to socialize and lend emotional support to one another (Glick & Kessler, 1980). The increase in the number of working women has meant an acceleration of the rate at which women leave home to work to escape social isolation and to receive tangible rewards for their service by which they can measure their own worth.

There is often a complete reversal of roles in relation to parents during the period of early adulthood. There is a progression from dependence on parents to mutual acceptance as adults, followed by a reversal of roles as parents become infirm and depend on their children for physical and financial support.

We do not know the effect on women's development of choosing a career instead of marriage and child-rearing. In the past, being unmarried was often equated with being undesirable or inadequate. A single life as a career woman is now a clear option attended by little stigma, but with many drawbacks. The greatest drawback is the absence of a formal tie to another person and the social isolation with which single women must deal. A wide range of social and recreational interests and a meaningful job help single women to cope effectively. Viewed in this context, for many women marriage may result from their inability or failure to cultivate their own resources, but it is obvious that acquiring sufficient emotional, social, and economic resources to live as a single person is difficult for any woman or man.

Biologically, middle adulthood begins around the time of the female menopause (Notman, 1980). There is no comparable biological marker for males, who experience a modest lowering of sexual drive and physical energy. Metabolic processes slow, and food intake must be watched to stave off extra girth. The onset of a mild chronic illness such as hypertension calls for regular checkups, further attention to diet, such as salt and cholesterol restriction, and medication. The use of medication for hypertension or female hormones for menopausal symptoms stirs conflicts over dependency and autonomy, and also necessitates living with side effects.

Psychologically, middle adults usually come to grips with the fact that their career has advanced as far as it can. The exceptions are women who dropped out of the labor market to have children, or women who decide to enter the labor market at mid-life. In many instances, educated or talented middle-adult women are able to begin successful careers, or resume a career that had been interrupted. This may result in marital turmoil when husbands see their wives outdistance them professionally or when the balance of power in the family shifts as wives become breadwinners and begin to assert themselves as equals in other respects.

At a social level, a network of friends has usually been established, and friends begin to take the place of the children, who have now begun moving away from home and parental domination. The parents of middle adults have often restricted their social activities, may be retired, and have developed chronic health problems that frequently require the involvement of their children. That role reversal, in which for example, a mother needs her daughter to take her to the doctor, may be a source of tension for children who want to remain dependent on their parents, or for parents who cannot allow themselves to be dependent or to regress.

Erikson suggests that the basic conflict at this stage of life is *generativity versus stagnation*; whether one is willing to become involved with raising the next generation of adult co-workers or whether one chooses to wallow in one's decline or to defend oneself against the younger people by whom one fears displacement.

Middle adults must look forward to and prepare for late adulthood if they are to prevent loneliness and boredom in their later years. Middle adults, if they have not done so before, need to cultivate physical, social, and intellectual interests compatible with aging.

In middle adulthood, grandchildren come on the scene. Grandchildren offer middle adults the opportunity to relive aspects of their child-rearing, much as early adults relive aspects of their own childhood through their children. Because grandparents see young children less as a part of themselves and less as likely to act on their own forbidden impulses than do parents, grandparents are often more nurturing than parents. This, of course, is a source of potential conflict with the parents who react angrily to grandparents' refusal to set limits that parents feel are so necessary for their own children, but vigorously opposed when they were children themselves.

The difficulties of female middle adulthood are highlighted by a woman's cessation of menses. For males, it can be seen in the reaction to an illness such as a heart attack (Cassell, 1979).

Postmenopausal women grieve for their youth, for loss of reproductive capacity, and for the children they will never have. The syndrome of involutional melancholia (severe unipolar depression in a postmenopausal woman) was formerly related to postmenopausal changes in metabolism. It now seems more likely that postmenopausal depression ordinarily has less to do with hormonal imbalance than with women's ability to accept or to change their role. The depression that frequently follows hysterectomy is partly a reaction to loss of an organ for which there is no adequate substitute.

Turning to men with a serious illness, we frequently find that an illness such as a heart attack strikes at a point when ceaseless striving to accomplish more and more in less and less time has become increasingly frustrating and unrewarding (Friedman & Rosenman, 1974). Nevertheless, men may have difficulty allowing themselves to regress long enough to recover adequately. It is as if they feel that a moment's let down will allow life to get completely out of hand, and cherished goals will become unattainable (Weiner, 1976a). One cherished goal that must be abandoned is the illusion of living forever. A heart attack can be the hard knock that awakens men to the fact that they will not live forever, and that the quality of their lives is more important than the amount of material goods they accumulate.

Having been sobered by menopause, by illness, and by the death of parents, middle adults make the transition to late adulthood.

Erik Erikson describes the central issue of this stage of life as *integrity versus despair*; the sense of one's life having had meaning, and the challenge of continuing a meaningful existence. Late adulthood begins as early as one's state of physical and emotional decline forces withdrawal from many activities.

Biologically old persons suffer motor and sensory impairment. Bones and muscles weaken. Joints grow stiff. Taste, smell, sight, and hearing fail, and speed of learning and recall slow. As in early childhood, the unfamiliar is frightening and confusing. Sexual drive diminishes, but old people generally continue sexual relations as long as they retain their health and their mates (Busse & Blazer, 1980).

Beginning in middle adulthood, most people feel the need for a certain amount of orderliness and routine. In late adulthood, order and predictability become more important because of old persons' reduced ability to adapt physically or psychologically to change. Confusional states occur frequently when mildly demented old persons change their place of residence or enter unfamiliar surroundings, such as a hospital, because familiar sensory cues are lost.

The psychological state of old persons depends on the intactness of their body and brain, and on their ability to tailor their environment to meet their needs. Helpless, incapacitated older persons may despair and find their lives meaningless, especially if invalidism leads to social isolation. Invalided old people who have developed good social skills and a wide range of interests often maintain good spirits.

In our society, older people tend to become isolated from younger persons. They are often forced to retire at age 65. Their children leave and establish homes in other parts of the city or country, and because of increasing infirmity, elder persons are unable to travel to be with their families. Those who own their own residences gradually become unable to keep them up, and move to sheltered living arrangements with other older people, thus removing them further from purposeful activity and the mainstream of life. In my own discussions with older people, I find that their primary fear is not death, but helplessness and isolation in an indifferent world.

The old people who fare best maintain a high level of activity and involvement with others; enough to feel that their lives have some meaning to other people, or to a higher cause.

Death completes the life cycle. For the mature older person, it is an expected and sometimes welcome rest from the trials and labors of life (Roberts, Kimsey, Logan, & Shaw, 1970).

COPING AND DEFENSE MECHANISMS

The foregoing view of psychological development and life stages is intended to alert therapists to an important aspect of the diagnostic process—establishing patients' level of psychological and cognitive development in the context of the life tasks they face. Now we turn to the means by which people cope with and adapt to life.

Coping mechanisms are the psychological mechanisms that lead to positive, creative adaptations and for some people, to self-realization: becoming fully one's self. The classical mechanisms of defense (A. Freud, 1946) are psychological attempts to deceive one's self and others and to avoid facing the responsibility for one's decisions and one's behavior. In essence, they are means to deal with failure of positive adaptation and attempts to compensate, explain it away, or blame it on somebody or something else.

Coping Mechanisms

The most basic coping mechanisms are *decision, will,* and *responsibility*; deciding on a course of action, using free will to implement the action decided upon, and responsibly facing the consequences of the action taken. That frequently involves suffering short-term discomfort for the sake of a longer-term gain, and also makes use of denial, a mechanism we will discuss again later. As we noted earlier, the willingness to suffer short-term discomfort for long-term gain is termed the *reality principle*. One of the important tasks of psychological development is making the transition to the reality principle from the *pleasure principle*. The denial referred to above is *denial of imminent death*; denial of the possibility that we may not live to carry out our plans. Without that denial, we would say, "What's the use?" and make no effort on our own behalf. In spite of our denial that death may be imminent, an important coping mechanism is the *acceptance of eventual death*. Acceptance of our limited existence on earth provides a strong push toward self-realization.

Becoming a psychotherapist exemplifies the above coping mechanisms. It begins with a decision to help people, and with a search for a career that fulfills that decision. Having decided on a helping profession, the therapist-to-be secures the appropriate preliminary education and enters a professional school. The long educational process is endured so that one can eventually help people and little thought is given to the possibility one may not live through the years of education involved.

The following coping mechanisms, stimulus-seeking and mastery, are partly biologically determined, but are also shaped by the developing child's environment. *Stimulus-seeking* (including initiative-taking and risk-taking) is finding enjoyment in stimuli that have not been previously experienced. That mechanism, which can be reinforced or discouraged in parenting a child, is the basis for a sense of adventure in dealing with the world. It is the basis of play, and later, of creative activity.

Mastery is the urge to master one's own motor and sensory apparatus and to master some portion of one's world. The mechanism of mastery leads us to make the most we can of ourselves and helps us shape our immediate world in ways that enable us to survive.

Still another important coping mechanism is *attribution of meaning*. Humans need a sense that existence is understandable and meaningful. As long as we can make sense out of our lives and of the events in our lives, we can keep going in a productive manner. When our lives make no sense, we lose our will to live as social beings (Frankl, 1959).

Two other coping mechanisms are trust and hope. Trust is a coping mechanism developed in the first year of life, according to Erikson (1963). Basic *trust* is the sense that there is something positive in one's world that will comfort, nurture, and protect. Trust projected into the future is *hope*, the expectation that something good or positive will occur as the result of our actions, and is based on a past experience of a masterable, understandable environment. The coping mechanisms we have described are the basis of art, science, and religion, and enable people to live together in families and societies.

Vaillant (1977), who reported a long-term study of healthy men, has called our attention to five other coping mechanisms; sublimation, suppression, altruism, anticipation, and humor. *Sublimation* is acquiring and using skills that will allow the socially acceptable expression of one's inner drives. The urge to master, for example, is converted into the mastery of a profession. The aggressive and sexual drives can be sublimated into competitive sports and long-term love relationships. *Suppression*, which was also mentioned in our discussion of infancy, is willing oneself to wait until the best moment to undertake a particular act or course of action. *Altruism* is doing for others without expectation of gain. *Anticipation* is planning in advance; thinking ahead to problems that may arise and planning tentative courses of action should they arise. It is also anticipating opportunities that may arise and planning on how best to capitalize on them. The other mechanism that Vaillant found in his population of healthy men is *humor*; the ability to enjoy the uncertainty and reversals of life instead of being crushed by them. It's the ability to see that we're all in the same boat, to enjoy its rocking and to enjoy getting splashed. Humor is the ability to make light of one's own fumblings while taking them seriously enough to avoid repeating the damaging ones. Having a sense of humor enables us to laugh at our first bumbling efforts to make sense of a case history or to make a psychotherapeutic intervention instead of feeling overwhelmed by what we do not yet know as beginning professionals. It's also the ability of patients to laugh and reassure us we'll do better the next time.

Mechanisms of Defense

As noted earlier, the classical mechanisms of defense are means to avoid responsibility. They cause and are responses to failures of adaptation. They are employed by persons who are not mature enough to have developed adequate coping mechanisms or by persons who are fixated at or regressed to childish levels of function. Vaillant (1977) has divided defense mechanisms into three categories: *psychotic, immature,* and *neurotic.*

Psychotic defenses. The psychotic mechanisms are used by severely regressed or fixated persons with great impairment of *reality testing,* the ability to distinguish between what is real and what is wished for, feared, or imagined. Psychotic mechanisms occur in the ordinary process of dreaming, when ego relaxes its guard over the unconscious. They include denial of external reality, distortion, and delusional projection.

Denial of external reality is evident in the psychotic person's refusal to believe that the reason he was fired was his chronic lateness and uncooperativeness. Denial of external reality necessitates the substitution of fantasy for reality. The man who is fired for lateness, for example, may believe that he is the victim of a conspiracy against him. The fantasies of psychotic people are not dispelled by reasoning with them, and because of the fixed nature of these fantasies, they are called *delusions*, or false beliefs.

Distortion is reshaping one's perception of reality to suit one's needs. People who feel powerless distort their feelings of helplessness and instead feel as if they have special powers. They explain their failures in life as being due to people who are jealous of those special powers. Distortion also occurs normally in dreaming. The characteristic distortions in dreaming are displacement, symbolization, and condensation. *Displacement* is the mental substitution of one person or object for another. It is the chief psychological mechanism in the formation of phobias. *Symbolization* is the mental substitution of one person or thing for another, usually based on a quality they have in common. The quality shared in common may be a personality trait, such as meekness or quietness, so that in a dream a mouse may symbolize a meek, quiet person, or the mousy aspect of one's own personality. While there are probably a few dream symbols that many people have in common, most dream symbols can only be understood by knowing something of the dreamer as a person and of his experiences on the day he had a particular dream (Freud, 1900/1960). *Condensation* is a process by which two or more symbols represent the same thing.

Delusional projection is the attribution of one's own thoughts and feelings to others. A psychotic person may feel that the President of the United States is jealous of his or her special powers, and that the President is trying to steal those powers. Or psychotic people may deal with homosexual impulses by hallucinating voices that tell them they are queer, thus avoiding the responsibility for feeling their own homosexual urges.

Immature defenses. The immature mechanisms of ego defense are common in children up through the teenage years, and include projection, fantasy, hypochondriasis, passive-aggressive behavior, and acting out.

Projection is attributing one's own feelings to someone else. Projection is one of the most common causes of marital discord, where it takes the form of blaming. The husband says, "I stayed out last night because I knew you were angry with me." The wife says, "I'm not affectionate because I know you're sexually interested in other women."

Fantasy is a means of mentally gratifying one's self without running the risk of failing. Children use fantasy to prepare for manhood and womanhood. They pretend to be moms and dads, and play at having their own homes and careers. Fantasy is a pathologic defense when it becomes a habitual substitute for action in reality. A man who stays home and imagines a relationship with a woman instead of attending a social event and starting a real relationship is making self-defeating use of fantasy.

Hypochondriasis is focusing on bodily sensations and a sense of being unwell or in pain as a means to attract attention, to enable dependence, and to express anger toward those on whom we depend. It is a means to fulfill needs that are not otherwise met. A woman whose husband is inattentive focuses on multiple physical symptoms and succeeds in getting the attention of many doctors, and is getting revenge on her spouse by being too sick for sexual intimacy. It differs from *conversion*, a mechanism that makes symbolic use of symptoms to express and deal with unconscious conflict. Conversion usually symbolizes a wish and its prohibition. Paralysis of the legs may occur, for instance, when the wish to escape a frightening situation is thwarted by fear of being considered a coward. The conflict is settled by becoming paralyzed. No conscious decision to stay or to flee is made, and one is rescued by someone else.

Passive-aggressive behavior is aggression directed passively or indirectly against others that often worsens an uncomfortable situation. For example, a teenage boy asserts himself against his mother's domination by staying out past his curfew and thereby provokes a more stringent curfew. Passive-aggressive behavior is frequently reinforced by the mechanism of *rationalization*, offering of a reasonable excuse for one's behavior. The teenage girl who comes in late really couldn't help it because her date had a flat, the movie started late, and, besides, nobody else had to be in that early.

Acting out was originally a technical term in psychoanalysis that referred to living out important themes from childhood outside the therapy hour instead of remembering them in therapy and giving them up (Greenson, 1967). As presently used (Vaillant, 1977), the term means the direct expression of an unconscious wish or impulse without recognizing the feeling that goes along with it, and giving in to impulses instead of learning to bear the frustration of delay. Examples from adolescence are very common, and include premature entry into sexual relations to deal with the fear of adult sexuality and to avoid the tension of frustration.

Neurotic defenses. The neurotic defenses are everyday mechanisms for dealing with stress by unconscious avoidance of responsibility for certain desires and impulses. Symptomatic neuroses develop when they are overused and when they are heavily reinforced by the environment. A neurotic defense, like any other defense, has the *primary gain* of defending against an uncomfortable thought, feeling, or urge. There may also be *secondary gain*; that which one can gain from the environment as a result of having symptoms. For example, the anxious hovering of parents over a child who is uncomfortable returning to school after a holiday may reinforce the child's anxiety and facilitate the development of a school phobia. Thus, the most important part of treating school-phobic children may be eliminating the secondary gain by returning them to school. After that, the symptoms often subside dramatically.

Repression is an unconscious mechanism by which thoughts and feelings are pushed out of the conscious mind into the unconscious portion of the mind. Repression is part of the normal process of forgetting, without which we would be hopelessly mired in the random clutter of information that passes through our brains each day. Thoughts, feelings, and memories do not slip out of our minds and become lost once they have been recorded. Studies using hypnosis indicate that the intact brain can recall many supposedly forgotten experiences (Crasilneck & Hall, 1975). The active forgetting process is overused by many people who thereby avoid awareness of emotionally important information. Ordinary instances of repression are forgetting appointments with a person with whom one is angry or whom one finds frightening. Repression is a part of most neurotic defense mechanisms, and other neurotic defense mechanisms often come into play when repression becomes ineffective as a defense. For example, a girl whose repression deals with her sexual impulses very well while attending a girls' boarding school may need to use additional mechanisms to deal with her sexual impulses when she begins to attend a coeducational school.

Intellectualization is a defense that allows one to discuss the most frightening or painful aspects of one's self without feeling the fear or pain. A sexually inhibited woman may say that she avoids men because they're only interested in sex, and that she has other priorities. A man who is ruining his life by dealing with others in a passively aggressive manner may state blandly that his behavior stems from his fear of his father, and that he cannot change that behavior now. It's his father's fault, and that's that.

Isolation is a more specific term for separating feelings from thoughts. People who use isolation can be aware that a clenched, white-knuckled fist and tight jaw occur when a person is angry, but they don't recognize their own anger when their own fists are tight and their jaws are clenched. On the other hand, such a person may recognize that he or she is in a situation that others experience as frustrating or irritating, but doesn't feel the frustration or the irritation himself.

Displacement was mentioned as a mechanism in dream formation, and is also a defense mechanism during the waking state. Displacement involves the substitution of a less emotionally charged person, event, or thing for one that has a very high emotional charge. Anger toward one's parents is readily displaced onto friends or the family pet. Fears of one's own drives can be displaced onto places that symbolize them. Dependent people who are fearful of their sexual urges may develop a fear of social situations that enables them to avoid sexual stimulation.

Reaction formation is acting in opposition to a wish or fear that a person does not want to consciously recognize. It is a very common mechanism in young adults who deal with fear of leaving home by doing the opposite and going to college at great distances from home. It can also occur as exaggerated considerateness and politeness to someone toward whom one's negative feelings must be repressed.

Dissociation is a mechanism that allows the temporary forgetting of aspects of one's personality, or of one's entire identity. It is the basis for dissociative or fugue states (so-called amnesias), multiple personalities, and also is the basis for rash decisions that are later regretted. In a minor dissociation, a woman may forget about her financial state and buy an expensive dress, only to "wake up" emotionally the next day and be in very genuine distress over having overspent. A major dissociation can involve forgetting one's name and one's past.

A list of psychological defense mechanisms is potentially endless. It would include every possible psychological maneuver to avoid dealing fully and responsibly with life's problems. In Chapter 3, we will see how various defense mechanisms cluster to form diagnostic entities, taking into account that the presence of certain defense mechanisms in various forms of mental illness, such as the presence of projection in paranoid schizophrenia, does not mean that the illness is a result of that mechanism. The use of psychotic mechanisms may be the ego's only means to cope with acute or chronic structural or functional immaturity or disorganization of the nervous system.

SUMMARY

In this chapter, I have presented a group of highly simplified schemata. Human psychological development and adaptation are far too complex to be adequately described and categorized by any existing system of inquiry or theory of development. Rather than aiming at completeness, I have attempted to establish a frame of reference for therapists to understand the context in which symptoms arise and the psychological mechanisms by which they develop. Given the same dynamic constellation and defense mechanisms, therapists' treatment approaches will vary in relation to their patients' present life tasks and demands. Given patients with similar life tasks, therapists' treatment will depend on their patients' dynamic constellations and the adaptive and defense mechanisms they are able to mobilize. Early traumas and failures or inadequacies of development may be overcome in later life or may constitute a nucleus about which psychopathology develops. Viewing patients dynamically in the context of their life experiences and life tasks helps differentiate between psychopathology and ordinary psychosocial development, and between healthy or creative adaptation and reversible or irreversible psychopathology.

CHAPTER 3

Psychopathology

Most emotional disorders result from interacting social, psychological, and physical or chemical forces in persons with certain cognitive, emotional, metabolic, or genetic vulnerabilities. To understand the role of psychological treatments in emotional disorders, it is helpful to view emotional disorders as states of imbalance.

Figure 3 shows that a certain degree of symptomatology or malfunction falls within the range of expected or normal discomfort or dysfunction; fatigue after a long day's work, a headache after a trying day at the office, and tension before making an oral presentation to a class or before confronting a superior. More severe symptoms that do not subside once the immediate precipitant is removed fall within the range designated as illness, and are diagnosed and treated by mental health professionals; persisting fatigue unrelated to physical effort, or disabling headaches and anxiety.

Lessening the load on one end of the scale by reducing or counterbalancing any or all of the social, psychological, or biological contributing factors can reduce symptoms. A tension headache that begins with muscular tension in the head and neck can be relieved by aspirin, which blocks perception of pain. It thereby reduces the reflex muscular spasm that results from the initial muscle tightening. The same headache can be relieved by removing people from a tension-producing situation, by distracting them from the source of their tension, or by facilitating the expression of pent-up feelings.

The same principles apply to the treatment of major mental disorders. The symptoms of schizophrenia can be treated by chemical blockade of midbrain dopamine-mediated pathways, by removing symptomatic persons from highly stressful environments and placing them in less challenging and more supportive milieus, and by helping them to find effective ways to suppress and avoid dealing with feelings. Usually, mental disorders are treated by combining all these approaches into a biopsychosocial treatment.

PSYCHOLOGICAL HEALTH AND ILLNESS

Observing human systems in action permits an operational definition of psychological health and illness. *Psychological health is creative psychological problem-solving in a social context. Psychological illness is applying stereotyped or inefficient problem-solving mechanisms to situations that change in nature and complexity.*

Psychologically healthy persons, having to deal with problems they have never faced before, seek needed help, decide what to do, and follow their course of action until it is obvious that it works or it doesn't work. If it doesn't work, the problem is reformulated and approached differently. Immature or emotionally unhealthy persons try to find a way to avoid dealing with the problem, to use in unmodified form a course of action that worked in some closely related problem, to blame somebody else for the problem, or to find an excuse, such as a symptom which prevents dealing with the problem. Psychotic persons believe they can't succeed because there is a conspiracy against them. Immature persons find they can't succeed because too much is expected of them, and neurotic persons develop symptoms that divert their attention.

Certain attitudes and behaviors are prerequisites to creative problem-solving. They are: feeling able to influence one's environment, feeling reasonable responsibility for one's self and others, and willingness to assume different roles vis-à-vis one's self and others as required in daily living (Lewis, Beavers, Gossett, & Phillips, 1976). Those attitudes lead to the healthy behaviors of constructively attempting to alter one's environment, assuming appropriate responsibility for one's self and others, and assuming different roles toward one's self and others as needed to meet the demands of daily living.

As we have noted, there are multiple sources of one person's inability to fit a square peg in a round hole, and the ability of another to modify the peg or the hole so that they do fit. Some of the roots are biological. Some people's nervous systems are more biologically intact than others. Other people have been deprived of generally available learning experiences. Still others are victims of their own fantasy lives. All of those sources have a final common pathway; inefficiency at solving intra-

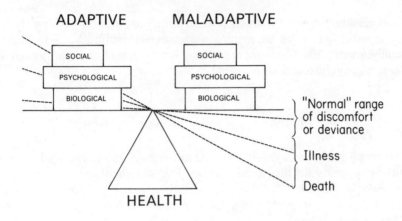

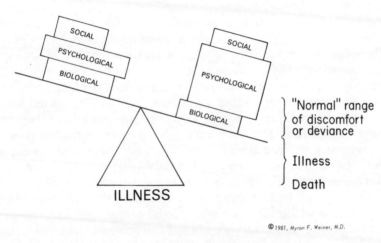

© 1981, Myron F. Weiner, M.D.

Figure 3. A Model of Health and Illness

psychic and interpersonal problems. Guilt, ordinarily a useful internal braking system, runs amok, and part of the mind becomes an enemy, torturing at every turn. Or, those who are loved best, who are major sources of support, are treated as enemies and therefore withdraw their support, reinforcing alienation.

The final common pathway described above manifests psychologically as a sense of helplessness to deal with, or to control, some aspect of one's environment or of one's own thoughts, feelings, or behavior. The sense of helplessness may be experienced directly, or it may be dealt with by developing delusions of exaggerated potency, while actually becoming less potent in the real world. People may also develop physical symptoms or delusions of persecution that explain why they cannot do what they want to or feel they ought to do. A sense of helplessness is partly determined and partly reinforced by a fear of dire consequences expected if one acts in one's own behalf (Miller, Rossellini, & Seligman, 1977). The expectation of painful consequences may result from past experience or from anticipating one's own projected rage. In many instances, a sense of helplessness translates into self-defeating behaviors that guarantee the expected outcome.

There are many ways to deal with feeling helpless. Delusions and physical symptoms may be used to account for feelings of helplessness or, indeed, to assert that one is very powerful, but is prevented from acting by circumstances beyond one's control. On the other hand, one can give in to a sense of helplessness and be morbid. Or, one can attempt to compensate. One means to compensate is to shrink one's world to an area so small that it can be almost entirely comprehended, and to deal with the rest of the world as if it were irrelevant or unimportant. This is the restrictive approach – "If it hasn't anything to do with my immediate world, it doesn't matter." An approach adopted by alcoholics might be described as perceptual modification. Drink until the world looks the way you want it. One can also struggle to control the thinking and behavior of the important persons in one's life.

PSYCHOPATHOLOGY

Individual psychological development occurs within the context of a family (Beavers, Lewis, Gossett, & Phillips, 1975; Lewis, Beavers, Gossett, & Phillips, 1976) but for the sake of convenience will now be considered out of that context, as if the individual psychic apparatus had an existence independent of family and social setting.

A simplified schema of psychic development was presented in Figure 1, entitled The psychic apparatus through life (see Chapter 2). The size of the circle depicting the ego shows the amount of psychic energy available to the ego in relation to the other parts of the psychic apparatus at certain points in the life cycle. For the sake of simplicity, the boundary between the conscious and the unconscious portions of the mind is indicated only for the ideal adult. The ego ideal is also only shown for the adult. Dysphoria experienced at the ego's boundary with reality is experienced as fear. Dysphoria at the boundary of the ego with the id is felt as anxiety, or objectless fear. It is objectless because its origin is unconscious. Dysphoria at the ego's boundary with the superego is experienced as guilt.

Figure 4, entitled Ego Strength, graphically compares the ideal ego with the ego that is chronically impaired, poorly developed, or still in the process of development, and also compares an ideal ego with a temporarily impaired ego. As depicted in Figure 4, an ideal ego has enough energy available after dealing with reality, with the superego's demands, and with the id's drives to allow for creative activity, for play, and for coping with unexpected events. When the ego has little energy in relation to the demands of reality and the other parts of the psychic apparatus, a person often develops uncomfortable symptoms or maladaptive behavior by using psychological mechanisms that save energy, but can have devastating consequences for interpersonal relations.

The amount of available ego energy, or ego strength, is an important consideration in psychotherapy. When there is little surplus ego energy, psychotherapy that requires self-observation cannot be employed because it requires the ego to use part of its energy for self-observation. When the ego is greatly compromised, the psychological measures employed must be directed toward helping the ego repress the contents of the id, avoid guilty rumination, and focus on the demands of reality. When greater ego energy is available, a reflective or interactive approach may then become appropriate.

Assessment of Ego Strength

The ability to assess ego strength is an important tool for the psychotherapist. Assessment of ego strength does not end with the initial evaluation of patients for therapy. It is an ongoing process that helps therapists determine whether they are helping or doing harm.

Ego strength can be evaluated both longitudinally and cross-sectionally; as trait or state. Patients can be assessed in terms of their lifelong ability to deal with themselves and the world, or can be assessed on the basis of how they are functioning that moment in the context of their relationship with a particular therapist. Therapists' interventions are based on patients' ego state *at the moment*, and not on a past history of high ego function. A past history of poor ego function suggests a need for caution. Patients' longitudinal ego strength, if high, may lend a positive prognostic note to the treatment, but does not indicate the nature of the treatment that needs to be administered. Many persons

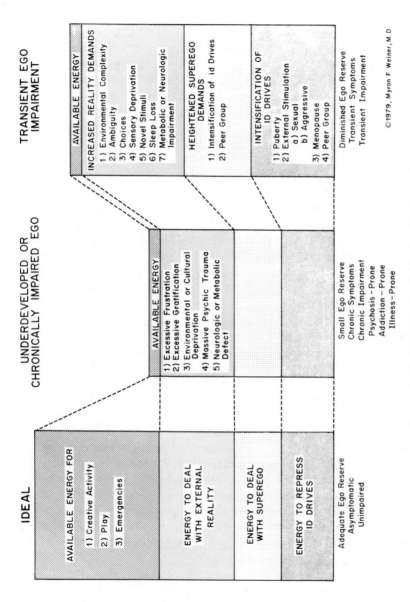

Figure 4. Ego Strength (Available Psychic Energy)

with strong premorbid personalities become severely ill and unresponsive to psychological treatment techniques.

Attractive, verbal, intelligent, and successful (AVIS) are the hallmarks of longitudinal ego strength in young adults and middle-aged adults. Attractive suggests the ability to care for one's self, a sense that one is worth the time and effort, and an interest in positive responses from others. Overconcern or an exclusive focus on appearance may suggest problems of self-esteem or excessive narcissism. Severe self-esteem problems make it difficult to invest psychologically in oneself. Highly narcissistic persons, although they may be successful, are difficult to treat because it is difficult for them to invest in anything outside themselves.

Verbal skills refers to the ability of persons to communicate information about their thoughts, feelings, and behavior to therapists. Many persons are extremely verbal, but do not communicate coherent or useful information. Thus, the critical aspect of the verbal dimension is not the quantity of talk, but its meaningfulness. Verbal skills also refers to use of secondary process communication. While patients' verbalization of primary process thought allows therapists to know what is going on at an unconscious level, the contents of the material cannot be used to shape psychological interventions. Instead, the form is observed (i.e., rambling, tangential, circumstantial, loose, derailed, autistic, neologistic, or word salad) as a means of gauging progress in treatment.

Intelligence refers solely to intelligence within or above the range of average. Most psychotherapeutic techniques can be used with persons of average intelligence, but therapists become sharply limited in dealing with cognitively impaired persons (see also Chapter 10 on repressive therapy).

Successful refers to success in several different areas; educational, occupational, and interpersonal. Educational success is a person's becoming educated to the degree commensurate with his or her native ability, opportunities to become educated, and peer group. Occupational success means working regularly, assuming responsibility on the job, and dealing effectively with job crises. Interpersonal success refers to the ability to develop and sustain interpersonal relationships, both casual and intimate.

More important for therapists' immediate interventions are the cross-sectional indicators of ego strength. They are:

1. *Intactness of biological systems.* Disturbances in vegetative functioning are often clues of marked impairment of ego strength. They in-

clude profound *changes* in appetite (too much or too little), weight (too much or too little), sleep (too much or too little), and energy (too much or too little). Because many young women with anorexia nervosa fit all of the AVIS criteria, it is easy to assume they have great ego strength, but the life-threatening changes in biological systems found in such individuals suggest that such is not the case *at the moment*. The same is often true of manic patients.

Intactness of biological systems also includes cognitive intactness. Organic impairment of the ability to receive, process, and express or act on information all profoundly affect ego strength. Thus, one cannot engage in psychotherapy with a delirious person. Mildly demented persons still have the ability to learn, and may profit from a therapy that deals with problems of living on a concrete manner. Persons who are intoxicated with alcohol or other drugs, on the other hand, are not able to integrate new information and are best excluded from treatment sessions when intoxicated. Therapists must also consider that persons who are physically ill may be severely ego-depleted despite their premorbid high level of function.

2. Ability to concentrate. Ability to concentrate depends partly on biological maturity and intactness of biological function, but also operates as an independent variable. Defects in concentration are evident in the tangentiality of the manic, the intrusiveness of primary process thought in schizophrenia, and the flightiness of the immature histrionic personality.

3. Contact. Therapists' ability to treat depends on their ability to make meaningful contact with each patient. This is not possible with profoundly depressed, psychotic, mistrustful, or extremely narcissistic persons. Degree of contact is usually measured by patients' responsiveness to therapists' communications and to therapists as human beings. The flow of interviews gives important information about contact. When the flow (after the initial few minutes) continues to be awkwardly paced, when patients do not respond to therapists' requests to continue (or to allow interruption), when eyes do not meet, and smiles are not exchanged, there needs to be concern about the adequacy of contact for verbal psychotherapy.

4. Impulse control. Impulse control is partly a function of physical maturity, partly a function of psychological maturity, and partly a function of biological integrity. Lack of impulse control precludes verbal psychotherapy as a primary treatment modality. Lesser degrees of impaired ego control may allow for combined environmental and verbal therapy. Impulse control seen cross-sectionally is reflected in patients' ability to sit still, to communicate without pacing or gesticulating wildly, and to resist violent impulses toward self or others.

5. Reality testing. Reality testing refers to the ability to clearly identify and accept responsibility for one's own thoughts, feelings, and actions. Persons with impaired reality testing blur the distinction between their own inner experiences and external events, between their thoughts and the thoughts of others, and between their own feelings and feelings they claim have been induced by outside influences over which they have no control. Impaired reality testing is often associated with primary process thinking, but also occurs in persons with severe personality disorders. It includes the ability to recognize that one is ill, that one's thoughts and feelings are peculiar or dangerous, and that the therapist is a potential ally.

6. Ability to assume responsibility. Ability to assume responsibility depends on several of the factors listed above, including intactness of biological systems, cognitive integrity, ability to concentrate, to control impulses, and to test reality. The ability to assume responsibility becomes progressively more impaired as one descends the ladder from mature coping mechanisms to psychotic defense mechanisms, which are essentially the ego's reactions to its inability to effectively encode, process, and act upon the information it receives. Instead, the ego simplifies the encoding and processing functions, reducing the significance of all input to a more easily manageable delusional system or sometimes to incoherent babble.

Clinicians need not rely solely on clinical judgment in estimating ego strength. All of the aspects of ego strength mentioned above can be rated by various means. There are medical tests of biological function ranging from vital signs to vitamin B_{12} levels in plasma. There are tests of cognitive function, such as the Wechsler Adult Intelligence Scale for general intelligence or the Mini-Mental State Examination (Folstein, Folstein, & McHugh, 1975) (see Appendix) to detect organicity. The Minnesota Multiphasic Personality Inventory (MMPI) can provide an overall index of ego strength, as can the Rorschach Test. Instruments such as the Beck Depression Inventory or the Geriatric Depression Scale (Yesavage, Brink, Rose, Lum, Huang, Adey, & Leirer, 1983) (see Appendix) can be used as self-rating assessments.

Changes in ego strength can be evaluated by clinicians' assessment of changes in the parameters listed above and can be confirmed by instruments such as the MMPI, the Brief Psychiatric Rating Scale (Overall and Gorham, 1962) (see Appendix), and the Hamilton Scale for Rating Depression (Hamilton, 1962) (see Appendix). While such quantifications are crude, they give clinicians a more stable and reproducible frame of reference than their purely subjective evaluation.

A note of caution regarding rating scales. They are only as good as the care taken by therapists instructing patients in filling them out (MMPI, Beck, Geriatric Depression Scale) or the expertise of the therapist in administering and scoring them. Even tests that are as simple as the Brief Psychiatric Rating Scale, the Hamilton Rating Scale, and the Mini-Mental State Examination require practice and knowledge of the common conventions in scoring.

The Mental Disorders

The present accepted classification of mental disorders defines them by symptom clusters (American Psychiatric Association, 1980). It does not presuppose underlying dynamic factors, and as such, lacks the uniting thread of earlier classification systems that are less descriptively precise. A dynamic understanding of these disorders is necessary for the psychotherapist, and therefore necessitates moving away from a purely descriptive catalog of symptoms to an inferential system of dynamic factors that form a part of all emotional disorders.

Organic mental disorders. Organic mental disorders such as delirium and the changes in cognitive ability and personality that result from dementia are caused by physical, metabolic, or chemical impairment of ego functioning. They are reversible to the extent that the cause of physical ego impairment can be reversed. They can also be made less symptomatic by reducing environmental, cognitive, and emotional demands on the ego, usually by reducing the complexity of the patients' environment and by encouraging or helping patients to accept their limitations.

Figure 5 shows compromised ego function leading to delirium, the physically-impaired ego's attempt to deal with an incomprehensible environment by using psychotic mechanisms. Note that from a dynamic standpoint, delirium is identical to an acute functional psychosis, whether schizophreniform psychosis, schizophrenia, or mania. Indeed, the

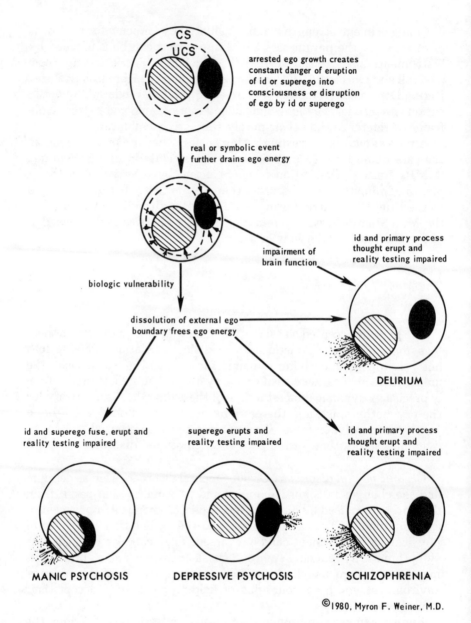

Figure 5. The Psychosis-Prone Ego

treatment of acute functional psychosis is similar to the treatment of delirium; simplifying the environment, reducing the need for decision-making, orienting patients to reality, and administering medications that reduce emotionally induced ego disruptions without clouding the sensorium.

Figure 5 also shows that when there is insufficient energy for repression, id contents erupt at the surface of the ego in the form of primary process thinking, thus impairing the ego's ability to deal with external reality.

Psychotic disorders. Psychotic disorders can be understood dynamically as failure of the ego to repress the contents of the id or the unconscious portion of the superego, which then erupt and impair the ego's ability to stay in contact with culturally determined reality and to distinguish its own contents from external reality.

Whether a schizophreniform psychosis, schizophrenia, or a bipolar affective disorder, psychosis begins with ego impairment that may be acute or chronic and psychological or biological in origin. As shown in Figure 5, when the factors that impair ego function become sufficiently strong, or when real or symbolic psychological events provide the last straw, the compromised ego conserves its energy by releasing unconscious thoughts and feelings that are pressing for discharge. Thus, we see that the circle indicating available ego energy increases in size as the ego abandons its attempts at complete repression of this material, accepts it as reality, and continues to function at a compromised level instead of being totally paralyzed in its attempts to deal with internal and external reality simultaneously.

From a dynamic standpoint, undifferentiated schizophrenia is acceptance by the ego of the id's primary process thinking. In less regressed schizophrenics, the primary process is cloaked by ego-elaborated delusions and hallucinations that explain in secondary process the ego's experience of primary process thinking while removing the responsibility from the ego and projecting it outward on the world in delusions of persecution and in hallucinated accusatory voices.

Affective disorders. When of psychotic proportions, affective disorders can also be described as in Figure 5. When the ego is not so greatly impaired and patients are aware that their mental state is compromised, affective disorders can be understood as an altered relationship between ego and superego, based on predisposing factors in the structure of the superego, as shown in Figure 6, entitled Two Varieties of Normal Character.

The self-satisfied character differs from the self-critical character in the means by which the superego deals with the ego; whether its predominant method of regulating the ego's discharge of id impulses is rewarding self-esteem or punishing guilt. The mechanisms used by the superego are partly composed of introjected parental attitudes, but may also be reactions against those attitudes. It is useful to regard the adult superego's tendencies to reward or punish as relatively fixed (although modifiable) and to see fluctuations in mood as reflections of the ego's reward or punishment by the superego rather than as change in the superego. In the case of self-satisfied character, there is little need for the ego to defend against the superego, but these persons may get into difficulties because they have little motivation for self-examination. Part of the ego's self-examination stems from a need to establish a stable identity, part stems from existential concerns, such as the meaning of one's life, and part of the ego's self-examination is for the purpose of insuring that it is adequately defended against the superego. Total agreement between the superego and the ego is part of the pathology of the narcissistic character.

The self-critical person depicted in Figure 6 often finds the superego a source of difficulty in maintaining self-esteem. The extremely self-critical, nonpsychotic person is often diagnosed clinically as a dysthymic disorder or masochistic character. The fluctuations between exaggerated self-acceptance and self-criticism seen in persons with cyclothymic disorders can be seen as changes in the ego's ability to defend itself against the punishing aspects of the superego.

The pathways that lead to depressive disorders are presented in Figure 7.

The beginning substrate of depression may be a self-critical or masochistic character, a person who can be thought of as characterologically depressed. Depression is often triggered by a real, symbolic, or anticipated failure to live up to a highly cherished goal. An athletic woman who develops arthritis may become depressed because of failure to maintain her former level of activity. Failure to be promoted can devastate a person for whom professional advancement is an important ego ideal. Loss of prestige can be as much a blow as loss of income, and the anticipation of any of these may be treated by the ego as if the event really took place.

Pathological grief extends the mourning process that normally accompanies loss of a loved one into self-reproach and self-accusation.

"IDEAL"

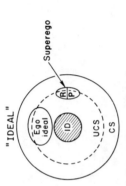

UCS = Unconscious portion of ego

CS = Conscious portion of ego

R   = Rewarding superego attitudes

P   = Punitive superego attitudes

SELF-CRITICAL

Ego development unimpaired

Conformity to ego ideal reinforced by guilt

Behavior compatible with ego ideal

Mildly self-doubting and self-critical

Recognizes standards as one's own

SELF-SATISFIED

Ego development unimpaired

Conformity to ego ideal reinforced by reward

Behavior compatible with ego ideal

Self-accepting

Recognizes standards as one's own

©1979, Myron F. Weiner, M.D.

Figure 6. Two Varieties of Normal Character

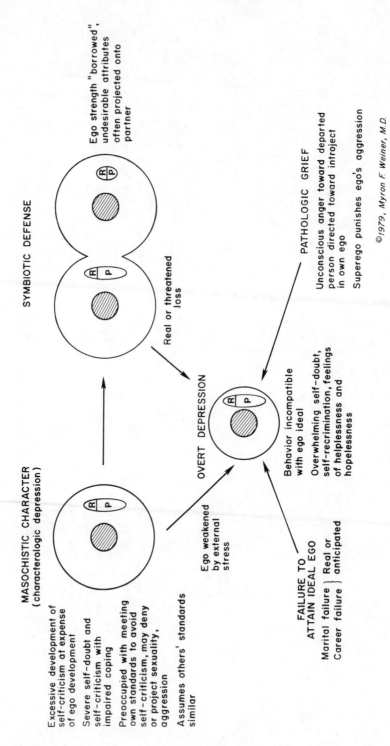

Figure 7. Pathways to Depression

MASOCHISTIC CHARACTER
(characterologic depression)

Excessive development of self-criticism at expense of ego development

Severe self-doubt and self-criticism with impaired coping

Preoccupied with meeting own standards to avoid self-criticism, may deny or project sexuality, aggression

Assumes others' standards similar

SYMBIOTIC DEFENSE

Ego strength "borrowed", undesirable attributes often projected onto partner

Real or threatened loss

OVERT DEPRESSION

Behavior incompatible with ego ideal

Overwhelming self-doubt, self-recrimination, feelings of helplessness and hopelessness

Ego weakened by external stress

FAILURE TO ATTAIN IDEAL EGO
Marital failure } Real or
Career failure } anticipated

PATHOLOGIC GRIEF

Unconscious anger toward departed person directed toward introject in own ego

Superego punishes ego's aggression

©1979, Myron F. Weiner, M.D.

Dynamically, this stems from an attack by the ego on itself. The ego attacks itself because it is punished by the superego for feeling anger toward the person who has departed, and the ego's anger is displaced onto itself, and in particular, those aspects of the self that are introjects of the lost person (Freud, 1917/1957). A manifestation of this process is survivor guilt in which the survivor says, "I was the one who should have died because I have so many less desirable attributes such as generosity, kindness, and so forth."

Figure 7 also points out a frequently adopted defense against a punishing superego: acquiring a friend or mate whose superego serves to balance one's own. A real, symbolic, or threatened loss of that person can also reactivate the punitive aspect of one's own superego and lead to overt depression.

Guilt is frequently associated with depression. It is difficult to know if guilt is a causative factor in depression, or if it results from the paralyzing depressive mood rendering the person unable to satisfy the superego, which then punishes the ego with guilt. Research studies show no strong association between guilt and depression (Silverman, Silverman, & Eardley, 1984). The efficacy of antidepressants suggests that in certain persons guilt results from depressed mood and is not the cause. When antidepressants alleviate depressed mood, guilty rumination stops and patients find it difficult to understand why they were previously so hard on themselves. On the surface, it would appear that psychotherapy might have little to offer where guilt is secondary to altered mood. However, several studies indicate that one type of psychotherapy (cognitive therapy) is as effective as antidepressant medication in moderately depressed outpatients (Murphy, Simons, Wetzel, & Lastman, 1984). Thus, psychological measures can help the ego become aware that the guilt it suffers is irrational, and is possibly the result of a biological predisposition and/or chemical malfunction, and can facilitate a person seeking treatment instead of continuing to suffer or deciding to end the suffering by suicide.

Neurosis. From a dynamic standpoint, neurosis is an acute or chronic compromise by an already compromised ego between the demands of the id and the superego. The ego cloaks the expression of id drives so that they are unrecognized by the superego, and the ego thereby conserves some of the energy that would have been required for repression. The price, however, is the development of a symptom that is alien and uncomfortable to the ego, such as a compulsion, an obsessive thought, or a phobia. For example, a woman who fears punishment by her superego because of her sexual attraction to men may develop a fear of contamination by germs (symbolizing sperm). She may not only avoid dirt phobically, using the mechanism of displacement but may become obsessed with the thought that she is contaminated, and may wash her hands repeatedly and ritualistically to be certain that she has gotten rid of all germs (the mechanism of undoing).

Figure 8, entitled Two Pathways to Neurosis, shows temporary impairment of ego functioning leading to the development of neurotic symptoms such as transient phobias and compulsions. The ego conserves its energy for adaptation by allowing symbolic partial discharge of formerly repressed strivings in a manner acceptable to the superego. The ego bypasses the superego by disguising the impulse, or bribes the superego by suffering guilt for discharge of unacceptable impulses. If partial symbolic discharge does not relieve the pressure of the id on the ego, the ego experiences anxiety. If the impulses discharged are inadequately disguised, the ego feels guilt.

Figure 8 also points out that the ego's energy may be acutely or chronically inadequate to the task of mediating between id and superego. In neurotic disorders, the ego is thought to regress to the defenses and coping styles of the developmental era at which the ego is most strongly fixated (Brenner, 1973).

Psychologically, anxiety disorders and panic disorders can be viewed as the ego's chronic or temporary inability to repress id drives. The resultant pressure of id drives on the unconscious portion of the ego produces anxiety, or if sufficiently intense, panic. In part because there has been no cultivation of additional defense mechanisms and in part because anxiety disorders frequently result from chronic ego weakness in persons with a small repertoire of coping and defense mechanisms, these disorders are often best treated by drugs or by psychological means that reinforce repression.

Chronic ego inadequacy may result from constitutional, environmental, or psychological factors, and is more common than acute ego impairment produced by a traumatic event, for which the new classification of posttraumatic stress disorder is the appropriate term (American Psychiatric Association, 1980).

Posttraumatic stress disorder. These disorders, formerly known as traumatic neuroses, are the simplest (after anxiety disorders) to describe from a psychodynamic point of view. In theory, every person is subject to posttraumatic stress disorder given stimuli of sufficient intensity and duration. However, posttraumatic stress disorders occur rarely in civilian life without significant premorbid predisposition. They are most

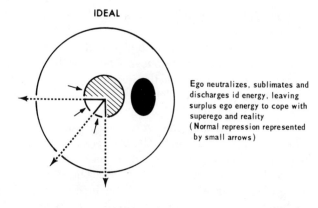

IDEAL

Ego neutralizes, sublimates and discharges id energy, leaving surplus ego energy to cope with superego and reality (Normal repression represented by small arrows)

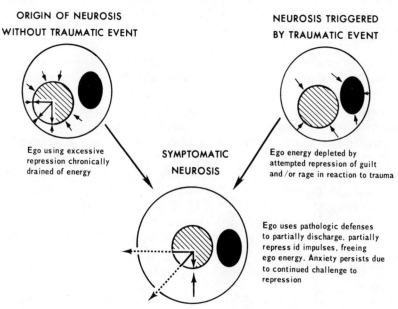

ORIGIN OF NEUROSIS WITHOUT TRAUMATIC EVENT

Ego using excessive repression chronically drained of energy

NEUROSIS TRIGGERED BY TRAUMATIC EVENT

Ego energy depleted by attempted repression of guilt and/or rage in reaction to trauma

SYMPTOMATIC NEUROSIS

Ego uses pathologic defenses to partially discharge, partially repress id impulses, freeing ego energy. Anxiety persists due to continued challenge to repression

Figure 8. Two Pathways to Neurosis

common in military combat, civilian disasters (such as fires or tornados), and concentration camps (Baker, 1980). In all of these situations, the ego is acutely or chronically flooded with overwhelming affects, including anger, fear, and hopelessness. The overwhelming affects are also accompanied by real physical danger and often by actual physical injury. The ego's energy is often depleted by loss of sleep and inadequate nutrition.

The inability of the ego to repress is manifested by repetitive dreams of the traumatic situation as the ego seeks to master the trauma (Freud, 1920/1955). Mastery of trauma by repetition is in part a process of intrapsychic desensitization that reexposes the ego to the same stimuli and attempts to integrate the experience into mental life. If repression occurs before the overwhelming stimulus is adequately integrated, there may be unconscious repetition of the traumatic event in the form of tics or other habitual patterns of behavior.

Personality disorder. When the ego accepts and accommodates itself to id drives that are unacceptable to society at large, when it permanently changes the aim and object of certain drives, or when it adopts styles of interpersonal behavior that further cripple personality development by narrowing its repertoire of interpersonal behaviors or failing to develop an adequate repertoire, we may speak of the existence of a personality disorder (see Figure 9).

Personality disorders generally solidify in early adulthood. Reality testing in the individual with a personality disorder is basically intact, and any discomfort suffered by the ego is indirect and secondary to the effect that the personality disorder has on the individual's interpersonal relationships. People with personality disorders are often distressed by the fact that others shun them, but more often they are pushed into treatment by other persons who find their behavior particularly distressing.

Thus, a passively agressive teenager may be referred for treatment because of failure to do homework assignments, resulting in academic failure; similarly, a passively aggressive adult factory worker may be referred for treatment because of chronic absenteeism or tardiness.

A diagram of the psychic apparatus found in all personality disorders resembles the diagram of the prepsychotic personality depicted in Figure 5. Despite compromised ego function, persons with personality disorders are probably not prone to psychosis unless they have a genetic predisposition for schizophrenia or an affective disorder. Persons with personality disorders can develop transient psychotic symptoms (such

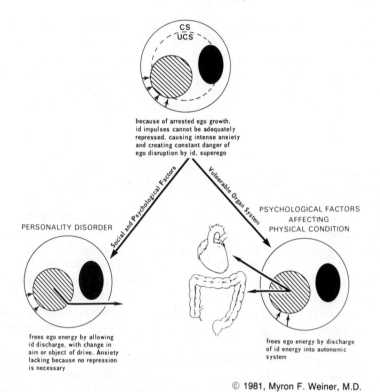

because of arrested ego growth,
id impulses cannot be adequately
repressed, causing intense anxiety
and creating constant danger of
ego disruption by id, superego

PERSONALITY DISORDER

PSYCHOLOGICAL FACTORS
AFFECTING
PHYSICAL CONDITION

frees ego energy by allowing
id discharge, with change in
aim or object of drive. Anxiety
lacking because no repression
is necessary

frees ego energy by discharge
of id energy into autonomic
system

© 1981, Myron F. Weiner, M.D.

Figure 9. Personality Disorder and Psychological Factors
Affecting Physical Condition

as schizophreniform psychosis) under severe stress, but reconstitute when the stress is removed.

Each personality disorder reflects a different psychological or interpersonal dynamic. The general dynamic schema is presented in Figure 9. Paranoid personalities change the source of their aggressive drive, seeing themselves as the object of others' aggression and justifying their own aggression against others as appropriate self-defense. The schizoid personality defends against id drives by failing to develop the capacity for forming interpersonal relationships; the avoidant personality averts narcissistic injury by withdrawing from situations of potential risk to self-esteem. The histrionic personality is comfortable with self-dramatization. Narcissistic personalities have the complete approval of their superego and are unaware that others can be troubled by their behavior or demands. The antisocial personality's underdeveloped superego allows the discharge of all impulses under any circumstance and his or her insufficient ego also makes conforming to others' standards of behavior difficult. The dependent personality discharges aggression by clinging, while the passive-aggressive personality converts aggression into its opposite. The compulsive personality employs the mechanism of undoing as a means to combat undesirable impulses, and the masochistic character turns his or her aggression against the self either directly or through stimulating the aggression of others. The borderline personality maintains its fluidity and uses the entire range of mental mechanisms and coping styles, but with little success because of their inconsistent application.

In considering the treatment of personality disorders, therapists raise four questions. What is the nature of this patient's motivation for treatment? Is the individual seeking personal help or relief from the complaints of others? How severely is the ego compromised? Absence of psychosis does not mean that adequate ego strength exists. Can the person's means of defense or coping be made sufficiently ego-alien to make them susceptible to change through behavioral means or insight? Finally, is there sufficient support for change in the individual's environment?

Paraphilias. The paraphilias change the aim or object of the sexual drive. In the voyeur, the aim of the sexual drive is changed from sexual penetration to visual penetration, while in the exhibitionist sexual display is substituted for penetration. Transsexualism is a complicated disorder in which the person seeks to change his or her entire self into a person of the opposite sex; this disorder thus constitutes an identity disorder and not merely an alteration in aim or object of libidinal drive. Transvestism and fetishism almost always occur in men. In the former, heterosexual excitement is enhanced by dressing in women's clothing; in the latter, the aim and the object of the sexual drive is changed from penetration of the female genitals to possession of an article of clothing. Sexual sadism and masochism result from fusion of the sexual and aggressive drives which are then directed against others or the self, and in pedophilia and zoophilia the aim of the sexual drive is changed and redirected toward children and animals, respectively. Homosexuality can be viewed as a fear of the genitals or other attributes of the opposite sex that is dealt with by a learned attraction to the genitals of same-sexed persons which is exactly analogous to the development of heterosexuality.

The paraphilias are difficult to treat not only because they are ego-syntonic but because they involve alternate sources of sexual pleasure that substitute for pleasure blocked by fear of heterosexual adult genital union.

Psychological factors affecting physical condition. There is little doubt that emotions play a significant role in precipitating many physical disorders, and often help to sustain or aggravate them. A linear model of the role of emotions in physical disorders is presented in Figure 9. However, it is unlikely that a simple linear relationship occurs between an emotional state and a physical disorder, or between a specific emotional conflict and a physical disorder. (Reiser, 1975). In all physical illnesses, there is an interaction between physical, genetic, metabolic, environmental, and psychological factors, as depicted in Figure 10. The pathways by which emotions influence organs outside the central nervous system are indicated in Figure 11. The neuroendocrine concomitants of emotional states that occur in reaction to ideas or events result from input from the cortex to the limbic system of the brain, which in turn stimulates the autonomic and/or endocrine system. Emotional states are thus translated into altered organ function, such as the increased pulse and blood pressure that accompany rage. The different effects of emotional arousal on various organ systems is explained in part by genetically determined susceptibility. For example, serum pepsinogen level, important in peptic ulcer formation, is genetically determined (Mirsky, 1958). Without high serum levels of pepsinogen, peptic ulceration of the stomach and duodenum is unlikely.

Whether prolonged emotional states can cause permanent tissue alteration has not yet been proved, but there is evidence that psychological treatment can influence the course of asthma, ulcerative colitis, and early essential hypertension (Karasu, 1979).

At this stage of our knowledge, it is probably better to consider emotional factors as aggravating rather than causing physical disorders; the influence of a chronic disease such as asthma on psychological development is probably just as important as the influence of emotions on the asthma.

The complex interaction of psychological, social, and physical factors can be shown in obesity, a physical disorder whose development is largely under conscious control (Figure 12). While the cause of obesity is overeating and its cure is reducing food intake, obesity is a complicated disorder. Hunger and unknown genetic factors together with sociocultural, sensory, and emotional factors determine eating behavior. Eating relieves some emotional tensions, but creates others due to the

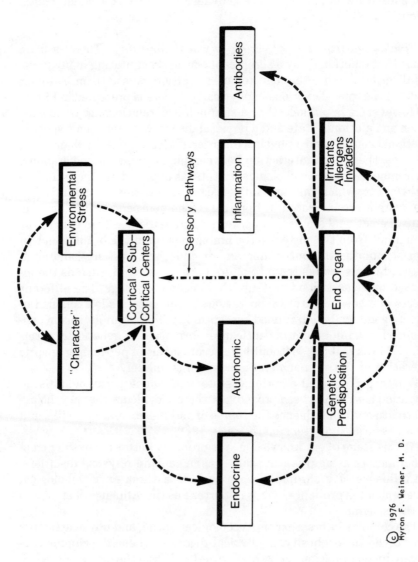

Figure 10. Modifiers of End-Organ Activity

© 1976
Myron F. Weiner, M. D.

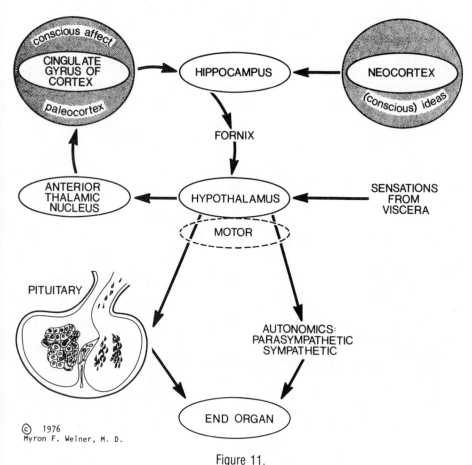

Figure 11.

resulting obesity. However, obesity may represent other gains (see below) in the form of large size and reduced sexual drive, and may also satisfy the ego's need for punishment. Given these complicating factors, it is not hard to understand why the treatment of obesity fails so often.

Substance use disorders. It is tempting to ascribe deep and significant psychopathology to persons who develop dependence on alcohol or other substances. However, studies of alcoholics show that their psychopathology is as much a product of their alcoholism as it is a predisposing factor (Vaillant, 1981). Other forms of substance abuse such as paint-sniffing or heroin abuse seem more related to complex

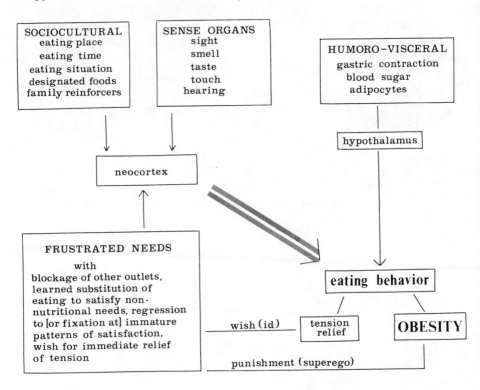

© Myron F. Weiner, 1977

Figure 12. Factors in Overeating and Obesity

social issues than to individual psychopathology (Pattison & Kaufman, 1979). Once use of the substance, whether it is innately addicting or heavily socially reinforced, becomes established, the disorders seen clinically stem from that substance abuse. The initial treatment, then, is not dealing with the psychopathology that underlies the symptom of drug use, but bringing about withdrawal of the substance through whatever means are available and acceptable.

Returning to the definition of psychological illness, we find that there is an adaptive gain to the compromise that is reached by the psychic apparatus. Certain problems can be dealt with, although less flexibly. The gain of reducing intrapsychic conflict has been referred to as the *primary gain* of the altered psychological state. In addition, all illnesses present the possibility of *secondary gain*; some positive influence on the environment or input from the environment that results from the illness, such as the entrapment of certain people and the reassurance of their continued nurturance. Monetary compensation is often available as well. In many instances, the secondary gain is a more important sustaining factor than the primary intrapsychic cause of the psychological disorder.

THERAPEUTIC AXIOMS

I find the following axioms useful guides in assessing psychopathology and treating patients.

1. Ego development does not occur spontaneously. It requires stimulation by reward, frustration, and modeling. Persons who are unrewarded and unchallenged by their environment, and who lack models of appropriate coping, may fail to develop their psychological resources.

2. Intrapsychic change is generally not possible unless environmental change is possible. An intrapsychic change cannot come about unless the environment will support that change, and when there is great secondary gain, that may need to be addressed before the psychological disorder can be treated.

3. The form of a symptom is a less important predictor of change than the person's baseline ego strength. Well-functioning persons who suffer a transient psychotic disorder under extreme stress may be more amenable to psychological treatment than slightly anxious persons with few work or interpersonal skills.

4. Psychopathology is almost never entirely fixed. Chronic schizophrenics have been enabled to leave institutions after many years through stimulation of hope (Rogers, Gendlin, Kiesler, & Truax, 1967). Chronic alcoholics have rehabilitated themselves and led exemplary lives (Vaillant, 1981). Much of the intractability of illness depends on the context in which it occurs and in which help is sought. Much of treatment success depends on a unique patient–therapist interaction. Therefore, it is frequently not possible to predict who will respond to what kind of treatment, and these guidelines can be regarded only as rough rules of thumb.

5. Patients influence their therapists more than we would like to believe, and therapists attempt to avoid certain issues by disapproving of their expression or ignoring them so patients will stop bringing them up (Singer & Luborsky, 1977). The central issue for therapists is less one of whether patients have treatable psychopathology, but by

whom patients can be treated, by what method, and under what circumstances.

6. Psychotherapy does not cure. Psychotherapy shifts intrapsychic forces that can always shift again toward maladaptive patterns in life's flow of intrapsychic and interpersonal events. A positive psychotherapeutic result is a new equilibrium. Given enough force of the right type, that equilibrium can be disturbed.

CHAPTER 4

The Elements of Psychotherapy

All psychotherapies involve a designated helper who is accepted by and meets with a help-seeker in a series of formal, structured meetings.

In addition, there are elements common to all psychological therapies; they are listed in Table 2. When blended differently, these elements form treatment techniques that vary greatly in their conduct and application. After having decided to emphasize certain therapeutic elements, therapists use the other elements of therapy as they seem indicated to expedite the flow of the general type of treatment chosen. And, of course, no choice of therapeutic technique is absolute. Therapists can change their technique, after properly dealing with their patients' reactions, to one they both expect to be more useful.

Although several therapeutic elements, such as catharsis and giving patients encouragement to face emotional issues, are highly valued by many therapists, there is no objective evidence that any single therapeutic element has greater potency than others. As noted in Chapter 1, there is a persistent tendency to regard interpretations that lead to patients' development of insight into their unconscious dynamics as the only truly mutative element of psychotherapy (Wallace, 1983). The other elements of the psychotherapeutic process are held to be stepping stones toward preparing patients to accept interpretations and develop curative insights. Patients whose symptoms are relieved by catharsis are no more or less cured than persons who develop insight or who respond to a program of behavior modification. A more balanced (and more realistic) view of the elements of psychotherapy is that one cannot predict for a given patient what element or what combination of psychotherapeutic elements will be most important. It is therefore imperative

TABLE 2
Elements of Psychotherapy

Interaction
Stimulation of hope
Stimulation of cooperation
Suggestion
Command
Manipulation
Education, including information-giving and role-playing
Encouraging the development of external support for new
    behaviors
Reframing
Encouragement to face emotional issues
Facilitation of catharsis
Positive reinforcement
Negative reinforcement
Desensitization
Feedback
Promotion of identification
Insight
Attribution of meaning
Testing of perceptions
Working through, including behavior rehearsal
Dealing with transference and countertransference

that therapists understand and be able to use each of the elements of psychotherapy to the extent that any given patient is able to profit from it.

INTERACTION

The basis of psychotherapy is cognitive, emotional, and behavioral *interaction* between therapists and patients. The quality and quantity of interaction are determined by therapists after evaluating patients' need for interaction, and the type of interaction most needed and best tolerated. They are also determined by the unique, specific blend of personalities that occur in a group or dyadic therapy, and are influenced by a host of environmental, physiological, psychological, and social factors.

There must be sufficient interaction for patients to feel involvement with their therapist, but sufficient sensitivity on the part of therapists to not traumatize persons for whom interaction implies the threat of destruction, engulfment, esteem-threatening competition, or seduction. The interaction must be sufficient to help patients produce historical information, feelings, or behavior that can be dealt with in the therapeutic situation. In some cases, interaction must be minimized to help patients contain their feelings and behavior, and in other cases to keep the thinking of patients from becoming disrupted by primary process material.

STIMULATION OF HOPE

All psychotherapies offer the *hope* of changing patients' thoughts, feelings, behavior, or environment. Hope is tacitly implied by accepting patients for psychological treatment, but hope may be actively cultivated at certain times by pointing out patients' gains in therapy or affirming that the possibility of change does exist. Active instillation of hope and reassurance that patients will improve are important in treating severe depression as a means of temporarily counteracting patients' sense of hopelessness until physical or chemical treatments take effect. Promises of cure, on the other hand, may contribute to patients' magical expectations of therapy and diminish their participation or raise their expectations to impossible levels. Hope may be defended against by patients who have had earlier hopes dashed. In these instances, it may be helpful if therapists point out patients' actual resistance to hope and help separate past situations from the present therapeutic situation (French, 1958).

COOPERATION

Cooperation is also part of all psychotherapies. Cooperation is often considered to refer to the patient's working within the therapist's conceptual framework, but this view of cooperation greatly limits the possibilities of the therapeutic interaction. Cooperation is better defined as the establishment by the therapist of a frame of reference that enables patients to cooperate. This means that therapists may need to have more than one frame of reference available for therapeutic use, and, on occasion, requires that therapists accept patients completely on the patients' own terms.

Some of the most dramatic examples of meeting patients on their own terms to therapeutic advantage have been reported by psychiatrist–hypnotist Milton Erickson. In one instance, a woman whose three marriages had ended in disaster sought treatment only for the purpose of eliminating a sensation of coldness in her buttocks. Erickson accepted her terms, and through concentration on eliminating that symptom was able to help her make widespread improvement in her life (Rossi, 1980).

Cooperation is based on therapists offering realistic hope to patients that they will change, coupled with a treatment approach that patients can understand or will accept. Patients need not always understand the treatment approach to cooperate adequately, as the following example indicates.

A female mental health worker who had been treated in a hospital by stimulating repressed affect and uncovering repressed childhood conflicts failed to improve after several months. She was then transferred to another facility in which she was engaged in the ward milieu and was treated with antidepressant medication. When referred for outpatient follow-up, she was told by her new therapist that they would not focus on her feelings or on her childhood conflicts at first. Rather, they would focus on her day-to-day problems and functioning. She was puzzled and wondered if this approach meant that she was too ill to develop self-understanding. The therapist replied that it was important to take first things first. After she was coping adequately with her day-to-day problems, they would tackle deeper issues if she wished, or if it seemed necessary. She agreed to focus on her current problems in living and was pleased as she felt more in control of herself instead of being overwhelmed by her feelings. She stabilized rapidly, and was soon able to return to work.

As indicated above, part of the process of cooperation is *focusing*; this refers to therapist and patient together selecting or agreeing on an area to explore or a behavior pattern to change. The patient's attention is thus concentrated instead of being scattered or diverted from important issues. The act of focusing is a positive coping mechanism. In addition, it gives patients a sense of direction and control. This control may be perceived by patients as self-control or as control by the therapist, depending on their need to feel in control or to feel guided.

When patients focus on unproductive subjects, therapists have to find a means to get them to focus on more productive topics, as was done in the case above. The simplest means of accomplishing this is to gently interrupt patients and to change the subject without an elaborate explanation.

Patients ordinarily appreciate expert guidance. Those who react negatively may need to examine their resistance to changing focus; especially, patients may need to note the areas in which they are unwilling to examine or to act. In the case of the mental health worker described in the above vignette, an explanation was necessary because the therapist's treatment technique differed so greatly from the patient's earlier therapy and the type of therapy that she valued most highly.

SUGGESTION

Suggestion refers to proposing to patients a course of action to be followed during or outside of formal psychotherapeutic sessions. It ranges from formal hypnosis to advice-giving. Patients can be encouraged to fantasize, or to feel a particular emotion deeply during a therapeutic visit, or therapists can suggest activities in patients' daily lives, such as increased socialization or becoming more assertive. Therapists' suggestion-making asserts that patients are in control of their behavior and have the final choice, but gives patients the benefit of therapists' expertise in determining a course of action.

For example, a socially inhibited woman who wished to date, but was fearful of men, was encouraged to first socialize with other women. By making female friends, she felt less pushed to date as a means to alleviate loneliness, and began to practice her social skills in a nonthreatening environment.

In making suggestions, therapists whose patients have adequate superegos generally avoid telling them what *should* or *ought to* or *must* be done. When therapists use those terms, patients' actions become governed by guilt (why didn't I do as I *should?*) instead of by choice, and self-punishment is increased instead of self-awareness and a repertoire of constructive behaviors. In promoting increased socialization, for example, therapists can assert instead that becoming more socially outgoing is a reasonable and less lonely alternative to social isolation, and that it might be worth trying. In all cases, when making suggestions therapists defer to patients' judgment and take into account patients' ability to follow the suggestions at the time they are offered.

Permission is a form of suggestion that takes advantage of patients projecting their superego onto the therapist. This projection is a common feature of all therapeutic relationships and occurs in mob formation (Freud, 1921/1955) to an even greater extent than in a therapeutic relationship. Just as a mob allows individuals to act out otherwise prohibited thoughts and feelings, therapists, acting as a surrogate superego, enable patients to express thoughts, feelings, and behavior formerly withheld because of guilt. Psychoanalysts ordinarily deal with superego projection by interpretation (Greenson, 1967). Nonanalytic therapists can take advantage of this opportunity to modify patients' superego by giving permission to do what was formerly forbidden (Pierce, Nichols, & DuBrin, 1983). Once the thought or feeling is expressed, or the act performed, and the ego finds itself unpunished, it feels freer to express itself; it is positively rewarded by the absence of guilt.

Permissions can be as simple as, "It's okay to think about sex," or "I give you permission to be angry," or "You have my permission to try out the assertive behavior that you have learned in your sessions with me."

Patients may be taken aback or may feel diminished by being given their therapist's permission. Noting the twinkle in the therapist's eyes, they usually understand the "as if" nature of the permission and are able to take it seriously without feeling belittled. The following case illustrates permission giving.

Mrs. A. A. C., a 73-year-old woman who had completed a successful psychoanalysis years earlier sought treatment because she was operating at a pace entirely too rapid for her own comfort and because she was becoming very irritable as well. The woman had maintained her feelings of self-worth by giving generously of her time to various volunteer projects. The therapist guessed that her overactivity was a form of expiating guilt, but instead of attempting to first discover and deal with the source of her guilt, he began grinning. The woman asked what he was grinning about and he replied, "All you need is permission." She was puzzled. He said, "I will give you permission to slow down." She failed to see how that would do any good. He explained that he was aware of a carry over of positive feelings from her physician-father and her former analyst that he could capitalize on to help her slow down.

She was pleasantly surprised to find that she was able to slow down and then began discussing the conscious source of her guilt, which turned out to be a romantic involvement.

The therapist chose permission-giving over analyzing because he felt that her analyzing would result in endless rumination and intellectualization. He made use of the transference situation, later explored with the patient the source of her guilt, and still later, the source of her irritation and anger.

COMMAND

In rare instances, therapists can take a step beyond suggestion and *command* patients to act or refrain from action. *Commands* are usually ineffective unless therapists have some physical or emotional control over their patients, or take patients by surprise. For example, a suicidal woman may be so surprised by a therapist's command not to jump from a window that she may hesitate long enough to be rescued or to allow the part of her that wants to live to act on her behalf. A therapist can command an obstreperous teenager to stay in the room and talk instead of running away or can command a psychiatric inpatient to stop agitating a fellow patient. In those cases, the control over patients may come from the institution to which patients are confined or from the force of therapists' personalities. Although useful in overcoming some forms of negativism, and on occasion, lifesaving, as in the above example, commands are seldom used in psychotherapy because a command sets therapists over patients and in opposition to them. Both positions can undermine the possibility of developing a cooperative relationship.

MANIPULATION

Manipulation has the advantage over suggestion that it does not require a cooperative relationship with patients, and has the advantage over commands that it does not openly set therapists against patients. It is a form of covert behavior modification. A manipulation is an indirect means to enable or to stimulate patients to act or to think in a certain way. A common manipulation is playing into patients' negativism. Teenagers who threaten not to go to school can be dealt with by saying that it's up to them if they pass or flunk, and that if they choose to stay out of school, nobody can stop them. If the therapist refuses to do battle over it, there is little strength to the patient's threat. Another type of manipulation is paradoxical intervention; encouraging patients to do something they claim not to want to do. In the following example, a teenager was encouraged to deny his own behavior.

A 13-year-old boy was told to clean his room thoroughly once a month. He invariably did a sloppy job but denied it, and felt angry and resentful that his mother called him a storyteller.

The therapist prescribed the same sequence of behavior with an important change. The boy was told to clean his room but leave one part dirty so that when his mother "caught" him he could do it over easily. The mother was told to do a military-style inspection. After her inspection she was to guess what the boy did not do properly. The boy had been told to make her job as difficult as possible by leaving something she would never guess, such as dirt in a corner, or a book out of place. The boy was told that even if his mother guessed correctly, he was to deny it and tell her it was something else which he was not to do over. By building denial into this situation, the therapist prescribed what happened and averted a power struggle. The boy could win by doing a good job of cleaning and leaving a less obvious part of the work undone (Weeks & L'Abate, 1982, p. 117).

Compulsive handwashers can be encouraged to wash their hands at fixed intervals at greater frequency than their ordinary handwashing routines. Washing hands at fixed intervals begins to bring patients' behavior under their own control, and as they feel more in control of their symptoms, the symptoms frequently abate.

Manipulation, like command, is of limited use because patients soon learn that they are being manipulated and come to mistrust their therapists. Therefore, manipulation tends to be most useful in emergencies or short-term treatment situations.

EDUCATION

Education is the imparting of information to patients for the purpose of augmenting ego function. That information can be used to improve ego function in many ways; as reassurance, or as a means of dealing with the superego, with id drives, or with the external environment. Patients can be educated to understand that their palpitations are due to emotionally determined anxiety attacks, and not dangerous cardiac disorders. Persons whose superegos demand self-reliance can be assured that seeking help is a sign of strength and not evidence of weakness. Fathers who are frightened by their attraction to teenage daughters can be assured that their feelings are normal; they need only control their actions. And, persons who lack social skills can be taught constructive ways to approach others.

To be effective educators, therapists need a variety of educational techniques and tools so that they can present information in a manner that patients can grasp. For some patients, that means therapists assigning reading or homework. These strategies are commonly employed by cognitive/behavior therapists in helping patients recognize and correct their cognitive distortions (Beck, 1976). Different therapists are better educators using one medium than another. Some are more adept at verbal explanations; others make better use of visually presented diagrams. Berne (1961) recommended using a blackboard to show ego states and to diagram transactions. Slides, videotapes, and movies can also be used.

Patients may be educated by direct instruction or by a process that encourages them to use their ability to understand. For example, patients can be taught that behaving courteously toward others facilitates others meeting their needs. Or, they can be allowed to experience the impact of their lack of courtesy by role-playing with their therapists.

Role-playing enables patients to gain an understanding of their impact on others, particularly if asked to play the role of people toward whom they have strong feelings they cannot express directly.

ENCOURAGING THE DEVELOPMENT OF EXTERNAL SUPPORT FOR NEW BEHAVIORS

Behavior is partially determined by the context in which it occurs. Observers of relational systems find that spouses (Martin, 1976) and other family members (Glick & Kessler, 1980) stimulate and help to maintain the maladaptive behavioral styles of the designated patients in their marital or family systems. Friends come to expect Jim to be a worrier or Julie to be shy, and thereby reinforce their behavior.

Part of the therapist's job is to encourage the development of supports for more adaptive ways of thinking and behaving outside of the therapeutic relationship. Supports outside the therapeutic relationship are important because they reduce patients' dependence on their therapists and enable patients to eventually separate from formal therapy. Masserman (1980) recommends that therapists actively intervene in their patients' families and social networks. Mobilizing external supports may mean that the patient works on developing new friendships, or may require making available to the patient the more formal support of a day hospital or a therapy group. Support can also be mobilized by helping those persons in patients' immediate environment to change their attitudes toward them and their expectations of them.

REFRAMING

Reframing is viewing a thought, feeling, or situation from a perspective that enables patients to be less self-critical and to take constructive action. In reframing, therapists may reinterpret qualities patients see as weakness as strength, those patients view as loss as gain, or those seen by patients as signs of crisis as being harbingers of opportunity.

From an intrapsychic standpoint, therapists' reframing statements enable patients' egos to avoid an aspect of the superego or the ego ideal that inhibits adequate functioning. For example, a woman who sought therapy because of phobic symptoms spent her sessions in self-criticism because of her weakness. Her ego-ideal of independence was threatened, and her superego criticized her for being less self-reliant. The therapist reframed her symptoms as a reaction to a traumatic event; her seeking therapy as a sign of strength, not weakness; and her coming to therapy as an opportunity to work out some long-standing interpersonal difficulties. Following is an example in which reframing was used to advantage.

> A mental health professional sought additional help from his ex-analyst to deal with a marital crisis that had developed after more than 20 years of what the patient had thought a successful marriage. His analyst was able to instill hope and to ease his ex-patient's discouragement by reframing the situation thus: "You and your wife have been courting for 20 years. Now you're trying to decide whether or not to get married."

ENCOURAGEMENT TO FACE EMOTIONAL ISSUES

Encouragement to face emotional issues is an important aspect of psychotherapy. The mechanisms of defense described earlier (see pp. 36–41) are all means by which the ego avoids facing issues. Therapists determine which issues patients have motivation and strength enough to face, which are relevant, and then decide how best to encourage their patients to face them.

CATHARSIS

Catharsis is the expression of thoughts and feelings that were formerly withheld from expression, and is the treatment of choice in some emotional disorders that result from temporary overwhelming of the ego by a massive psychological trauma, such as witnessing a fire in which one's best friend dies, causing an accident in which a loved one is severely injured, or the experience of rape. In these cases, the ego is flooded with affect that it cannot release. Catharsis is a good way to drain off dammed-up emotions, and gives immediate and dramatic relief (Lindemann, 1944).

A prerequisite for effective catharsis is that patients have sufficient superego development to force the ego to suppress or repress thoughts or feelings through stimulation of guilt. The confession of theft by persons with antisocial personalities has no psychotherapeutic effect, because there was no suppression of thought or feeling in relation to the act.

The process of catharsis embodies several other processes, including symbolic projection outward of unwanted aspects of one's self (Nichols & Zax, 1977), an appeal to a higher power for acceptance, and a hope for transformation by magic after symbolically offering up a part of one's self. It can also be the beginning of self-expression in an interpersonal context (Weiner, 1977).

Catharsis is initiated by establishing an atmosphere of acceptance and then asking patients to relive traumatic events in as much detail as possible. Caution must be exercised so that patients' egos do not become further overwhelmed. If therapists sense that patients' feelings are becoming too intense (signaled by hyperventilation, panic, or dissociation), patients can be asked to relax, to shut out the frightening thoughts, or to calm down by imagining a pleasant scene.

Catharsis is generally not encouraged in repressive therapies because the emotional intensity of catharsis temporarily blurs reality testing. Repressive therapies therefore generally avoid intense affect and encourage the development of rational solutions to problems in living.

By contrast, catharsis can be employed effectively at an ego-supportive or evocative level as the following example from feeling-expressive therapy illustrates:

Barbara: I'm not feeling that good about myself these days. I keep wondering if you're thinking critical thoughts about me. (Pause, then somewhat angrily.) If you could just say something reassuring to me, that would help!
Therapist: What would you like to hear from me?
Barbara: That you like me, that you like working with me. (Pause.) That you think I'm handling my grief very well. (Starting to cry.) That you think I'm doing well. (Crying harder.) That I'm doing well! (Barbara has been rubbing her head with her hand. She's crying fairly hard now, but not sobbing.)

Therapist: What's your left hand doing?

Barbara: (Still rubbing her head.) It's loving me! It's saying, "I'm doing well." (Barbara cries for a minute or two and slowly stops, sits quietly for 30 seconds or so and looks up.)

Therapist: What's up?

Barbara: I distracted myself. I started thinking about junk.

Therapist: What junk?

Barbara: Oh, what I'll do when I leave here, and about your bill. It's high this month.

Therapist: (Teasingly.) Hope you're getting your money's worth.

Barbara: (Suddenly angry.) I'm not today! I ask you for some reassurance and I get shit! "Reassure yourself," you tell me. Bunch of shit! (Reaching back and hitting the mat behind her vigorously and with both arms alternately.) Goddamn it! That's not what I wanted. It's not what I wanted! (Hits, flails, kicks, yells. Her anger no longer seemed to be focused on the therapist.)

Therapist: What's going on?

Barbara: (Still angry.) That's just the way *she* was. She was there most of the time, but when I needed her most, she wasn't there. Everybody said she was so good. I couldn't criticize her. When she wasn't there, I didn't even think "Where are you?" I just tuned out and got depressed. (Speaking rapidly.) I literally didn't know what hit me. (Pause.) I know what hit me! You did! (Talking to her mother.) With your goodness and all your compassion, where were you when I came home from camp? Off at some goddamn meeting saving the world! What about me? You sent me away for the whole summer and you weren't even there when I got home! (Rising tone, very angry, hitting the mat, kicking, yelling.) You weren't even there when I got home! You weren't there! Aunt Louise was there. That was supposed to make it all right. Well, it didn't! Where were you? (Now Barbara begins to cry and then sob. She continues to hit the mat, but more slowly, softly and aimlessly.) Where were you? Oh shit!

(Barbara cries for 5 to 10 minutes, saying only a few words: "Ohhh!" "I wanted you." "Where were you?" She was still lying on her back on the mat. She stopped gradually, sobbing less, crying softly. She opened her eyes, looked at her therapist, and said, "Hi." The tempo in the next exchange was much slower and quieter – the calm after the storm.)

Therapist: Hi. (Pause.)

Barbara: Jeeze. (Pause.)

Therapist: What?

Barbara: I sure was mad at her.

Therapist: Mm-hm.

Barbara: I didn't know. I needed her so much . . . that I actually hurt so much about the time she wasn't there . . . I guess the message was, "How could you find fault with your mother? Everybody knows how good she is." (Pause.) And she was, too, in lots of ways.

Therapist: If she hadn't been, you probably wouldn't miss her so much.

Barbara: Yeah. I guess so. (Starts crying again softly.) Boy, I do miss her. I can't get used to the idea that she's gone. She's just not here anymore. She's not in the hospital, she's not in Westfield, she's not in her house. She's not really in the cemetery. Just gone. (Pause. Then to the therapist.) I was pretty pissed at you for awhile! (Laughing.) Looks like you survived.

Therapist: Yeah. (Pause.) So my not giving you what you wanted brought you right back to the old days.

Barbara: Yeah, and more so probably cause you both (therapist and mother) did give me what I wanted most of the time. It's like a shock. (Pause.) Sounds like I have it in me to get very mad at people who take pretty good care of me most of the time – like you and her. That could be tough on those closest to me. Brian (Barbara's boyfriend) said something like that to me yesterday. He said most of the time I love him well, am appreciative of him, and everything, but then suddenly I'll fly off the handle and act like he was this big disappointment. (Pause.) Sounds like maybe I've got a little mother stuff with him.

Therapist: Could be. (Lightly.) Next time you're mad at him, you could explain that it's only 'cause he loves you so well that you get so mad. He's part of a very exclusive club.

Barbara: Right. "You only hurt the one you love." Lucky him!

Therapist: He is lucky. You have a lot to give (Pierce, Nichols, & DuBrin, 1983, pp. 7–9).

The vignette above also illustrates the notion that catharsis completes an interrupted emotional action sequence (Pierce, Nichols, & DuBrin, 1983). In the context of the relationship with her therapist, the patient relived in the present feelings she had experienced toward her mother. Catharsis in this situation was followed by the therapist's reframing statement, "Next time you're mad at him, you could explain that it's only 'cause he loves you so well that you get so mad. He's part of a very exclusive club." The therapist's last statement is a direct affirmation of the patient's ability to love – focusing on a positive attribute instead of her negative quality of distancing those whom she loves.

The example above also describes a physical component to catharsis. The patient was sitting on a mat which she struck repeatedly as she ventilated her anger toward her mother. The physical component of catharsis has been emphasized by many authors (Schutz, 1967; Keleman, 1971; Pierce, Nichols, & DuBrin, 1983) as an important way to help patients experience and express their emotions more fully. The same note of caution is to be sounded for physical expression of emotion as for catharsis in general. Engaging in action may temporarily suspend rational judgment and may result in acting out instead of the recognition and integration of feelings.

POSITIVE REINFORCEMENT

Most persons find affirmation such as the above affirmation by Barbara's therapist to be a powerful positive reinforcer, just as lack of affirmation or criticism is a powerful negative reinforcer. Patients' behavior during and outside of therapeutic sessions is partly regulated by therapists' positive and negative reinforcement. *Positive reinforcement* refers to therapists' rewarding or encouraging certain behavior. Patients may be encouraged to freely express feelings during a therapy session or may be encouraged to focus attention on the therapist–patient interaction. Positive reinforcement shapes patients' behaviors and is accomplished by therapists communicating their approval and interest in what patients are saying or doing. Therapists can also shape patients' behavior by *negative reinforcement*, which can be simple failure to provide positive reinforcement. Other types of negative reinforcement are actively changing the subject or telling patients that they are discussing unproductive topics and suggesting potentially more productive subjects for discussion.

Attempting to call patients' attention to maladaptive patterns of living before establishing a positive therapeutic relationship often serves as a negative reinforcer; not of the behavior, but of patients' communicating material to their therapists for which they might possibly be criticized.

DESENSITIZATION

Almost any approach in which patients discuss fears or anxieties contains an element of *desensitization*: reduction of the fear-producing quality of a thought, experience, or feeling through repeated direct or symbolic exposure. Persons who are frightened by the intensity of their anger may be partially desensitized by talking about their anger and by seeing that no damage has been done to themselves or anyone else through expressing their anger. Desensitization can also be carried out in a formal way as behavior therapy.

FEEDBACK

Feedback is an important aspect of ego-supportive therapy that entails therapists informing patients about their behavior as it affects the therapists in the here and now. That frequently involves disclosure of feelings, such as therapists telling patients that they are reacting to certain behaviors with anger. This type of feedback is specifically indicated for persons with interpersonal difficulties who have difficulty understanding the impact of their behavior on others (Weiner, 1982b). It is applied with the same caveat as positive and negative reinforcement; it must be presented in a context (usually a positive therapist–patient relationship) that allows it to be experienced as acceptance instead of criticism. If there has been no development of patient's capacity for self-observation, feedback is experienced as disapproval, as an admonition to stop a certain behavior, or as approval of that behavior.

The purpose of feedback is to stimulate reflection – to alert patients to the interpersonal antecedents and effects of their behavior. It encourages thinking in terms of interpersonal cause and affect and generally develops patients' ability to consider their thoughts and feelings before acting on them. In some cases, it develops their ability to communicate certain types of feelings, as illustrated in the following example.*

Patient: I'm tired of playing Superman!
Therapist: So why keep it up?
Patient: People don't really want to know what troubles you. They don't want to know when you feel down and weak.
Therapist: Do you ever feel that way?
Patient (softly): Yeah, most of the time.
Therapist: I see.
(a few moments later)
Patient: When I told you how emotionally helpless I feel so much of the time, I was surprised at your response.

---

*J. Schimel, personal communication. 1982.

Therapist: How so?
Patient: I expected you to be disgusted.
Therapist: And how did I respond?
Patient: You still seemed to like me.
Therapist: That's right, I do. In fact, I like you better when you can admit human feelings instead of playing Superman. I never really thought you were perfect, anyway.
Patient (laughs): I guess nobody else does either.
Therapist (smiles): Right on!

In the example above, the therapist responds positively to the patient's expression of feelings and opens the door for the patient to be more human with others.

IDENTIFICATION

Identification is a cornerstone of normal maturation (Bandura, 1971). The wish to identify with valued others persists throughout life. Identification with their therapists may be a crucial aspect of psychotherapy for patients who have misidentified or were unable to make constructive identifications at crucial points in their emotional development (Weiner, 1982a). Identification with therapists' acceptance and inquiring attitude allows patients to tolerate the deprivation of evocative therapies, and combined with positive transference, forms the basis of the therapeutic alliance.

Anna Freud (1946) noted that children take into themselves highly feared or admired qualities of the persons whom they most strongly love or fear. Identification is particularly useful in defending against external threat. By taking on some aspect of a dreaded person or situation, children convert anxious dread into pleasurable security.

Identification is the last step of a process that begins with introjection, taking into the self part of the external world. Identification transforms the self so that it becomes similar to the introjected object. Identification may begin with conscious imitation, but is an unconsciously mediated process (Greenson, 1954). Patients are enabled to discard old values and to replace them with new values based on their identification with therapists. This recapitulates the process of superego formation in which parental values are introjected positively or negatively by children, and form the nucleus of their adult value systems.

Identifications with therapists may be small and discrete or may involve patients' entire personalities. Transient partial identification with therapists is necessary for the eventual individuation of patients and their separation from their therapists.

To the extent that identification with therapists blocks further maturation, therapists can deal with it as a defense. To the extent that identification with therapists promotes facing life, it may be fostered.

INSIGHT

Insight can occur at many levels. In the strict psychoanalytic sense, insight refers to becoming aware of the unconscious meaning of thoughts, feelings, or behavior. Therapists bring this about through interpretation. *Interpretation* means "to make conscious the unconscious meaning, source, history, mode, or cause of a given psychic event" (Greenson, 1967).

The term insight also applies to awareness of patterns of behavior of which one was formerly unaware. It is likely that insight serves a number of functions. Its most important function is *attribution of meaning*; explaining a hitherto unexplainable symptom, feeling, or behavior. When therapists can attribute meaning to the material patients bring in, patients experience relief that they are understood, although they may not at that moment understand themselves. Therapists' means of conveying understanding will differ from patient to patient. For many people, insight means adopting their therapist's view of their symptoms. For others, it is becoming aware of the way they interact with people, and for a few it is coming to understand the unconscious forces in their own minds. The level of insight for which therapists strive with each patient depends on many variables, but primarily on the patient's ego strength. The less ego strength patients have, the more therapists must rely on active teaching. People with better coping skills can acquire insight through examining their experiences with their therapists, as in the example of Barbara and her therapist. Persons with better than average coping skills can become aware of unconscious forces in themselves through the medium of interpretation.

The process by which insight occurs often parallels the steps observed by Kubler-Ross (1969) in the process of dying: denial, anger, bargaining, depression, and acceptance. When first confronted with evidence of unconscious hostility toward a beloved person, patients deny it. If their therapists note similar evidence again, patients displace their anger onto their therapists, and still later may grudgingly accede that under certain rare circumstances, and to certain minimal degrees, they may have experienced angry feelings. With the emergence of more evidence of these feelings, patients become depressed as the superego seeks to maintain repression by the use of guilt. Finally, when the superego's sanctions are dealt with, patients are able to accept the interpretation and to recognize their formerly repressed feelings.

In dealing with ego-syntonic character traits, the process consists of patients encountering certain patterns of thought and feelings within themselves, realizing that they are not only irrational, but undesirable (making them ego-alien) and exploring the underlying fears or wishes responsible for them. As a result of these explorations, patients' self-views change; they begin to think and behave differently, and find the positive changes in themselves reinforced by their environment. When there is environmental resistance to patients' changes, they are obliged to assess the utility of the changes they have experienced and/or to seek means to influence their environment to support the changes in themselves.

The fact that insight into the childhood origins of certain behaviors often does not lead to change led to the designation of insight as emotional (from which change flows automatically) and intellectual (from which no change flows because the insight is not integrated into the patient's personality). It is possible to distinguish what patients feel is really true about themselves from what they parrot to please or mollify their therapists. Even when patients develop strong convictions about their behavior originating in conflict repressed during childhood, that is insufficient for change. For many patients, integration of insight into the personality requires active urging by therapists and active support by their environment. They require urging and support in part because of secondary gains that are not resolved by insight and are only relinquished by an act of will. For example, a phobic person may come to understand that her unwillingness to drive stems in part from reactivation of conflict repressed during childhood. However, she may never get behind the wheel of her car without pressure from the therapist or her family to relinquish the secondary gain of not driving.

ATTRIBUTION OF MEANING

Therapists attribute meaning to their patients' dreams, symptoms, behavior, and life problems. Attribution of meaning takes many forms. Making a diagnosis is a form of meaning-attribution. Ascribing behavior to unconscious motivation or dreams to unconscious forces are forms of meaning-attribution, as is labeling thoughts, feelings, and behavior as appropriate or inappropriate to a patient's life situation or stage of emotional development. Thus, diagnosis, interpretation, and reframing all have the common property that they are forms of meaning attribution.

The essential therapeutic aspect of meaning attribution is that it places patients' thoughts, feelings, and behavior into a frame of reference from which they can be approached by an internally consistent logical system. In different therapists' hands and with different patients, the logic may be quite different. For example, a person with episodes of high anxiety and palpitations who is not psychologically minded and who sees no possible connection between life events and symptoms might be best offered a diagnosis of panic disorder and be treated by prescribing a tricyclic antidepressant (Zitrin, Klein, & Woerner, 1978). A person with similar symptoms who expresses interest in their meaning and who relates symptoms to certain life events or conflicts might be offered the suggestion that anxiety results from intrapsychic conflict and may be therefore dealt with in an evocative psychotherapy.

The actual meaning attributed by a therapist to a patient's thoughts, feelings, or behavior is less important than the therapist selecting a meaning that can be usefully integrated by the patient at that time. Thus, it is more useful to first tell the mother of a provocative 14-year-old daughter that her anger is a normal reaction to being provoked than to tell her that she is concerned about being displaced from her husband's affections by the child. Having assured the mother that she is essentially a normal person reacting in a normal way to a difficult part of her daughter's growing up (i.e., her need to assert independence through defiance), it can later be pointed out that the child appears to be promoting disagreement between her parents.

Meaning attribution can be used to promote a particular course of action. For example: "Your symptoms of weight loss, poor appetite, sleeplessness, and suicidal thoughts tell me that you are severely depressed and that your life is in danger. Such an illness is best treated in a psychiatric hospital." Meaning attribution can also be used to alleviate anxiety, as in, "Your symptoms suggest to me a mild episode of depression related to your children leaving home. I think it will resolve quickly through us talking together and helping you to find some new interests."

TESTING OF PERCEPTIONS

Testing of perceptions designates patients' active attempts to validate their view of their world as it changes during psychotherapy. Patients test perceptions by soliciting the views of their therapists and using them to validate their own perceptions.

Testing of perceptions requires developing the ability to become detached from one's self and observe noncritically. In psychoanalytic psychotherapy, the process is described as making a therapeutic split in the ego that allows the ego to observe itself in action. This ego-split differs from self-criticism. It is not the guilt-producing action of the superego by which it induces the ego to confine certain id drives, nor is it the price the ego pays for discharging impulses disapproved of the superego. Examples of the latter are obese persons who loudly chastise themselves while in the act of overeating.

The following examples illustrate testing of perceptions at the three basic levels of psychotherapy.

Repressive

Patient: I think I'm handling things a lot better than I used to, don't you?
Therapist: I think so, too, but I'd like to hear what you think you're handling better.
Patient: I'm really studying hard. I get to class on time, and get my assignments done on time. And, I have the good grades to prove it.
Therapist: Seems to me you're absolutely right. You're doing a great job at school.

Note that the therapist also supplies positive feedback and positive reinforcement in addition to confirming the patient's perception.

Ego-Supportive

Patient: I think I'm a lot less hostile than I used to be.
Therapist: Perhaps so. What brought it to mind?
Patient: I usually get mad when you point out how I operate, but I didn't get mad at you this time.
Therapist: Come to think of it, you're right. Looks like you're on the right track.

Again, the elements of feedback and positive reinforcement are used in affirming the patient's self-perception.

Evocative

Patient: You know, I'm a lot less self-critical than I used to be.
Therapist: Tell me about it.
Patient: The other night, I yelled at the kids for coming in late and didn't

feel guilty about it afterward. And today, when I thought you were wrong about my feelings toward my mother, I wasn't afraid to tell you.

Therapist: So, you feel the self-doubting, self-punishing part of you is easing up and you're able to be more assertive.

Patient: That's right.

The therapist confirms the patient's perception that an intrapsychic change has taken place, but emphasizes the patient's self-affirmation instead of passing judgment on the patient's behavior as correct or incorrect.

WORKING THROUGH

Ultimately, patients must translate what they have learned into action. In behavior therapies, that begins with *behavior rehearsal* during therapeutic sessions. For example, patients practice being more assertive in the therapeutic sessions. They also keep diaries that indicate changes in behavior toward others. In therapies based on insight, the process is known as *working through*, the translating of intellectual insight into emotional insight. As patients become aware that they suppress angry feelings for fear of destroying others, and become further aware that their fear is irrational, they experiment with more direct expression of anger to give this insight real meaning in their lives. In the following example, a patient worked through inhibitions concerning her sexuality.

As Mrs. A. S. became more comfortable with her own sexuality, she began to take off her jacket at work and started wearing skirts instead of slacks. She also began enjoying the glances of the men at work instead of feeling offended or threatened by them. For Mrs. A. S., working through her acceptance of her femininity also involved dressing more femininely and enjoying the female sexual aspect of herself.

The impact of the therapeutic elements we have discussed depends on the quality of the therapist–patient relationship. A spirit of cooperation is usually needed before psychological work can proceed, but this can be blocked by therapists' or patients' fears or unrealistic expectations and by emotional reactions in therapist–patient relationship.

TRANSFERENCE

The term transference was developed in psychoanalysis (Fenichel, 1945). It refers to patients' attempts to relive in therapeutic sessions some aspect of their past lives that they found very frustrating or very satisfying. For example, a woman who experienced her mother as very frustrating and irritating may attempt to make her therapist into an ideal nurturing mother and may become enraged when the therapist shows only an ordinary professional interest. The transference wish for a nurturing mother and the patient's anger over the frustration of her wish can stalemate the treatment unless it is dealt with actively by the therapist in one of three ways. The therapist can explain the patient's frustration as a normal reaction to therapy, can indicate that the patient's attempts to stimulate nurturing interfere with the development of cooperation, or can help the patient to deal with unresolved feelings toward the frustrating mother. The type of approach to transference and to the patient's unconscious is based on the therapeutic method employed, as indicated in the following examples.

Repressive

Patient (angrily): This therapy is sure going slow. (Transference wish: I wish you could fix me magically.)
Therapist (sympathetically): I know. But you're doing a good job and we're getting there. (Accepts transference wish but refuses to accept role of omnipotent healer.)

Ego-Supportive

Patient (angrily): This therapy is sure going slow.
Therapist: How is it different from what you expected?
Patient: I hoped we'd be through in a few months.
Therapist: How'd you hope that would come about?
Patient: I guess I thought I'd tell you my problems and you'd give me the answers.
Therapist (grins): Well?
Patient (sheepishly): Well, I tell you my problems . . .
Therapist: And?
Patient: And you get me to assume responsibility for solving them.

Instead of attempting to alleviate the tension immediately, as in the example from repressive therapy, the therapist encourages the patient to reflect. Without exploring the origins of the transference wish, the therapist refuses to gratify it and instead turns the responsibility for the patient back to the individual.

Evocative

Patient (angrily): This therapy is sure going slow.
Therapist: In what way is it slow for you?
Patient: Not much change.
Therapist: What sort of change had you hoped for?
Patient: To be less inhibited in dealing with people; freer to be intimate.
Therapist: And . . . ?
Patient: And I'm still the same person.
Therapist: Any feelings about that?
Patient: Yeah, I'm angry.
Therapist: And . . . ?
Patient: . . . and disappointed in you.
Therapist: Because?
Patient: Because. . . . I don't know. . . . It's as if I expected you to make everything okay.
Therapist: As if I were . . . ?
Patient (irritated): I don't know. Like a god or somebody who could fix things almost like magic.

In this instance, the therapist uncovers the patient's transference wish to be healed magically. Sensitivity of therapists to transference is important because of the potential for transference to block or facilitate therapy. A transference-based expectation of a positive therapeutic outcome is usually helpful to therapy. Transference-based expectations of criticism must frequently be brought into the open and dealt with by explaining them away, e.g., "Almost everyone expects a therapist to be critical," by discussing therapist behaviors that seem critical of the patient, or by uncovering patients' general expectations of criticism and understanding their origins and their tendency to be applied to present-day interactions.

The best means for therapists to detect transference is to assume that they are at the center of their patients' emotional world; that all behaviors and thoughts of their patients are directly related to the person or the behaviors of the therapist. When all of the patients' thoughts, feelings, and behaviors are viewed in this context, transference reactions are most likely to be uncovered. The caveat here is that no therapist is entirely at the center of any patient's emotional world, and the impact of other events and relationships cannot be dismissed.

Transference Resolution

Therapists often speak of recapitulating and working through in the transference relationship aspects of early interpersonal relationships. The little available research evidence on the subject shows that family reenactment is rarely regarded as significant by patients and that the most valued therapeutic experiences are here-and-now interpersonal events that often do not refer to the influence of the past on the present (Yalom, 1975). Often, one such important event is the therapist's simple acknowledgement of the patient as a person (Malan, 1976; Yalom, 1980).

The author compared 12 categories of therapeutic factors developed by Yalom (1970) and applied them to four different groups of patients. The categories were interpersonal output, interpersonal input, catharsis, insight, existential factors, cohesiveness, guidance, altruism, identification, instillation of hope, universality, and family reenactment. Interpersonal output means risking new behaviors. Interpersonal input is learning the reactions of others to one's own behavior. Catharsis is expressing formerly withheld feelings, and insight is discovering formerly unknown aspects of one's self. Existential factors designate coming to grips with the realities of life, such as the need to assume responsibility for one's self. Cohesiveness refers to mutual acceptance and a sense of mutual belonging. Guidance is being offered suggestions. Altruism means doing for others without self-interest or a sense of obligation. Identification refers to acting like, or following the lead of others. Universality refers to being comforted by seeing that others have the same problem. Family reenactment designates reexperiencing aspects of one's own earlier life.

Using Yalom's 12 categories, the author compared patients' appraisal of the most important therapeutic factors in four groups: a group of 8 patients preparing to enter long-term group therapy, a group of 9 patients assessed after a time-limited group of 10 sessions, Yalom's sample of 20 patients (75 sessions each), and a group of 10 patients each with more than two years of experience in a group (Weiner, 1984a) (see Figure 13). The author found that patients rated 11 of Yalom's 12 categories as important. Family reenactment was not considered important by any group.

The two insight items that connect past with present that appear in the pregroup expectations drop out in the treated groups. In addition, the number of noninsight factors increases as the length of group treatment increases. Prospective patients expected insight to be the most

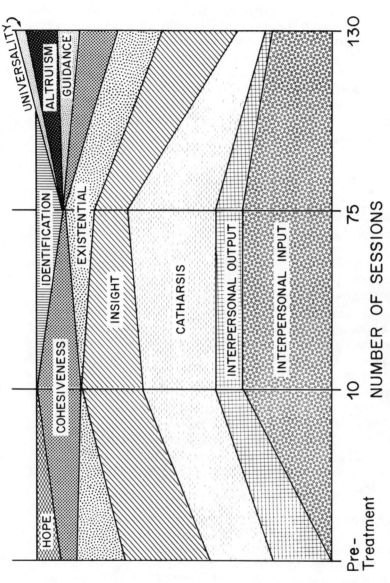

Figure 13. Therapeutic Factors and Length of Psychotherapy:
A Comparison of Four Groups of Patients

(Adapted from Weiner, M. F. (1984a). *Techniques of group psychotherapy*. Washington, D.C.: American
Psychiatric Press.)

important therapeutic vehicle, with catharsis, learning to trust others, and learning how one relates to others running close behind. However, persons who completed the same questionnaire after periods of group therapy ranging from 10 sessions to more than two years indicated that interpersonal learning (feedback about their behavior from other group members and the ability to express themselves) was first, and insight was rated second in importance. If we are willing to believe what our patients tell us, we must agree with Yalom's (1970) earlier finding that insight is not the primary therapeutic vehicle, at least in group psychotherapy, even in group psychotherapy whose aim is insight.

COUNTERTRANSFERENCE

In addition to the distortions of the therapeutic process produced by transference and non-transference-based irrational attitudes of patients, there is also distortion by the emotional attitudes of therapists. Countertransference, another term borrowed from psychoanalysis, is frequently used to describe the emotional reactions of therapists to patients (Little, 1951). Countertransference originally meant therapists' reactions to patients' transferences or the development of transference in therapists toward patients; for example, female patients' transference wish for an ideal father may restimulate male therapists' wish to be idolized by the women in their present lives to make up for their mothers' lack of interest or their critical attitude toward them. In current use, the term countertransference has been broadened to encompass all of the emotional reactions of therapists to their patients (Langs, 1973).

Countertransference plays an important role in therapists' emphasis on the use of one therapeutic element over another and on the effectiveness of the therapeutic element(s) they employ. The extent of therapists' interaction with their patients shown in the next two vignettes exemplifies this point.

A therapist was unusually interactive with his attractive female patient, who told him how much she appreciated his activity and how much better she felt with him than her last therapist, whom she experienced as depriving. In this situation, the therapist's unusual degree of activity may well have been a sublimated sexual involvement that was reinforced by the patient's pleasure and by her favorable comparison of him with her former therapist, which appealed to her present therapist's competitive strivings and narcissism.

Another male therapist was very passive with a male patient who had been detected in fondling his young stepdaughter. The patient's reported desperation over the possibility of losing both his wife and stepdaughter did not stimulate the therapist to greater interaction even after the patient made a suicide attempt (Weiner, 1983a). In this situation, the therapist was acting out his anger toward the patient and simultaneously repudiating the possibility that he could be sexually interested in a child.

Countertransference can disrupt or block therapy because it involves fulfilling therapists' emotional needs in the therapeutic process. When severe countertransference difficulties arise, they are dealt with by therapists' recognition of them and by refraining from countertransference-based behavior such as attempting to cultivate patients' admiration or friendship. If therapists are unable to alter their behavior, they can seek supervision or personal therapy.

THE PSYCHOTHERAPIST AS A PERSON

The person of the psychotherapist is an element of psychotherapy not included in formal lists. Certain personal attitudes of therapists usually facilitate psychotherapy. They are therapists' willingness to be actively involved with their patients, a positive attitude toward and acceptance of both themselves and their patients, and a certain amount of interpersonal warmth. Those qualities are perceived by patients as genuineness (i.e., the therapists believe what they say and believe in what they are doing), acceptance, and compassion or empathy (Mitchell, Bozarth, & Kraufft, 1977).

Patients (and people in general) respond poorly to persons whom they perceive as emotionally uninvolved who are merely manipulating them to obtain a certain type of response, and who lack compassion. In fact, it is probable that the failure of many professionally unqualified healers to heal is readily overlooked because they establish a warm empathic relationship with the people they treat. Their patients may go away sick, but they don't go away mad.

The interpersonal skills basic to any psychotherapeutic endeavor are cultivated through active involvement with patients and through discovering that even the most immature or dilapidated person is unique. Spending time talking with people in any kind of life crisis enables us to see them as persons in distress instead of as individuals with disorders. In talking to people in many kinds of distress, one learns how to approach sensitively or to avoid painful issues and how to be with another person during a time of distress. Patients are most grateful and respond best to persons who listen, try to understand, and offer hope through their attitude or suggestions.

While listening, therapists communicate interest verbally and non-verbally. They acknowledge hearing what patients have to say, and their posture and attitude are attentive. They may reflect or rephrase certain portions of patients' comments to be certain that they understand what patients are saying, thus giving patients a chance to correct therapists' distortions of their communications. Finally, therapists offer guidance by suggesting the most profitable subject for discussion during therapeutic sessions, urging patients to examine certain behavior with others, or giving patients advice on the conduct of their lives.

All this is done with sensitivity to patients' ability to tolerate the involvement of other persons in their lives and is based on therapists' calculations of how their attitudes and interactions with patients will be perceived and reacted to. This will be partially determined by transference, partly by ordinary role expectations, and partly by the role played by therapists in patients' intrapsychic economies; i.e., whether they symbolize punitive superego introjects, or nurturing superego introjects; whether they oppose the discharge of instinctual drives, or facilitate such discharge.

SUMMARY

The science of psychotherapy identifies and attempts to determine the mode of action of the elements of psychotherapy. The art of psychotherapy skillfully modifies and blends those elements. Often, elements are combined that seem contradictory; e.g., encouraging catharsis in a patient in repressive therapy, or stimulating a person in an evocative therapy to act on his or her own behalf. Practiced psychotherapists develop a sense of how much of each element to blend into the therapeutic action at any given point in time, recognizing that the flow of therapy or unavoidable external circumstances may require a completely different blend during the next session.

Although therapists develop a basic frame of reference for treating patients generally, and for the treatment of each individual patient, therapists come to each session prepared to alter or stand firmly by the therapeutic course they have taken, based on the patient's therapeutic needs at that point in treatment.

CHAPTER 5

Goals and Process
of Psychotherapy

There is much disagreement about the goals and process of psychotherapy. Some form of self-awareness is universally held to be important for resolving emotional problems, as is the ability to take constructive action, but the paths to and nature of the needed self-awareness
and eventual constructive action are the subject of great controversy.
On reviewing the psychotherapy literature, one is struck by the paucity
of careful observation and the tendency to generalize from a few patients with particular problems to all persons who seek psychological
help. In addition, much more attention is paid to the process of psychotherapy than to its outcome.

GOALS

The goals of psychotherapy have been described in educational, functional, structural, and dynamic terms. Freud (1940/1964) described the
goal of therapy in educational terms, as helping to undo the educational
blunders made by one's parents. Saul (1958), a psychoanalyst, suggested
that therapy develops the capacity to enjoy loving and being loved, and
fosters a balance between work and recreation. He also described the
goals of therapy in structural and dynamic terms. New choices are
opened. Adaptability and flexibility are increased. As patients deal with
their drives or reduce their frustrations and conflicts, they free bound
energy and diminish emotional tension. Childhood patterns of id and
superego are softened and lessened. Ego is expanded and is less at the
mercy of automatic unconscious patterns, less tyrannized by infantile
impulses and purposeless guilt and compulsion. Patients become able

to make their decisions and live their lives according to reason. Because patients often try to gratify childish wishes in their adult lives, they experience ever-present guilt and self-punishment. To the extent that psychotherapy ameliorates this inner frustration, it increases patients' satisfaction in life.

Strupp (1969), a researcher in the field of psychotherapy, views psychodynamic psychotherapy as a process from which patients learn new beliefs about themselves and others and new strategies for handling interpersonal experiences, both abetted by subsequent reality testing.

According to Strupp, patients learn that the world is not so bad, that people are relatively reliable and trustworthy, and that people react negatively to demands and exploitation. They learn to scale down childish demands and expectations, give up some aspirations, reduce their narcissism, and accept limitations in themselves and others.

Patients learn to find self-satisfaction sufficient reward for their achievements, and learn that expecting praise and applause leads to disappointment, which in turn breeds resentment. They learn that gratification must often be delayed or accepted in a different form and amount from what they want; that tension, frustration, and privation must often be endured for the sake of a greater good. Although painful, frustrations are usually bearable, and do not last forever.

What is worth having is worth working for. Realistic action is needed to reach a desired goal, but some goals are unattainable, and symbolic gratification may need to suffice.

It does not usually help to avoid painful, difficult, and anxiety-provoking situations. Avoidance may provide temporary relief, but intensifies problems instead of solving them.

Feelings are not the same as acts. Angry feelings in oneself and others are neither lethal nor dangerous. They will not destroy other people or, via retaliation, oneself. Ingratiating oneself with others usually does not lead to approval and, when it does, it is at the cost of self-depreciation. On the other hand, negativism usually does not coerce other persons to do one's bidding.

The talion principle in interpersonal relations is self-defeating. Cooperation with others generally brings the greatest returns. One cannot "buy" others, but one can cooperate with those who are willing to cooperate. Other people, however, are not obligated to cooperate, nor are efforts to subjugate them likely to work. Attempts to fuse with another person do not work. All people ultimately have to stand on their own feet.

Honesty about one's feelings and motives is a good policy, but it is not necessary to broadcast one's less desirable traits – although they are universal – or wallow in guilt or self-pity because one is not perfect. People are judged by their actions, not their fantasies. By recognizing one's motivations, one can often take useful action. On the other hand, one is responsible for one's actions; they cannot be blamed on others, nor can therapists absolve patients from guilt. Patients have to forgive themselves.

All people have their rights, and need to stand by them. By respecting others and themselves, often people can also gratify their own wishes more effectively.

There is need to respect, accept, and be subordinate to higher authorities, but their power is never complete, and it is often possible to leave oppressive settings for a more congenial climate. However, accepting authority does not entail abandoning freedom. On the contrary, accepting authority can reduce conflict with others.

The past is irreversible, but there is considerable latitude in shaping the present. Blaming others for one's predicament is self-defeating.

Finally, it is useful to have a clear understanding of one's identity and role functions and to develop enough flexibility of role to function from time to time as an authority or as a subordinate, to be dependent or independent, to assert or submit, and to compete or abstain from competition.

THE PROCESS

There are many descriptions of psychotherapeutic process, usually couched in terms of theoretical constructs that are hard to validate. Carl Rogers's (1961) observations, however, describe the process without resorting to a metapsychology or diagnostic label. Rogers hypothesizes that individuals move from rigid structure to flow, from stasis to process; that the qualities of patients' expressions may indicate their position on such a continuum and indicate where they stand in the process of change. Rogers suggests seven stages of change:

In *stage one*, the individual is not likely to seek therapy. There is no willingness to communicate about self, and communication is only about externals. Feelings and personal meanings are neither recognized nor owned. Personal constructs are extremely rigid. Close and communicative relationships are construed as dangerous. Problems are not recognized or perceived. There is much blockage in internal communication, and there is no desire to change. The following vignette is an example of a person at this stage.

Mrs. O., a mildly depressed 45-year-old divorcee, was referred for therapy by her family doctor. She had no interest in seeing a psychiatrist. Her physician had recently completed a hospital work-up, including studies of her gastrointestinal tract, her thyroid function, her glucose metabolism, and her brain waves. A slight abnormality was detected on her electroencephalographic tracing. She was given diphenylhydantoin (Dilantin) 100 mg four times a day. Her depression, feelings of hopelessness, and suicidal ideation waned rapidly on this regime, and at the time the therapist saw her she said that she was nearly well. She then recounted some of the chaotic ways in which she had lived her life, but saw no connection between that and her unhappiness, which she was altogether willing to attribute to abnormal brain metabolism. She cried at several points during the session and was surprised to find herself doing so because of the fact that she had been "doing so well." Since she had told the therapist at the beginning of the session that she thought she probably could not afford to see him, either from a psychological or a financial standpoint, he told her he would leave it as her decision to enter or not enter therapy with him, and that he would not try to "sell" her. Later, at a time of greater distress, she did seek and accept therapy.

In *stage two*, there is communication about nonself topics. Problems are perceived as external; one's self is perceived as a passive object. There is no sense of personal responsibility for problems. Feelings may be exhibited, but are not recognized as such or owned. Experiencing is bound by the structure of the past. Personal constructs are rigid and experienced as facts instead of constructs. The differentiation of personal meanings and feelings is very limited and global. All is seen as black or white. Contradictions may be expressed, with little recognition of them as contradictions, as seen next.

Mrs. R., a 23-year-old-woman being divorced by her husband, was brought to a psychiatrist against her will by her parents, with whom she was currently living. Her first visit was a three-way session including her parents. They said that they had been rescuing her from one difficulty after another since her teenage years. Her most recent difficulty had been severe weight loss (down to 65 pounds). Her parents had been contacted by the people with whom she had been living, and they had hospitalized her under the care of an internist.

When the therapist asked Mrs. R. if she were interested in talking to him at another time without her parents present, she said, "I don't care." The therapist commented to the parents that she seemed to want them to decide. They asked her if she would come to the office if they left her off at the entrance to the building. She then began to sulk and remonstrate against them because they treated her like a baby. She screamed, "You're the crazy ones, not me!"

In the individual session that followed, she portrayed herself as totally self-sufficient, denied the implications of her severe weight loss, or the fact that she played any part in permitting her parents to "interfere."

In *stage three*, there is freer communication about the self as an object. There is also expression about self-related experiences as objects. There is expression about the self as a reflected object, existing primarily in others. There is much expression about, or description of, feelings and personal meanings not now present. There is little acceptance of feelings. For the most part, feelings are revealed as something shameful, bad or abnormal, or unacceptable in other ways. Feelings are exhibited, and then sometimes recognized as feelings. Experiencing is described as in the past or somewhat remote from the self.

In *stage four*, patients describe more intense feelings of the "not-now-present" variety. Feelings are described as objects in the present. Occasionally, feelings are expressed as in the present, sometimes breaking through almost against the patients' wishes. Although there is a tendency toward experiencing feelings in the immediate present, patients distrust and fear their feelings. Experiencing is less bound by the structure of the past, is less remote, and may occasionally occur with little postponement. There is a loosening of the way experience is construed. There are some discoveries of personal constructs; there is a definite recognition of these as constructs; and there is a beginning questioning of their validity. There is an increased differentiation of feelings, constructs, and personal meanings, with some tendency toward seeking exactness of symbolization. There is a concern about contradictions and incongruities between experience and self. There are feelings of self-responsibility for problems although such feelings vacillate. Though a close relationship still seems dangerous, patients risk themselves, relating to some small extent on a feeling basis.

In *stage five*, feelings are expressed freely as in the present and are very close to being fully experienced. They "bubble up," or "seep through," in spite of the fear and distrust which patients feel at experiencing them with fullness and immediacy. There is a beginning tendency to recognize that experiencing a feeling involves a direct referent. There is surprise and fright, rarely pleasure, at the feelings that "bubble through." There is an increasing ownership of self-feelings and a desire to be these, to be the "real me." Experiencing is loosened, is no longer remote, and frequently occurs with immediacy. The ways in which experience is constructed are much loosened. There are many fresh discoveries of personal constructs as constructs and a critical examination and questioning of these. There is a strong and evident tendency toward exactness and differentiation of feelings and meanings. Contradictions and incongruencies in experience are faced more clearly. There is an increasing quality of acceptance of self-responsibility for the problems being faced, and a concern as to how patients have contributed to their own difficulties. There are increasingly freer dialogues within the self, and reduced blockage of internal communication, as the following example illustrates.

> Mrs. I., who had completed six years of twice-a-week individual psychotherapy six months previously, called her ex-therapist and said she was experiencing some difficulty. As they briefly reviewed her therapy experience, she said she had learned a great deal, but tearfully complained that she was having difficulty with her husband. She thought he resented the fact that she had started to college several years before, and had nearly completed an undergraduate degree. In addition, she wanted to obtain an advanced degree to become a mental health professional. Her husband complained that she was "always analyzing him" and that she was using her education to belittle him. As she talked, the therapist noted that she used the phrase "verbalizing to him" rather than "talking to him," and concluded that to a certain extent her husband was probably correct. Somewhat angrily and defensively, the patient shifted to dealing with her feelings that her termination from therapy was a desertion by her therapist. Now that the spring semester of college was over, she had again begun to experience the sensation of being let down. After her second session, she said that she would again like to deal with her problems on her own. Her therapist made no reply to this, but suggested that she call him in the fall and let him know how things were going.

In the *sixth stage*, a present feeling is directly experienced with immediacy and richness. This immediacy of experiencing, and its feeling content, are accepted, not denied, feared, or struggled against. There is a quality of living subjectively in the experience, not feeling about it. Self as an object tends to disappear. Experiencing, at this stage, takes on a real process quality. Another characteristic of this stage is the physiological loosening that accompanies it. Moistness in the eyes, tears, sighs, and muscular relaxation are frequent. The incongruence between experience and awareness is experienced vividly as it disappears into congruence. The relevant personal construct is dissolved in this experiencing moment, and the patients feel cut loose from their previously stabilized framework. The moment of full experiencing becomes a clear and definite referent. Differentiation of experiencing is sharp and basic. In this stage, there are no longer "problems," external or internal. The patient is living, subjectively, a phase of his problem. It is not an object.

In the *seventh stage*, which occurs as much outside of the therapeutic relationship as in it, new feelings are experienced with immediacy and richness of detail, both in the therapeutic relationship and outside. The experiencing of such feelings is used as a clear referent. There is a growing and continuing sense of accepting ownership of these changing feelings, a basic trust on the part of patients in their own process. Experiencing has lost almost completely its structure-bound aspects and becomes process experiencing; that is, situations are experienced and interpreted in their newness, not as repetitions of past experiences. The self becomes increasingly the subjective and reflexive awareness of experiencing. The self is much less frequently a perceived object, and much more frequently felt confidently in process. Personal constructs are tentatively reformulated or validated against further experience, but even then to be held loosely. Internal communication is clear, with feelings and symbols well-matched and the use of fresh terms for new feelings. Patients experience being able to effectively choose new ways of being.

Rogers' seven stages reflect an ideal course of psychotherapy in which patients move from externalizing their difficulties to accepting themselves and their responsibility for themselves. They also embody the essence of psychopathology and enable us to look at psychopathology in functional terms.

Stages one and two in many ways resemble the psychological state of persons who are psychotic or who have severe personality disorders. The later stages remind us of persons with less severe character and neurotic problems. Rogers's schema, then, allows us to see the flow that occurs in the process of therapy, whether that process consists of work with severely ego-impaired persons or persons with mild neurotic problems who are psychologically unaware.

Rogers's process model of psychotherapy does not include a regressive experience in which patients reexperience their past in the relationship with the therapist. Has Rogers overlooked something, or is it possible that the emphasis placed on patients' regression in therapy is a complication instead of a normal concomitant of therapy or an important therapeutic mechanism?

THE ROLE OF REGRESSION

Regression is held by many therapists to be a necessary part of the therapeutic process (Tuttman, 1982). Because regression so frequently occurs in psychotherapy patients (whether or not it is actively sought by the therapist), the subject warrants extensive discussion.

What Is Regression?

Regression is the reappearance of types of mental functioning characteristic of a person's earlier development (Arlow & Brenner, 1964). The concept of regression in the service of the ego is an important aspect of modern psychoanalytic psychotherapy (Scheidlinger, 1980). Through a carefully controlled and monitored process of ego regression, the analysand in classical psychoanalysis develops insight, and reworks self-defeating coping and defensive mechanisms that have been fixated at immature levels for many reasons, including conflict, overgratification, or unavailability of appropriate objects for identification. The vehicle for insight and constructive change is the analysis of the transference that develops as the analysand's ego regresses. The analyst has the technical problem of insuring that the analysand's regression is sufficient to enable the development of the transference neurosis, but not so great as to stimulate the destructive acting out of unconscious drives and conflicts (Greenson, 1967).

The distinction between an ego incapacitated by regression, and regression in the service of the ego was first made by Kris (1952) in connection with the regulated, creative use of primary process material by artists. He was speaking of a creative process, however, not a therapeutic one.

Balint (1968) studied regression in analysis and concluded it was helpful when the analysand's motivation for regression was for the sake of sharing with the analyst and to further his or her own and the analyst's understanding. That type of regression was held to differ from regression to enable libidinal gratification or acting out.

Tuttman (1982) views regression as making crucial material accessible to the observing ego allied with the analyst, and eventuates in dealing with the unfinished business of earlier development.

The problem for therapists is determining which patients will develop useful regressive states and which will not. At present, our tools are a history of patients' level and quality of function in love and work relationships and our evaluation of their use of mature coping and defensive mechanisms in their daily lives and in the relationship with the therapist.

What's Harmful About Regression?

Whether or not regression is harmful depends on the amount of difficulty it causes for the regressed person or his environment. We can obtain some idea about the mixed blessings of regression from the Menninger Foundation Psychotherapy Research Project.

The Menninger Foundation's Psychotherapy Research Project (Kernberg, Burstein, Coyne, et al., 1972) concluded that psychoanalysis produced greater positive change in well-integrated patients than expressive or supportive techniques produced in less well-integrated persons, but the use of psychoanalysis and expressive techniques resulted in hospitalization for half of the patients so treated. Less well-integrated patients who were treated exclusively by supportive (i.e., non-regression-promoting) measures showed less global positive change, but required hospitalization half as often. In short, the treatment techniques that fostered greater regression had more potential for doing damage and required augmentation by substantial amounts of environmental structuring and manipulation.

At this point, I take certain liberties based on my experience in treating and supervising patient treatment in many settings and construct a hypothetical "ordinary" outpatient. This is not a retrospective view of persons who successfully completed long-term therapy. Rather, it is a retrospective view of those who sought help.

The views of many therapists are skewed because they consider only those persons who have responded positively to their therapy. In reading about treatment, we find very little about the nature of persons who were not able to tolerate and cooperate with the therapy prescribed; the differences between those who sought psychological help unsuccessfully and those who were able to respond to the help offered. The author, by contrast, has devoted considerable study to failures in psychotherapy (Weiner, 1982b), and suggests that ordinary persons seeking outpatient therapy (unless specifically seeking psychoanalytic treatment by a psychoanalyst) are very different from what therapists might like them to be.

The ordinary patients to whom I refer have never been psychotic. They have suffered some impairment of function in work, social, and intimate relationships in addition to low self-esteem and a few functional complaints such as indigestion, lightheadedness, nervousness, fatigue, or insomnia. In addition, they may suffer ego-dystonic emotional symptoms such as anxiety or depression.

Ordinary patients believe that their past life experiences have some bearing on their present state of mind, and often attribute symptoms to stresses in work or personal relationships. They have heard of psychoanalysis and frequently think that mental health professionals will blame their troubles on upbringing or on unfortunate childhood experiences. Patients are usually aware that there is a connection between mind and body, and frequently say that they or some family member think that their physical symptoms are products of worry or psychological tension.

Encouraging these persons to undergo ego regression in the therapeutic relationship is usually counterproductive. If anything, ordinary psychologically troubled identified patients need to overcome a functionally regressed style of living instead of regressing further.

Ego regression would be necessary to treat ideal, autonomously functioning individuals. In order to be effective participants in psychotherapy, they would need to have faith in the therapist and in the process of therapy. Patients would therefore need to suspend part of their critical judgment and give greater weight to the therapist's words and actions than to the words and actions of ordinary peers. Patients would need to regress into fantasy to become aware of the sources of disturbance in their unconscious mental lives because they manage their real lives so well.

Ordinary patients do not need to regress because they have already suffered a developmental arrest or have regressed in response to intrapsychic or interpersonal pressures. They do not relinquish their autonomy to include the therapist in their lives. They substitute a (hopefully) healthier dependency on the therapist for less healthy types of dependent relationships. In Kohut's (1971) terms, the therapist becomes a selfobject to aid the patient's transition from archaic modes of selfobject relationships to mature self-object relationships (Wolf, 1983). Patients substitute the reasonableness of the therapist's judgment for their own unreasonableness toward themselves or others. They do not need to enter fantasy because their unconscious problems manifest in their dealings with others.

Therefore, the stimulation and working through of transferences cannot be the main therapeutic tool of the nonpsychoanalyst working with the ordinary troubled person who seeks professional help. Transferences are dealt with when they interfere with the learning and practice of constructive interpersonal attitudes and behaviors. Idealizing and mirroring transferences are allowed to stand unless they block patients' progress toward adult relationships.

In the author's experience, encouraging ego regression is an inefficient technique for ordinary patients and may result in destructive acting out or psychological worsening due to overwhelming of the weakened ego by the superego. With severely disturbed patients, regression must be actively opposed.

Normund Wong (1980), in a symposium on treating narcissistic and borderline patients, suggests adjunctive group therapy to avert a transference psychosis because it provides reality testing and support. The terrifying transferences of the borderline and the idealizing transferences of narcissistic patients can be modified by the shared perceptions of peers. Group members encourage infantile and narcissistic characters to express and deal with their needs in ways that can be more readily responded to by others, and borderline patients find models for identification and internalization in groups.

Roth (1980) concluded that the idealizing transference might best be undisturbed with borderline and narcissistically impaired persons. Kibel (1980) noted that when allowed to regress, severely disturbed patients became vulnerable to their wishes for and fears of engulfment by others.

Regression has taken its toll of many psychotherapy patients, especially those whose unconscious mental lives severely disrupted their daily functioning. The most blatant examples are patients with borderline personality disorders or psychotic disorders who were treated by probing unconscious motivation. For example, a manic-depressive woman's suicide was precipitated in part by her therapist's pointing out her identification with her parents, both of whom had suicided. A patient with a borderline personality disorder whose transference regression could not be controlled attempted suicide to express her anger and fear of desertion when her therapist took a brief trip.

Less severe reactions have occurred in people who were less disorganized and maladjusted, in the form of protracted stalemates in the case of people who overidealized their therapists or felt overly criticized by their therapists (Weiner, 1982b).

A Nonregressive Therapy Process

If relatively healthy people in classical psychoanalysis with experienced analysts frequently require hospitalization to shore them up (Kernberg, 1972), it is clear that ordinary patients require a treatment that is progressive instead of regressive, that concentrates on function in reality instead of immersion in fantasy, and that solidifies the ego instead of fragmenting it.

A progressive treatment accepts patients at their presenting level of function and helps them to avoid further regression by focusing on their present behavior and thinking. It accepts idealizing and mirroring transferences as part of the normal growth process, attempts to alter maladaptive behavior by direct teaching or modeling, and uses the positive feelings engendered by small constructive steps in the therapeutic relationship to encourage patients to take similar steps in their outside lives. If applied with respect for the individual patient's ability and motivation to change, an inexperienced or naive therapist is less apt to do harm with a progressive therapy than with active probing of patients' unconscious. In addition, symptomatic improvement stimulates the curiosity of many patients, who then develop an interest in insight-oriented therapy and the capacity for tolerating it because of improved impulse control and increased capacity for self-observation and for forming a therapeutic alliance.

I believe that a blend of therapeutic activities proposed by Carl Rogers, Heinz Kohut, and Irvin Yalom offer an alternative to stimulating regression. Rogers focused on therapist-offered conditions, Kohut on integrating the patient's sense of a unified self, and Yalom on teaching coping skills and self-observation through interpersonal interaction and feedback.

Carl Rogers (1957) proposed that the therapist feel with patients, accept them as they are, and let patients experience the therapist as a real person in the here-and-now.

Kohut (1971, 1977) advocates therapists' nonjudgmental acceptance of preoedipally fixated patients' idealizing and mirroring transferences. Kohut recommends that therapists first become patients' needed selfobjects and gradually help patients make the transition from less mature to more mature types of selfobject relationships. Kohut and his followers stress the importance of the real interactions between therapists and patients and find that interpretations are often therapists' means of blaming patients for therapists' failures to understand or empathize (Tolpin, 1983).

Yalom (1975) emphasizes the therapist's technical operations, focusing on the interaction between patients and therapists in the here and now, showing the self-defeating nature of the patients' maladaptive interactions, and emphasizing the development of better coping skills, which are reinforced by the therapist. He fosters a sense of reality and has a concrete focus for therapeutic activity – helping patients to learn how to react and behave more constructively. He relies heavily on interpersonal feedback, on modeling, and on identification. For work with inpatients, Yalom (1983) also encourages the therapist's openness in the here-and-now.

The approaches of Rogers, Kohut, and Yalom may be criticized as psychologically superficial, and, therefore, less likely to produce permanent cure. On the other hand, there is much evidence that deeper probing can be disruptive. Ego-supportive therapies can be criticized because they do not encourage patients' exploration of themselves at the deepest possible level. That is true, but therapists need not discourage patients in ego-supportive therapy from taking a deeper look if they so wish and if they can tolerate it.

At first glance, Rogers's, Kohut's, and Yalom's notions may also appear inadequate because they do not emphasize abreaction or working through of conflict. But when the author examined his own most successful interventions and his best outcomes, he found that the patients who did best were not those who had the most profound abreactions or developed the greatest insight into their psychodynamics, but those who accepted his esteem for them and who became able to understand his communications most clearly. They were regressed and somewhat childish on entering therapy. As they matured in therapy, they became more confident of themselves and relied less heavily on the therapist, as we see in the next example.

Mrs. A. Y. was a 30-year-old married professional woman whose complaints were excessive worry, overconcern with pleasing others, and a sense of general tenseness.

She was an only child. Her mother died when she was a freshman in college. After her mother's death, her father put considerable pressure on her to quit college and take care of him, but she had resisted. In his relationship with her mother, Mrs. A. Y.'s father had been very dependent. Three years after her death, he married a woman who was less tolerant of his dependent clinging and seemed to do much better.

Mrs. A. Y. had dated her husband for five years before their marriage, and had married four years prior to her seeking treatment. She seemed to have transferred her own dependent needs to her husband at about the same time her mother died without having had a period of living on her own. As she put it, she drifted into marriage with him.

At the time she entered therapy, Mrs. A. Y. maintained a state of childish dependency on the approval of others, and was afraid to stand up for herself in reasonable ways on the job and in other interpersonal relationships. In therapy, Mrs. A. Y.'s passive means of expressing aggression were explored, as were her wishes to be more sexual and to touch people. She noted that she was warm and positive to the children with whom she worked, but that she became inhibited with their parents and her husband. Over time, she gave up protecting other people at work from doing unpleasant tasks, which was the way her father was treated by her mother until her mother died. Later, she dealt more effectively with her anger toward her father and her resentment of him butting into her business. She became able to see her confusion of her husband with her father. As she started dealing with the sadness left over from her mother's death, she became better able to face and deal with other people about emotional issues. As she became more sexually comfortable, she also became more aggressive with her husband. Actually, she overshot the mark and discovered after a year of therapy that she was becoming too aggressive with him. Later in therapy, she found that her husband did not respond any better to being berated than other people did, and she began reinforcing him positively rather than criticizing him for what he failed to do for her. She had three separate periods of being very angry with her husband during therapy, especially with the playful, childish part of him. After a year and a half of therapy, she was able to see people less in terms of all good and all bad. After nearly two years, she was able to see the difference between being snobbish and selective in making friends, and when she terminated therapy felt much more comfortable in interpersonal relationships, was less stiff and tense, and was considerably less worried than when she had presented two years previously. Her father had just had a heart attack, and she found his illness added a whole new dimension to their relationship. They were able to talk to each other as people more than they had been able to before.

Most of this woman's therapy was carried out at a there-and-then level and did not involve working through transferences directly with the therapist. Rather, transference issues were addressed through her relationship with her husband, her real father, and with the parents of the children she worked with.

With successful patients, transferences were interpreted when they interfered with the progress of therapy, but more important were increased self-acceptance based on acceptance by the therapist, realistic feedback from the therapist and others, recognition of immature or self-defeating behavior, risking more mature behavior in and outside of therapeutic sessions, and taking the responsibility for one's own behavior. No transference interpretation was useful without the solid support of the therapist, friends, and family members, in changing old behaviors and ways of thinking for more adaptive behavior. That support generally consisted of praise for positive activities instead of criticism for immature attitudes. Dreams were dealt with by tying them to events in the therapeutic interaction instead of to the patient's childhood experiences and memories.

The patients who regressed in therapy tended to do the most poorly in life. Those who progressed from the fixated or regressed states in which they entered therapy had the best results. Successful therapy is therefore not a process in which patients get worse so that they can get better, although regressive storms do occur even in well-conducted therapies. Successful therapy for ordinary patients enables them to progress from a regressed state to a state of more reasonable dependence and independence, or more adequate expression, and also of more adequate restraint.

In the author's experience, the most helpful technical procedures were not the development of a regressive transference and its resolution by interpretation, but the presence of the therapist as a real person (instead of a transference screen), acceptance by patients of feedback about interpersonal behavior in the here-and-now, identification with healthy aspects of the therapist, the therapist's praise for constructive behavior and failure to reinforce undesirable behaviors, the therapist's encouragement of patients to face issues, and the therapist's willingness to lend his or her special expertise when advice was needed and could be accepted.

SUMMARY

Psychotherapy is an educational process that in many ways parallels the normal process of psychological maturation. The general trend in maturation and successful psychotherapy is toward the development of a flexible, broadly based adaptive repertoire that changes in response to inner and to environmental demands.

There is little evidence that regression is often a necessary or important part of the psychotherapeutic process. One does not need to take one step backward before taking two steps forward. Except in psychoanalysis, therapists actively interrupt patients' tendencies toward regression and encourage them to progress instead.

CHAPTER 6

Levels and Types of Psychotherapy

This chapter presents an overview of the three levels of psychotherapy. It also describes in detail the general principles of the three levels of psychotherapy that apply regardless of the specific method of psychotherapy employed at that level. The various techniques described under each of the three levels have more commonalities than differences, and their separation into different methods is more an issue of emphasis than a qualitative differentiation.

To ascertain the most fitting level and type of psychological treatment, the therapist needs to establish:

1. The ego strength of the patient. How well is the patient able to deal with the combined pressures from reality, superego, and id? That will indicate the level of therapeutic approach and therapeutic interventions.

2. The area in which the ego is weakest or is suffering the most distress. Is the source of stress primarily environmental or intrapsychic? If intrapsychic, does the difficulty stem from the demands of superego or id? Although most symptomatology has multiple determinants, deciding on the most important source of stress for the ego gives the therapist a starting point.

3. The patient's ego structure. What are the patient's most important defense and coping mechanisms? Which of these can be mobilized most readily and which most need to be worked through or altered?

4. A biopsychosocial diagnosis, if possible. This means taking a history adequate to establish the probable role of biological factors in patients' difficulties (Is the patient manifesting the depressed stage of a manic-depressive illness or a situational problem?). In addition, the

history assays the points in life at which the patient made or failed to make appropriate maturational steps and became fixated or developed immature defenses. In the history-taking, the therapist also examines the patient's past and present interpersonal environment. Who provided the patient's earlier satisfactions and frustrations and how? What persons constitute the patient's present sources of satisfaction and stress, and in what way do they support, frustrate, irritate, or gratify the patient?

5. The direction the transference will probably take. The therapist attempts to determine the characteristic transferences made by the patient in other relationships and the behaviors or attitudes on the part of others that have tended to trigger positive and negative transferences on the part of the patient. The therapist also uses this information to avoid falling into transference traps that will distract from the main thrust of therapy, and to capitalize on transferences that can make the therapy more effective.

6. The state of the patient's object relationships. Are there sufficient environmental supports or will the therapist be required to supply them personally or through placing the patient in a more supportive environment? Can the patient accept the therapist as a separate, real person, or are the patient's object needs and ego boundaries such that he or she will fear engulfment or will wish to be incorporated by the therapist?

Table 3 provides an overall frame of reference for comparing and contrasting the elements used in the three levels of psychotherapy. The three levels are based on differing views of dealing with unconscious mental processes — reinforcement of repression, circumscribed exploration of ego defenses, and exploration of repressed mental content (see Table 4). Patients' object needs also play a role.

Object relations, the establishment of which we deem a mark of maturity, exist to circumvent the pain of separateness. Object relations and ego differentiation occur only because the child and the mother cannot remain fused. Everyone, whether normal or neurotic, seeks to return to that period of symbiotic bliss through identification and object relations. Patients relinquish their hold on therapists as real persons so that they can learn more about themselves. Each time therapists treat patients as real persons (loaning them money for parking, or giving directions to the office), they temporarily ease patients' interpersonal loneliness and, ultimately, their feelings of abandonment by their parents. Patients and therapists basically wish to regard each other as real people, but most therapeutic approaches are more effective when therapists deliberately impose a barrier that keeps them, as people, out of the therapeutic interaction (Tarachow, 1963).

TABLE 3
Levels and Elements of Psychotherapy

Levels	Elements
Repressive	Interaction Stimulation of hope Attribution of meaning Reframing Command Suggestion Education Desensitization Reinforcement External support Behavior rehearsal Manipulation Dealing with transference and countertrans- ference
Ego-supportive	Interaction Stimulation of hope Attribution of meaning Reframing Feedback Identification Suggestion Education Desensitization Reinforcement Catharsis Facing emotional issues Testing of perceptions Working through Dealing with transference and countertrans- ference
Evocative	Interaction Stimulation of hope Attribution of meaning Reframing Catharsis Facing emotional issues Interpretation Insight Desensitization Identification Testing of perceptions Working through Dealing with transference and countertrans- ference

TABLE 4
Levels of Dynamic Psychotherapy

Repressive	Ego-Supportive	Evocative
A. Primary focus on problems in external reality.	A. Primary focus on problems in external reality, therapist–patient relationship.	A. Primary focus on patient's thoughts and feelings.
1. Therapist is voice of reality.	1. Patient encouraged to think out own problems with guidance.	1. Assumes patient can deal with reality.
2. Focuses on life outside the therapeutic hour.	2. Confronts behavior during therapy hour.	2. Deals with fantasies, free association.
B. Encourages dependence on therapist as authority.	B. Encourages moderate self-reliance.	B. Encourages full self-reliance.
1. Therapist actively directs sessions, may use agenda.	1. Therapist helps patient focus.	1. Patient usually takes the lead.
2. Therapist *explains* patient's symptoms, behavior, dreams.	2. Therapist encourages reflection.	2. Patient explains own behavior, dreams.
3. Therapist gives opinion about best courses of action.	3. Therapist gives occasional opinion.	3. Therapist follows patient's course of action.
4. Therapist often makes judgments for patient.	4. Encourages patient to use own judgment in most instances.	4. Therapist refrains from attempting to influence patient's judgment.

(continued)

TABLE 4 (*continued*)

Repressive	Ego-Supportive	Evocative
C. Stimulates positive transference.	C. Stimulates positive transference.	C. Stimulates full range of transference.
1. Therapist explains away negative aspects of transference.	1. Therapist allows limited negative transference to develop in specific sectors.	1. Transference development unrestricted.
2. Transference relationship static.	2. Transference partially developed.	2. Transference developed as fully as possible.
3. Therapist otherwise avoids becoming transference object.		
D. Stimulates use of secondary process.	D. Stimulates use of secondary process.	D. Encourages temporary lapse into primary process.
1. Patient explains what he or she means.	1. Active use of controlled imagination (guided imagery).	1. Free association—explanation not required.
2. Patient urged to communicate thoughts and feelings directly.	2. Patient urged to communicate thoughts and feelings directly.	2. Patient urged to communicate thoughts and feelings directly.
3. Session highly structured.	3. Intermediate level of structure.	3. Unstructured session.
4. Therapist's activity helps keep patient in reality.	4. Therapist remains active.	4. Often few sensory clues, but therapist may be active.
5. Therapist urges patient to ask questions instead of making assumptions.	5. Therapist urges patient to ask questions instead of making assumptions.	5. Therapist encourages patient to make assumptions.
6. Therapist encourages patient to think before acting.	6. Therapist encourages patient to think before acting.	6. Therapist encourages patient to verbalize without forethought.

TABLE 4 (continued)

Repressive	Ego-Supportive	Evocative
E. Therapist presents as real person (counterprojective), different from transference source.	E. Therapist gives feedback on impact of patient on therapist.	E. Therapist is transference object only.
1. Therapist teaches.	1. Therapist provides feedback.	1. Therapist interprets.
F. Therapist often intervenes actively in patient's life.	F. Therapist occasionally intervenes actively in patient's life.	F. Therapist seldom intervenes actively in patient's life.
1. May place in controlled environment to make environment more simple and predictable.		
1.1 May use coercion.		
2. Sets limits on actions.		
3. May instruct family, friends.		
G. Accepts patient's inability to tolerate intrapsychic sources of dysphoria.	G. Increases patient's capacity to tolerate intrapsychic sources of dysphoria.	G. Increases patient's capacity to tolerate dysphoria.
1. Focuses on control of symptoms by avoidance of triggering situations, and so forth.	1. Explores symptoms as they occur in interpersonal contexts.	1. Explores meaning of symptoms.
2. Avoids emotionally painful thoughts, feelings.	2. Deals with emotionally painful thoughts, feelings in the present.	2. Encourages facing present and past painful thoughts, feelings.

(continued)

117

TABLE 4 (*continued*)

Repressive	Ego-Supportive	Evocative
3. Chronic use of drugs to relieve dysphoria.	3. Short-term use of drugs to relieve dysphoria.	3. Rare use of drugs for dysphoria.
H. Accepts patient's defects in self-observation.	H. Stimulates patient's awareness in here-and-now of feelings and behaviors.	H. Increases patient's dynamic and genetic awareness.
1. Substitutes observations of therapist and concerned others.	1. Encourages awareness of feelings that lead to behavior.	1. Encourages awareness of feelings that lead to behavior.
2. May confront patient with behavior and its effects.	2. Confronts patient with effects of behavior on others.	2. Confronts patient with effects of behavior on others.
		3. Focuses on complex unconscious motivation for behavior.
I. Accepts defensive operations.	I. Challenges defensive operations in certain sectors of life and thinking.	I. Challenges defensive operations in many sectors of life and thinking.
1. Generally does not directly challenge projection, denial. Uses them as index of progress.	1. Challenges dysfunctional interpersonal defenses.	1. Challenges dysfunctional interpersonal defenses.
2. Family and couples therapy does challenge projection, denial at an interpersonal level.		2. Challenges dysfunctional intrapsychic defenses.

TABLE 4 (*continued*)

Repressive	Ego-Supportive	Evocative
J. Encourages accurate perception of reality. 1. Distracts from psychotic ideation. 2. May point out patient's role in creating interpersonal problems when patient is psychologically stable.	J. Encourages accurate perception of reality. 1. Actively points out patient's misperceptions of interpersonal reality. 2. Points out patient's role in creating here-and-now problems.	J. Encourages accurate perception of reality. 1. Points out patient's role in creating here-and-now problems. 2. Deals with the impact of patient's intrapsychic reality on perceptions.
K. Facilitates ego development or reintegration through teaching or modeling coping skills.	K. Facilitates ego development through encouraging patient to develop coping skills via participant observation.	K. Facilitates ego development through insight into maladaptive defensive reactions.
L. When the patient has an un-identifiable mental illness, patient may be encouraged to accept self as ill, and to see certain behavior as the result of illness.	L. Patient viewed as regressed or conflicted, not ill.	L. Patient not viewed as ill. Free will emphasized.

REPRESSIVE THERAPIES

Repressive (guidance, inspirational, educational) methods maintain repression of unconscious material because it is irrelevant to the therapy or because the therapist determines that exploring material from the unconscious may be destructive to the patient. Repressive techniques use *command, suggestion, education, desensitization, positive and negative reinforcement,* and *encouragement to obtain external support for new behaviors.* Repressive therapies conducted by lay therapists also facilitate *catharsis* and *identification.* Repressive therapies teach coping techniques, help develop social skills, and focus on problems of daily living – coping with reality.

Repressive approaches are used with persons who have little capacity, need, or motivation for insight or self-awareness. They are indicated for persons with little ego strength, in acute situational crises such as marital disruption, for individuals who want symptom relief more than self-understanding, and for persons who are not psychologically minded. Psychological-mindedness refers to the patient's ability to associate remembered or anticipated thoughts and feelings with actions.

In repressive techniques, patients' positive aspects are emphasized and their negative or self-defeating qualities are minimized. The sessions are highly structured, employ an agenda planned in advance, and often incorporate homework assignments designed to help patients implement what has been taught in therapeutic sessions (Ellis & Grieger, 1977). Therapists actively cultivate a positive relationship with patients and try to avoid transference formation by leaving little room for patients to use their imagination in an undirected way. When transferences that block the treatment do arise, therapists deal with them by explaining instead of exploring them or encouraging their continued development.

Regression is discouraged because of its potential for arousing material from the unconscious. Patients are encouraged to adopt slogans such as "think positively" or "move your muscles" (Low, 1952), which help them toward positive alternative behaviors. Repressive measures include reassurance that certain thoughts are normal. Assets and basic health or goodness are stressed, and attention is diverted from the unconscious toward problems of daily living. The repressive style ordinarily makes use of the therapeutic barrier; patients' vulnerability to their own object needs would lead them into unsuccessful attempts to incorporate the therapist as a real person. Repressive measures are useful in the early stages of all types of psychotherapy. They facilitate cooperation with the treatment and minimize anxiety until a bond is established between patient and therapist. Repressive measures are also appropriate in ego-supportive and evocative therapies when patients' anxiety becomes so intense that it works against the treatment process.

In the following example, the patient's intense anxiety made a repressive approach the only approach possible.

Mrs. A. A. B., a bright professional woman, was urged to have therapy by her supervisor because her difficulty interacting aggressively greatly hampered her work. Mrs. A. A. B. indicated that she had difficulty dealing with others' aggression in all areas of her life, but most of all at work and with her husband, by whom she was extremely intimidated.

She was very quiet and passive during sessions, awaiting the therapist's lead. She was extremely uncomfortable during their quiet periods and found herself feeling worse after particularly inactive sessions, during which she silently criticized herself and her therapist for not having more to say.

Finally, she became able to tell the therapist that she would find it helpful if he were to ask more direct questions instead of allowing long silences. Having previously failed to make headway by interpreting her silences as defenses against her aggression, the therapist became more active and focused on events in her daily life over which she had control and found that she was considerably more aggressive in her daily life than in the therapeutic session. She was pleased to agree that she was indeed more aggressive than she felt herself to be and listened attentively to the therapist's ideas as to how she could construct interpersonal interactions so that she was more in control and less vulnerable. For example, the therapist suggested that she present a controversial issue to her husband as an opportunity instead of a problem; that she start out with a firm voice when discussing important issues with other professionals.

This woman was better able to use a repressive approach than an insight-oriented approach despite her high intelligence, her professional training, and a character problem that was only moderate in degree.

EGO-SUPPORTIVE THERAPIES

Ego-supportive (counseling, interpersonal, interactional) methods are less highly structured than repressive therapies. They selectively reinforce repression of aspects of unconscious mental life that would overwhelm the ego and help to alter certain ego defenses so that they are less crippling. Patients are confronted with their projections (usually in the form of blaming others), denial (of responsibility for their own actions), and rationalizations (I can't help what I do) as they occur in day-to-day relationships. Ego-supportive approaches encourage the awareness of and taking responsibility for feelings and behavior, but their unconscious roots are not probed.

The chief therapeutic mechanisms of ego-supportive therapies are *feedback* and *identification*; feedback about the impact of the patient's behavior on the therapist and identification with healthy aspects of the therapist.

Feedback leads to the development of insight in interpersonal relations. Patients become more aware of the effects of others on them and the effects of their behavior on others, as the following vignette illustrates.

> Mrs. A. A. B. was unable to deal effectively with co-professionals because of her need to please and her fear of expressing her anger. Presenting herself to others in a meek, mousy way tended to irritate them instead of having the desired ingratiating effect.
>
> She maintained her same mousy demeanor with the therapist. During one session, however, he noted that her voice sounded fuller and more resonant and indicated his positive response to that. Calling attention to a positive behavior helped her to rehearse and to thereby present herself more effectively to her co-workers. It also helped the therapist avoid responding to her negative behavior in a way that she would have construed as critical and that would have undermined her self-esteem.

The feedback illustrated above differs from the intellectual insights achieved in repressive therapies, in which people learn to label aspects of themselves as sick or healthy, and the intrapsychic insight of evocative therapies in which patients become aware of the push and pull of unconscious emotional forces. Suggestion, education, reinforcement, facilitation of catharsis, encouragement to face emotional issues, and working through are also important elements of ego-supportive therapies.

Repressive therapies can be used with persons who have a wide range of ego strengths. Ego-supportive therapies are best used with people who have sufficient ego strength to cope adequately on a day-to-day basis. Ego-supportive therapies also require tolerance for a higher level of interpersonal tension than repressive therapies because they involve considerably more give and take between therapist and patient. Transferences are treated as distorted perceptions and are dealt with by helping the patient to see and correct those distortions in the here-and-now without tying them to the important persons in the patient's past.

Most once-a-week therapies conducted by professional psychotherapists are ego-supportive. There are too many special ego-supportive techniques to mention them all. Almost every therapist develops a personal vocabulary and many treatment techniques available are restatements of other widely used techniques.

Examples of ego-supportive therapies are Carl Rogers's (1951) client-centered therapy, Malan's (1976) and Davanloo's (1977) dynamically oriented brief psychotherapies, Transactional Analysis (Berne, 1964), Gestalt therapy (Stevens, 1975), and Psychodrama (Yablonsky, 1976).

EVOCATIVE THERAPIES

The evocative therapies (psychoanalysis, psychoanalytic psychotherapy) promote the emergence of material from the unconscious to shed light on the origins of present-day thinking and behavior in patients' childhood wishes and experiences. This is accomplished by stimulating partial ego regression through an unstructured therapy hour, lack of interpersonal cues, free association, and frustration of patients' object needs. The ego regression results in the development of transferences (Brenner, 1982) through which patients experience their basic instinctual drives, their infantile conflicts, and their fixations as though they were part of the present-day interaction with the therapist (Tarachow, 1963). Patients attempt to rework their defenses against their instinctual drives, to resolve their infantile conflicts, and to overcome their fixations. This type of approach requires a stable life adjustment, intact reality testing, and a capacity for a nondestructive partial ego regression.

Patients reverse their ego regression at the end of each session and become aware of their feelings during sessions rather than acting them out. Self-observation comes about through a "split" of the ego, one side caught up in the transference, the other observing itself in the transference relationship. The ego must also have sufficient strength to cope with the superego, so that it can observe its own defensive operations objectively instead of becoming self-accusatory.

An analytically oriented method requires that therapists frustrate their own, as well as patients' object needs. After their initial encounter, patient and therapist separate as people. It is the patient's initial contact and partial identification with the therapist that makes the resulting frustration bearable. Obviously, there are points in the therapeutic process when therapists must assure patients that they are working with a real person.

Analytically oriented therapies constitute, in a sense, a process of deprivation. The patient is deprived of infantile gratification through interpretation ("it looks like you're trying to make me into an all-giving mother") to free patients to pursue adult gratification. Viewed from this perspective, *every interpretation is a deprivation* (Greenson, 1967).

The psychoanalytic model is generally not suitable for therapists who need patients to regard them as real people instead of fantasy-generators, but that does not mean that the analytically based therapist is always neutral. The reality of the therapist is an important factor in maintaining ongoing analytic therapy. At times, it is necessary for analytic therapists to introduce some aspect of themselves as people, not only as a tension breaker, but also to correct the patients' fantasies and distortions (Greenson, 1967).

Evocative techniques have no place in treating persons with markedly impaired reality testing or impulse control, except under controlled circumstances in an institution.

The main tools of evocative therapists are facilitation of *catharsis, encouragement to face emotional issues*, the development of *insight* through a series of steps that culminate in interpretation of the present in terms of the past, and *working through*. Elements of desensitization and identification are probably also of some importance.

Evocative therapies usually require that patients be seen three to five times a week in 45- to 50-minute sessions. A couch is used in formal psychoanalysis, but may not be used in psychoanalytic psychotherapy. The frequency of sessions has some influence on the level at which patients' unconscious can be probed, but patients can also be seen frequently and dealt with by ego-supportive or repressive means through shortening the sessions and focusing on daily activities and occurrences.

SUMMARY

Treatment approaches can modify patients' environments so that they can function more effectively, can enable them to function within their current limitations, or can modify patients psychologically so that they function more effectively.

In determining the most applicable approach, one considers not only the patient but the interpersonal milieu. Treatment of children, for example, is frequently ineffective unless some change occurs in the family's interaction. Treatment of patients of any age can disrupt their most important relationships (Weiner, 1975).

Psychological methods are only a part of the larger armamentarium of treatment techniques that can be brought to bear on emotional problems. The choice of treatment method applied to the individual patient (physical, chemical, or psychological) depends on many factors, including the patient's biological vulnerability, the social milieu, the patient's emotional resources, and the treatment resources available, including the personal and professional limitations of the professional who carries out the treatment. Additional factors include the way the patient conceives of his or her difficulty; as an illness or as a psychological problem. The patient's ability to cooperate and motivation to do so also figure prominently in the decision as to choice of treatment method.

Finally, it must be stated that combined psychological approaches are often effective (Levitz & Stunkard, 1974; Liebman, Minuchin, & Baker, 1974). Psychotherapy, chemical treatment, and modification of the patient's life situation are also combined frequently. No decision about the main therapeutic method need be permanent. As the patient and his or her life situation changes, so can the treatment approach.

CHAPTER 7

Level and Timing
of Interventions

Patients often complain that their psychotherapists are too passive. On the other hand, therapists with highly structured active treatment techniques are criticized by their peers for imposing their frame of reference on patients without listening. The main issue, however, is not inactivity versus activity. It is what kind of activity, how much, and when. The danger lies in therapists' stereotyped use of any one type of treatment.

Lack of overt action does not always constitute therapeutic inactivity. Psychotherapists need not act the first time they make an observation about a patient or the first time a patient engages in a particular type of interaction with them, unless the patient is a clear danger to self or others. If the observation made or the interaction noted is dynamically important, the opportunity will present again and its recurrence may point to specific patterns of thinking, feeling, or behavior. Therapists are therefore not silent in order to frustrate their patients. They are silent because they have insufficient data, opportunity, or means to warrant or enable them to make an intervention at a particular time. They await a better opportunity or actively construct that opportunity.

Once therapists have decided on a therapeutic level or technique, they use the elements of psychotherapy accordingly, selecting a level of intervention that fits with their techniques and goals.

LEVELS OF INTERVENTION

The level at which therapists make observations and psychological interventions helps shape patients' conceptualization of their problems and provides a focus of investigation. The three levels are day-to-day reality (there-and-then), the emotional forces currently operating within the individual (dynamic or here-and-now), and the relationship of a patients' past thoughts, feelings, and experiences to their present perceptions of, and reactions to, their interpersonal and intrapsychic worlds (genetic) (Weiner, 1970). There-and-then interventions are part of repressive, ego-supportive, and evocative therapies. Here-and-now dynamic interventions are most useful in ego-supportive and evocative therapies. Genetic interventions are usually reserved for evocative therapies.

The use of these three levels of intervention is illustrated by vignettes from the treatment of Mrs. A. T.

Mrs. A. T. was a 43-year-old woman who had suffered from rheumatoid arthritis since the age of 10. She had been in once-a-week psychotherapy in another state for 13 years. She made good use of her therapy, and was dealing well with her husband, her child, and her illness at the time her husband was transferred to Texas.

After a year in Texas, her arthritis flared up. She was started on anti-inflammatory steroid medication and her arthritis improved, but she became extremely dysphoric. As a result, she again sought psychiatric treatment. Her new therapist consulted with her former therapist over the telephone and also reviewed his written summary of her treatment with him. Mrs. A. T. had been treated at an ego-supportive evocative level. Her transference to her former therapist was that of a preoedipal child to an idealized parent. The therapist's countertransference appeared to have been a helpful sublimation of his nurturing urges.

Mrs. A. T.'s new therapist thought that her therapy should now be focused on working through the idealized parental transference toward her former therapist and becoming her own parent.

There-and-Then

There-and-then interventions deal with some aspect of the patient's real life situation and do not involve the patient's reactions to the therapist or the antecedents of present-day behavior.

Mrs. A. T., for example, saw her former therapist and former rheumatologist as having been responsible for her receiving the best possible care for her arthritis. When her case was reviewed, it turned out that she had taken much initiative on her own behalf, had often correctly gone against her doctors' advice, and had not actually been carried over life's burdens by them.

Here-and-Now Dynamic

Here-and-now dynamic interventions deal with the therapist–patient relationship and suggest psychological cause and effect.

> Mrs. A. T. was aware of a difference in treatment approach by her former therapist and her new therapist. Her former therapist thought that lifelong once-a-week therapy might greatly alleviate her emotional ups and downs and thereby mitigate the course of her arthritis. Her new therapist thought that psychotherapy would not alter the course of her arthritis and that working toward dependence on herself, her peers, and her other physicians would be more useful to her, especially because she and her husband were to move again in a few years. He worked toward this goal at a here-and-now dynamic level by encouraging her to express her anger with him for not assuming a nurturing role toward her and for pushing her to stand on her own two feet, and to interact with others who suffered from arthritis instead of holding herself apart from them as she had formerly done.

Genetic

Genetic interventions tie present to past, elucidating unconscious themes held over from childhood. Bringing affective material from the past into the transference relationship with the therapist allows the reworking of feelings or thought patterns in the here-and-now of the patient–therapist relationship.

> Mrs. A. T.'s former therapist was presented to her new therapist as the perfect parent she wished she had instead of her nagging, superstitious parents who had preferred her brother. She was helped to relinquish her grudge toward her own parents, relinquish her former therapist as an idealized parent, and mobilize the adult part of her own ego.

As a result of work at all three levels, Mrs. A. T. decided to lessen the strain on her joints through reducing her physical activity, and to seek additional orthopedic consultation.

MODES OF INTERVENTION

Therapists often delay their responses to their patients' behavior. They may await further information. Even if they have sufficient information, they may delay until the patient is able to make use of a particular kind of intervention. With Mrs. A. T., the genetic intervention actually preceded the there-and-then intervention. It was not until her idealization of her former therapist was partly worked through that she could assess her own role in the treatment of her arthritis.

The four basic modes of intervention are *acceptance, suppression, facilitation*, and *exploration*.

Acceptance

Acceptance is a nonjudgmental response of the therapist that denotes a rational or intuitive understanding of the patient. It is an acknowledgement that, at a given moment, the therapist has entered the patient's emotional world. It may be signaled by a nod of the head, or by the therapist saying, "I see," "I hear you," or the traditional therapeutic, "Uh huh." The basic unspoken message is the therapist's recognition of and respect for the patient as a person. Acceptance is often the first step in the patient's opening up to the therapist. It is only after having felt accepted by the therapist that many patients go on to reveal their private concerns.

Suppression

Suppressive interventions aim to inhibit thoughts, feelings, or acts. Certain suppressive interventions are mandatory, such as suppressing physical violence. Therapists may request that patients reconsider a contemplated behavior, warn them that the behavior will not be allowed, or physically restrain patients.

> After Mr. D. threatened on several occasions to kill his brother, the therapist became alarmed. Because Mr. D.'s impulse control and judgment were questionable, the therapist indicated that he would warn Mr. D.'s brother if Mr. D. intended to carry out the threat. Mr. D.'s anger was then turned toward the therapist and was worked through.

Safety dictates the form of intervention in the presence of physical danger. In some cases, it may involve calling a security guard or the police.

In an evocative therapy, therapists may wish to suppress other forms of activity, such as casual person-to-person conversation, after explaining to patients that therapy progresses best if they stick to business. In repressive or ego-supportive therapies, therapists may allow social interchange to ease emotional pressures during the therapeutic session, to limit the transference potential of the relationship, or to help with the development of conversational and social skills.

Facilitation

Facilitative interventions bring psychological material to awareness or make material available for discussion.

Psychological facilitations range from requests that patients talk to confrontation, clarification, and interpretation. A confrontation establishes that something is being avoided, for example, "You're not looking at me today. What do you feel?" A clarification aims to establish a sharp focus on a particular psychological event. One might say, "You have been talking about other people being angry. Maybe that's what I'm reacting to. Perhaps you're angry." Confrontation and clarification refer not only to content, but also to the direction of communication. For example, the therapist may say, "You're treating me as if I weren't even here." Confrontation and clarification are utilized in repressive, ego-supportive, and evocative therapies.

Interpretations may be made early to defuse a rapidly building transference, e.g., "You're reacting to me as though I were as harsh as your father." Such interpretations do not make unconscious material conscious. They help patient and therapist label the patient's behavior and indicate its incongruity by tying it to the patient's past instead of only calling attention to its inappropriateness, and thus reinforcing the patient's view of the therapist as punitive and judgmental.

Exploration

Explorative interventions link thoughts, feelings, and behavior. In repressive therapies, therapists make new connections by suggesting alternative behaviors. For example, a therapist may respond to the patient's question regarding how to stop nail-biting by suggesting that the patient chew gum or engage in other forms of physical activity. Attributing meaning to thoughts and behavior is a valuable device in supportive therapy, or when any therapy is at a supportive level. For example, in dealing with a phobic patient, a therapist might say, "Irrational fears such as yours can be useful clues to self-understanding." Thus, the therapist indicates that the phobic symptoms are meaningful and that the patient can come to understand their meaning. This answer also points toward the unconscious symbolism without involving primary process. In evocative therapies, the patient explores himself through free association. Therapists can also stimulate patients' self-exploration by asking direct or open-ended questions, encouraging patients to express fantasy, or by offering fantasies of their own that emerge during the therapy hour (Singer & Pope, 1978).

TIMING

The timing of therapists' interventions is determined by the real therapist–patient relationship, the patient's ego strength and structure, the nature of the patient–therapist alliance, the patient's level of trust, the patient's object need, the patient's feelings about the therapist, and the therapist's feelings about the patient.

The Real Therapist–Patient Relationship

The real (nontransference) patient–therapist relationship includes the context of their initial contact, the purpose of their relationship, their working conditions, and how they experience each other as people.

Two issues concerning the context of the initial patient–therapist contact are: who has the problem, and the extent of the patient's motivation to deal with the problem. When patients are referred because their behavior troubles others but does not trouble them, therapists decide whether to point out the problem to the patients or to communicate information about the patients to the referring individual(s) so that they can better cope with patients. In either case, the therapist points out their real relationship, stating whom he or she serves and in what capacity. If patient and therapist agree that the therapist's primary alliance is to the patient, they need to agree on the goals toward which they will work.

The patient and therapist together establish how much the therapist will decide what is best for the patient. That includes how much the therapist will actively interfere with, or attempt to manage, the patient's life, as well as the degree of confidentiality of the relationship. With outpatients, these issues are usually dealt with implicitly. When patients require hospitalization or have borderline coping ability, they are made explicit.

The real therapist–patient relationship includes their experience of each other as real people. From the therapist's perspective, one may consider certain therapist-offered conditions.

From a study of the psychological treatment of hospitalized schizophrenic patients, Carl Rogers (1957) proposed three therapist-offered conditions that appeared to affect the length and frequency of patients' hospitalization; the therapist's genuineness, accurate empathy, and unconditional positive regard. The quality of genuineness refers to therapists' appearing to believe in what they say to patients; it is an absence of a manipulative quality in their interactions with patients. Accurate empathy is the therapist's actual ability to partially identify with and respond empathically to each patient. Unconditional positive regard means that the therapist conveys respect and positive feeling toward each patient as a person regardless of the patient's symptoms or behavior. While it has not been possible to confirm definitely the value of Rogers's therapist-offered conditions (Mitchell, Bozarth, & Kraufft, 1977), it seems likely that these qualities of the therapist are important components of the therapeutic process, while recognizing that there are some situations in which therapists must manipulate patients, that there are certain patient behaviors with which therapists cannot empathize, and that certain conditions exist under which the patient as a person cannot be accepted by the therapist. Manipulation may be necessary to induce patients to face situations they would rather avoid. Empathizing with dangerous or antisocial behavior might amount to condoning them, as might unconditional positive regard. On the other side of the coin, the therapist may have to actively withhold warmth and positive regard to keep from threatening schizoid patients with engulfment or stimulating borderline patients' wish to engulf.

The Patient's Ego Strength and Ego Structure

Before attempting to impart information to a patient, the therapist assesses the patient's ego strength at that moment. The relationship between therapeutic interventions by the therapist and the ego strength of the patient is multifaceted. The less the patients' ego strength, the greater will be their need to experience their environment as real, instead of experiencing it as a projection of their own fears and wishes. However, patients who have little ego strength are likely to misinterpret the therapists' actions or be unable to constructively integrate them into their thinking. For example, a female patients' wish for, and fear of, her therapist's sexual interest may increase when she learns her therapist sees her more often than other patients. That may stimulate a crippling regression. Suitable interventions with patients of low ego strength enhance reality testing, reinforcing impulse control, reducing fantasy, and augmenting the ego's defenses against disruptive aspects of the unconscious.

Although patients with more ego strength have less need to experience the therapist as a real person, they are also less likely to be damaged by the therapist. If the therapist's interventions stimulate fantasy or intensify unconscious impulses, the therapist may note a strengthening of resistances that signals the therapist to be more passive until the consequences of the intervention are worked through. A well-integrated patient is not directly damaged by most interventions. The damage is to the therapeutic relationship; intervention may undermine its effectiveness by changing the focus from patient to the therapist's activity.

Ego structure refers to the dynamic balance between the psychological forces that determine each person's characteristic responses to life events and psychological events. In addition, it also refers to alterations in that characteristic structure that occur with psychological decompensation. The following vignette provides examples of both.

A 55-year-old man was hospitalized for treatment of a life-threatening cardiac arrhythmia that followed a severe heart attack he had suffered six months before.

The patient's father had died of asthma when the patient was eight years old. As an adult, the patient was quite concerned that he might develop lung disease. Against the advice of his physician, he had taken a broad-spectrum antibiotic for years. In addition, he had jogged four miles a day for many years prior to his heart attack, and had successfully coached a number of children's athletic teams. In short, this man coped with his fears of physical helplessness by reaction formation involving intense physical activity.

Soon after he was hospitalized, he became delirious. During his delirium, he frequently expressed the idea that there was a plot to kill him. His notion that there was a plot against him alternated with him expressing his feelings of helplessness and hopelessness.

This man's delirium was largely due to the antiarrhythmic drugs with which he was treated. The paranoid content reflected his impaired ego's attempt to deal with his feelings of helplessness and his feeling that the body that he had worked so diligently to maintain was now betraying him. Because reaction formation was no longer available to him as a means to cope, his weakened ego dealt with his fear by projection.

As his delirium subsided, so did his paranoid ideas. He later apologized to the attending physician for having thought ill of him; this suggested that he was again able to make use of reaction formation.

There are many types of ego structure. Some are described phenomenologically as personality disorders in *Diagnostic and Statistical Manual of Mental Disorders, 3rd ed.* (DSM-III) (American Psychiatric Association, 1980), as indicated in Chapter 3.

Therapists learn to work within the context of their patients' personality structure. They avoid shows of friendliness to paranoid persons because paranoid persons experience a show of friendliness as a setup for attack. They avoid pressing schizoid and schizotypal persons to deal with the therapist as other than a neutral therapeutic instrument. And they structure the therapeutic hour when dealing with borderline personality disorders.

The Nature of the Alliance

The ideal alliance between therapist and patient is between the rational, health-seeking part of the patient and the rational, objectively observing aspect of the therapist. Other types of alliance are possible. Some patients hope to continue acting on their impulses instead of dealing with them and therefore seek out incompetent therapists. People who wish to reinforce the harsh aspects of their own conscience may seek a punitive, judgmental therapist. A person who wishes to enhance intellectual defenses may seek out a therapist who promotes rationalization.

Trust. Trust is a necessary part of the therapeutic alliance. Patients' trust may be based on transference expectations or the therapist's reputation, or patients may await evidence of therapists' trustworthiness before investing themselves in the therapist as a person or in the therapeutic process. Active attempts by therapists to cultivate trust are seldom helpful. Disclosure by therapists of their past successes or their good will toward patients have little influence on the development of trust. In the course of their regular contact, patients observe and experience their therapists' self-awareness, their self-confidence, and their capacity for understanding – and then decide whether trust is merited. Exaggerated trust or mistrust point to the operation of transference factors that may require investigation.

Object need. The object need of therapist and patient alike strongly affects the alliance. Therapists with strong object needs may repel schizoid persons, who feel engulfed or drained by human contact. Masochistic, self-sacrificing patients may be attracted by a therapist's need for admiration, but this type of alliance may perpetuate their psychopathology. Patients with great object needs may be seen as too draining by some therapists. Other therapists may see the possibility of mutual gratification during the course of therapy and do effective psychotherapy in a relationship that involves patient and therapist serving as real objects for one another.

The Patient's Feelings About the Therapist

In dealing with patients, therapists take into account patients' feelings toward them. That includes patients' probable unconscious feelings, as well as their consciously experienced and expressed feelings. Every patient has some transference feelings. Other feelings stem from the real situation – anger, for example, if therapists forget patients' appointments or keep them waiting. Still other feelings are based on nontransference expectations, such as the reasonable assumption that the patient will be accepted by the therapist.

Therapists can manipulate patients' feelings by various means. However, one cannot accurately predict the outcome. The same intervention with different persons who feel the same way about the therapist may have very different effects. If the therapist is active, activity on his or her part may be eagerly accepted by some patients; others, in spite of basically positive feelings, may feel the therapist is trying to control them.

In repressive therapies, positive feelings toward the therapist are accepted and are not explored. Therapists attempt to dispel negative feelings toward themselves by apologizing for or explaining away behavior by which they have antagonized patients. Negative transference feelings are also explained away. Therapists may reveal negative feelings of their own that developed under similar circumstances to promote the patients' identification with them and to indicate the essential normality of the patient's feelings.

Ego-supportive therapies explore the current factors in the patient's reaction to the therapist. Since the patient in an ego-supportive therapy has enough ego strength to feel and express his or her negative feelings toward the therapist without disrupting their relationship or acting self-destructively, awareness and expression of both positive and negative feelings are encouraged. The therapist stimulates the patient's expression of feelings by asking about feelings directly and also by asking if the opposite feeling also exists when one feeling is expressed. If the patient expresses liking the therapist, the patient may be asked if negative feelings are ever experienced.

In evocative therapies, therapists consider dynamic and genetic factors as they explore patients' feelings toward them. Therapists correct transference distortions only after patients have fully experienced the transference feelings and have explored all of their ramifications. In repressive and ego-supportive therapies, therapists begin to correct transference distortions early to prevent them from obstructing therapy. In an evocative therapy, the transference is allowed to become an obstruction and is then dealt with by an appropriate interpretation.

If therapists are seen by patients as the most important source of the patients' object needs, therapists must be careful not to stimulate intensely negative feelings toward themselves. Such interventions may precipitate a suicide attempt or withdrawal from treatment.

When the patient's object needs are well supplied outside the treatment relationship, there is greater likelihood that the patient's negative feelings will be talked out in the therapeutic situation and not acted out. On the other hand, stimulating positive feelings toward the therapist may reinforce a patient's masochistic demands to be dominated.

The Therapist's Feelings About the Patient

Every therapist develops feelings about his or her patients. Sometimes therapists' feelings enable them to do better work; at other times they are detrimental to the therapeutic relationship. If the therapist wishes to disclose his or her feelings to a patient, the therapist does well to first examine this wish. If the therapist is responding to the patient's urgings, the patient's motivation may be questioned by the therapist (at least internally) before a reply is given. This is especially important when the therapist or the patient feels that the disclosure is urgent.

Therapists try not to belittle a patient whom they dislike or to enhance themselves in the eyes of a patient from whom they wish positive regard.

The therapist's unconscious feelings and reactions to patients are of even greater importance than the therapist's conscious attitudes. These unconscious aspects of the therapist manifest themselves indirectly. To effectively deal with their own reactions, therapists observe their patients and themselves. Not all the therapist's unconscious reactions to the patient are countertransferences. Often, therapists are reacting to their anxiety about their own feelings or their ability to control their impulses.

Early in the treatment of a woman who had several extramarital liaisons, the therapist told her flatly that he did not intend to become physically involved with her. By employing that psychological overkill, the therapist confirmed the patient's view of herself as a malignant, destructive person. When the therapist, who was reacting to his own anxiety, felt in better control of himself and felt the treatment was progressing satisfactorily, he told the woman that he had reacted to his own sexual feelings rather than a sexual provocation on her part. This greatly diminished her sense of "badness" and facilitated a fruitful exploration of her sexuality.

SUMMARY

Decisions about the level and timing of therapeutic interventions are based on the active interplay between patient and therapist and not on arbitrary predetermined standards based on diagnosis or any other single criterion. The diagnosis in terms of the patient's ego strength determines the level of intervention. Patients' object needs and their reactions thereto determine how much therapists make their presence felt as people. The patient's coping and defensive mechanisms determine the nature and timing of specific interventions. Obsessive patients are encouraged to feel, while histrionic and impulsive persons are urged to think before they act. Paranoid persons' view of reality is unchallenged; depressed patients' view of the world is actively contested. In all cases, the level of interventions and their timing can vary widely as the patient–therapist interaction changes and as the patient's areas of vulnerability and assets change over time.

CHAPTER 8

The Therapist

The therapist is an important part of the therapeutic process. Although many aspects of the therapist's role change during the patient's therapy, one aspect generally does not. It is the therapist who directs the therapy, not in an arbitrary way that is based solely on the therapist's theoretical orientation, but rather in a way that is based on the patient's psychopathology, life situation, and unique personality.

In this chapter, therapists' responsibilities, their tools for working with patients, their interpersonal style, and the impact of their personal lives on therapy will be discussed, and an ideal therapist will be described. We will begin by reviewing therapists' responsibilities to their patients.

RESPONSIBILITIES

Therapists' responsibilities include establishing a therapeutic frame of reference, setting goals, establishing a level of participation, and developing awareness of their own personalities and styles, including dealing with their own personal needs as they are affected by outside events or events in the patient–therapist interaction.

Establishing a Therapeutic Frame of Reference

After taking an adequate history from patients and other pertinent sources, therapists establish a therapeutic frame of reference. They tentatively decide what direction therapy will take so as to be able to offer a therapeutic contract and to guide their interaction with patients after the contract has been accepted.

In order to establish a therapeutic frame of reference, therapists need to have been adequately trained in one or more therapeutic approaches. From their armamentarium, therapists choose an approach that most closely fulfills patients' treatment needs.

There are rare, very mature, well-trained therapists who can simply "go with the flow," making no conscious treatment decision, and following their instincts about what to say and when and how to say it. While existentially correct, and most likely to yield an authentic I–thou encounter between therapist and patient, most therapists treat patients more effectively if they develop a conscious plan for the therapy.

For trainees dealing with their first cases, the story is somewhat different. Because they lack an adequate frame of reference and adequate psychodynamic diagnostic skills, their cases are prescreened to insure that no immediate interventions are called for, and that the first sessions between fledgling therapist and new patient can be a gentle, extended history-taking that can be guided by a supervisor into a therapeutic interaction.

Setting Goals

The reduction of intrapsychic conflict is a reasonable technical goal for therapists to set for themselves, but is not ordinarily useful as a therapeutic contract to potential patients. Patients require concrete, measurable goals such as the reduction of unpleasant symptoms or self-defeating behaviors. As therapists attempt to formulate goals for patients, they concomitantly assess patients' ability to reach those goals. Therapists in a state hospital follow-up clinic may wish to help their patients achieve relief of symptoms through insight into unconscious mental processes or to achieve global personality change, but they are likely to frustrate themselves and to torment their patients by setting goals that are unattainable for the majority. If, on the other hand, therapists' patients are bright, verbal, and psychologically intact, these may be valid goals because of the candidates' innate abilities and because of the therapists' ability to identify with their patients (Berzins, 1977). It is also important that therapists be aware that their treatment goals do not always limit its eventual outcome. Many patients who have received short-term or supportive treatment make important changes in their lives.

In setting goals, therapists take into account their level of training and expertise in four areas; their ability to teach principles of psychologically healthy functioning, their sophistication about psychopathology, their mastery of psychological interventions, and their self-awareness. A good teacher with little sophistication about psychopathology and little formal awareness of therapeutic techniques can often conduct a repressive therapy well. Therapists who teach well, who have sophistication about psychopathology, and who are technically well equipped can conduct ego-supportive therapy well, even if they lack significant awareness of their own unconscious processes. By contrast, evocative therapists need not be talented teachers, because their therapeutic medium is confrontation and interpretation, not explanation or modeling. However, they must understand psychopathology well, must be able to facilitate the emergence of material from the unconscious, and must be sufficiently self-aware to help them guide the patient–therapist interactions without stimulating acting out.

In addition, setting goals requires that therapists know what support is available should patients require additional help through medication or hospitalization. If such support is not readily available and their patients have little ego strength, they will do best to conduct a therapy with limited behavioral goals. If such support is readily available, they can more reasonably strive for broader changes, anticipating that there will be occasional adverse reactions that may require biological treatment.

Therapists' Level of Participation

The nature of therapists' participation relates to the type and goal of treatment, the real therapist–patient relationship, patients' feelings about the therapist, and the therapist's feelings toward patients.

Type and goal of treatment. The therapist's participation varies in different types of therapy. In repressive therapies, the therapist is an active presence with an identifiable personality who instructs, advises, promotes discussion of important topics, and actively questions.

Therapists provide interpersonal feedback in ego-supportive therapy. By stating their reactions to patients, therapists enhance patients' awareness of their impact on others and validate or correct patients' perception of others' reactions. Therapists can model self-acceptance and acceptance of responsibility for their own feelings and behavior.

In evocative therapies, therapists begin as a neutral presence with a low level of interaction. Therapists' level of interaction changes as greater or lesser amounts of clarification, confrontation, and interpretation are required.

The real therapist–patient relationship. Frequently, therapists and patients are not totally unknown to each other. Therapists need not exclude all people whom they have ever met from their help, but should not undertake the treatment of persons over whom they have real influence (aside from hospitalized patients), or persons who have real influence over them, such as the manager of their professional office building.

Real relationships also develop during the course of therapy. Therapists and patients come to appreciate each other as real people. They learn to enjoy each other's company and, to a certain extent, learn to tolerate each other's interpersonal liabilities as each becomes important in the other's support network. For the above reasons, long-term therapies may sometimes lose their potency. When therapist and patient become stable parts of each other's emotional lives, it may be time to change therapists or mode of therapy.

Patients' feelings about therapists. Nontransference feelings toward therapists must be considered. Patients often feel abandoned when therapists are inactive, and their sense of abandonment may need to be offset by therapists' increased activity in asking questions or guiding the discussion. Patients are angered when their therapists are late and hurt when their appointments are canceled because of therapists putting their own needs first. Therapists often omit common courtesy in their desire not to contaminate a neutral therapeutic field, and in doing so often stimulate negative feelings. Failing to note that a patient has suffered a physical injury or appears ill, or failing to acknowledge that a patient has suffered an important setback on the job contributes to patients' sense of alienation and dehumanizes the therapeutic situation.

While many feeling reactions to therapists are partly rooted in transference, they often must be dealt with first as real events that call forth strong emotional reactions.

Therapists' feelings. Therapists' feelings during sessions can help them become aware of patients' resistances. If therapists' boredom or irritation indicates avoidance of issues by patients, they can interrupt silences by asking questions. Small talk can be steered to more profitable topics. After rapport has been established, therapists can express their own reactions to deal with resistances. For example, therapists can express boredom or restlessness in a kind way and suggest to their patients that more lively issues are probably being avoided. Accusing patients of being boring is scarcely ever productive, but therapists can reasonably say something like the following.

Something is different this session. Usually, I have no trouble following you, but today I'm really having trouble getting involved with what you're saying. Is it something in me, or have you noticed any difference in the quality of what's going on today?

THERAPISTS' TOOLS

Therapists' principal tools are their professional training, their innate empathic abilities, and their ability to use their own personalities as therapeutic instruments.

Professional Training

Adequate training involves didactic learning and supervised interaction with patients. It is not possible to state how many books of what kind need to be read, how many hours of lecture are required, or how many hours of supervised work with patients. For most psychiatrists, an additional several years beyond their four years of formal training are required to develop competence as a broadly based psychotherapist, and many seek an additional year or more of weekly supervision.

At the beginning, therapists in training require nearly hour for hour supervision of their cases. As trainees progress, many cases require only occasional supervision concerning specific problems that arise in the treatment. Each trainee needs the experience of videotaping sessions with patients and reviewing the tapes with one or more supervisors. The meta-language of therapy and the nonverbal communication during the hour can more readily be detected and dealt with in this way.

Empathy

Therapists need the capacity to put themselves in another person's place and imagine how this individual thinks and feels. The process of empathy occurs through two pathways—projecting the therapist into the patient (how would I feel if I were he?), and introjecting aspects of the patient (how would perceiving the world in that way lead me to behave?). These processes call for a certain fluidity of therapists' ego boundaries while still recognizing that it is only *as if* one is entering the psyche of another or allowing another to enter oneself.

The empathic process may be frightening to some persons, who fear the possible dissolution of their ego boundaries. Indeed, this diffusion of feelings across ego boundaries is responsible for many of the feelings that therapists experience in their interaction with patients. In addition, therapists' values and ego defenses make certain types of empathy more difficult. It is not difficult, for example, to empathize with loss of a lover. It becomes more difficult for many if the relationship was homosexual. It may be fairly easy to empathize with fear of the opposite sex based on a boy's intense oedipal rivalry with his father, but it is more difficult to empathize with the related perversion of pederasty.

Many therapists experiencing close emotional contact with persons who engage in what is for them feared or forbidden behavior also are frightened of contamination or possible entanglement in the feared or forbidden behavior. Thus, many therapists find that there are patients with whom their value systems block empathic contact. The same is true in terms of ego defenses. Some therapists tolerate aggression well, because they do not fear their own aggression. Others are so frightened by their own aggression that their defenses against it are too greatly threatened by aggressive patients.

Many of the problems of empathy can be dealt with in the supervisory process. What cannot be altered in supervision may be amenable to resolution in a trainees' group or in personal, individual therapy. What cannot be resolved needs to be noted by each therapist and to form part of the basis of each therapist's selection of patients.

In time, therapists use their own personalities as therapeutic instruments; sometimes through the process of self-disclosure, and sometimes by taking advantage of their own personality traits. That includes their ability to tolerate aggression or to be aggressive; their ability to be tender or accept tenderness, and so on.

Therapist Disclosure

I have discussed therapist self-disclosure at length elsewhere (Weiner, 1983a). Therapist disclosure may be employed in repressive, ego-supportive, and evocative therapies. In repressive and supportive therapies, it provides feedback at an interpersonal level, an avenue for identification, and a distraction from unconscious processes.

In evocative therapies, therapists provide sufficient information about themselves to adequately orient the patient and avoid the dehumanizing effect of total frustration. On the other hand, they do not present so much information about themselves that they obscure material from their patients' unconscious or help patients rationalize their transference distortions or their acting out. Inadvertent self-disclosures on the part of the therapist stimulate the development of transference. Deliberate disclosures may be useful in resolving transference distortions once an adequate working alliance has been established with patients' rational, observing egos.

As a general rule, therapists withhold their personal reactions until a constructive working relationship has been established. Using personal openness to seduce unmotivated patients into a working relationship frequently backfires (Freud, 1914/1958). Only with the most regressed patients is it necessary to "loan" a bit of one's self to supply sufficient hope and energy to spark a positive interaction. Most patients who push therapists to "show and tell" are usually trying to avoid self-exploration.

Well-timed disclosures can be used to cut through the projective identification and defensive splitting of object relations employed by borderline patients. Therapist disclosures can be used to establish that therapists have thoughts and feelings that differ from those of adolescent patients, who wish for and fear a return to the more nearly symbiotic relationship of earlier childhood, rather than face the uncertainties of becoming adults. Disclosing that therapists' thoughts and feelings differ from those attributed to them by patients can help persons who have difficulty seeing therapists as individuals rather than embodiments of their projected thoughts and feelings. They can also be useful with provocative patients who fail to understand the impact of their behavior on others, and for patients who see their therapists as extensions of their own fears and wishes.

Therapists must be aware of the impact of particular types of disclosures on patients with certain dynamic constellations. Disclosing feelings of friendliness to paranoid patients may heighten their suspicions. Expressing sympathy to severely depressed persons may increase their feelings of unworthiness. Patients must be able to integrate their therapists' disclosures in a constructive way.

When therapists make errors in treatment that are detected by patients, it is advisable for them to acknowledge their errors to confirm their patients' perceptions (not to expiate their own guilt). The patient's reactions to the error should then be explored in terms of the patient's own problems. Confessing shortcomings to patients who feel negatively about the therapist undermines the therapeutic relationship. Dealing with patients' negative feelings through expressions of friendliness may heighten guilt, intensify anger, and increase the distance between therapist and patient. Patients' hostile feelings should be acknowledged neutrally if possible. The performance of overtly hostile acts may necessitate physical restraint if therapist or patient is endangered.

On occasion, an overt emotional reaction by the therapist is the best means to indicate that he or she is not impervious and does react as a person to the patient. There are some patients who demand an overt reaction, and who will rage or sulk until they have provoked one. However, it is damaging to patients if therapists are contemptuous, hostile, and nonaccepting (Lieberman, Yalom, & Miles, 1973).

Style

Style refers to the quality of therapists' behavior with patients and the quality of interaction they stimulate or allow. Usually, therapists' style is more strongly related to their personality and personal needs than their theoretical orientation (Yalom, 1975). Narcissistic or interpersonally needy therapists find means to become the center of the therapy. Dependent therapists turn to patients for support of their decisions. Authoritarian therapists impose their judgments and formulations on their patients.

In a study of the therapists of schizophrenic inpatients, therapists who were rated as composed did best with anxious schizophrenics; those who were rated as comfortable with aggression did well with hostile patients; the ones rated as comfortable with depression did well with depressed patients; and those therapists who were rated as grandfatherly did well with seductive schizophrenics (Gunderson, 1978).

Over time, therapists come to accept their personal needs and to comfortably integrate them into the conduct of their therapy. Knowledge of their own personality and personal needs enables therapists to screen out and refer persons with whom they do not interact well and to refer them to professionals with whom they have a better chance.

At present, we probably know more about ineffective and damaging styles than we do about helpful styles. We know that sexual intimacy with patients is damaging (Dahlberg, 1970). We know that therapists' failure to recognize people as individuals is highly frustrating and generally nonproductive (Malan, Balfour, Hood, & Shooter, 1976). Studies of encounter groups show that group leaders who are highly intrusive, who offer little emotional support or cognitive framework, or who are controlling and highly idiosyncratic in their approach often damage people with little self-esteem, few coping skills, and high expectations (Lieberman, Yalom, & Miles, 1973). Studies of other aspects of leadership style are offered by Pope (1977).

GRATIFICATION OF OBJECT NEED

Kohut (1971) pointed out the need to gratify certain of patients' needs as a means to maintain the treatment relationship and as a means to establish a relational base on which to build a resolvable transference neurosis. He indicated the need of many patients to be admired by their therapists and the need of many patients to admire their therapists. Later, it became evident that maintaining a sense of self demands environmental reinforcement – the presence of people or symbols (selfobjects) that confirm one's selfhood (Wolf, 1982).

Selfobject functions are served by therapists smiling at their patients, by allowing patients to choose the chair they sit in if they wish to do so, or by indicating the chair to sit in if they would rather be seated in a designated chair. Offering to share a footstool or offering facial tissues to a crying patient also fills these needs. Failure to meet minimal object needs of patients results in therapist-induced fragmentation and defensiveness.

Therapists also have object needs, and usually see to it that their case load does not consist predominantly of persons who totally frustrate them. Therapists need sufficient gratification in the relationship to continue working with their patients, while taking care that such gratification does not stalemate the treatment, interfere with their lives away from the office, or undermine their professional judgment.

THERAPISTS' EMOTIONAL REACTIONS

The therapist as a person impinges importantly on the therapeutic process, regardless of his or her attempts to be a neutral therapeutic instrument. Therapists' reactions and interventions are colored by their values, their personalities, their personal needs, and the demands made by patients.

Through their experiences as therapists, and through their life experiences, supervision, and personal therapy, therapists become aware of their personalities and the impact of their personality on others (Weiner, 1983a). The best information about the impact of therapists' personality on patients and the impact of patients on therapists comes from direct observation of therapists' interaction with patients by a supervisor reviewing videotapes of therapy sessions (Gladfelter, 1970). All therapists evolve a style of interaction with certain kinds of patients. As therapists in training become aware of their style, they develop means for detecting unusual amounts of emotional tension in the therapeutic situation. Departures from a usual style of dealing with certain types of people and situations indicate to therapists that they must search themselves and their interactions with patients carefully to detect the source of the emotional pressure (or lack of pressure) and to ascertain if their change of style has an impact on therapy (Weiner, 1982b). In addition to changes in therapeutic style, there are other indications of unusual types or degrees of involvement by therapists, such as preoccupation with, or indifference toward certain patients and recurrent dreams about them (Langs, 1973). In this situation, the therapist's mental checklist should be:

1. What is the nature of my reaction?
2. What am I reacting to in the patient?
3. What am I reacting to in myself? Personal values? Personal needs? Countertransference?
4. Does my behavior need to be altered?
5. If it needs to be altered, in what way?

All therapists are excessively vulnerable to some patients. As therapists grow professionally, they become aware of their vulnerabilities and attempt to deal with them or compensate for them, sometimes by referring patients to other therapists, or by seeking personal treatment or supervision.

Being a therapist stimulates therapists' exhibitionistic urges and their defenses against them, and may lead to inappropriate activity or passivity. Therapists may respond to patients by saying, "What you say about me is true," instead of investigating the source of the patient's perception. In that way, therapists are vulnerable to psychological injury or manipulation by patients who are aware of their need for praise, acceptance, or other kinds of input.

One category of patients, those with borderline personality disorders, invariably create emotional storms in therapists as they project unacceptable parts of themselves onto their therapists and then react against these disowned, projected attributes. The therapist's emotional turmoil can be a valuable clue to the diagnosis of patients with borderline personality disorder. Therapists may be sensitive to patients because of events in therapists' personal lives; e.g., marital conflict, intergenerational conflict with parents or children, or losses through personal illness, divorce, or death. However, there are many times at which emotional reactions of therapists to their patients are appropriate responses to the material patients present.

Therapists must also be aware of the ways in which their patients conform or fail to conform to their cherished values, whether they be education, upward mobility, or interest in automobiles or athletics. It is difficult for many therapists to tolerate patients whose life values differ greatly from their own. For example, most therapists would have difficulty managing their feelings toward persons who regularly indulge in violent acts or criminal behavior that endangers the lives of others.

Finally, therapists must develop sufficient tools for self-exploration to recognize *countertransference*, the stirring up of their own unconscious conflicts by patients. The source of therapists' countertransference reactions can be sought in their dreams, the quality of their behaviors and feelings toward the person(s) in question, the therapists' associations, and the types of fantasy therapists can produce in relation to such individual(s).

If therapists' countertransference feelings do not alter their behavior with the patient(s) in question, nothing needs to be done about them for the sake of patients. Therapists, on the other hand, may wish to satisfy their curiosity or alleviate their own discomfort, which they can do by introspection, by discussing their feelings with a colleague, or by seeking supervision or personal therapy.

If therapists are behaving in a way they regard as nontherapeutic and cannot change their behavior, they have access to many routes of action. They can call their behavior to patients' attention and ask for their reaction as a means to help understand. They can videotape and review their sessions alone, with peers, or with a supervisor. They can seek supervision or personal therapy or, if all else fails, they can transfer the patient to another therapist.

Therapists owe themselves and their patients a satisfying life for themselves outside of the office. Otherwise, they are overly vulnerable to their own needs and to the transference expectations of their patients. Many needy therapists make extended families of their patients (Chesler, 1971), and in this way block the maturation of their patients and block opportunities for them to develop ordinary social outlets. Living vicariously through their patients is no better for therapists than for their patients. This tendency can be alleviated through the use of peer support groups for therapists (McCarley, 1975).

LIFE CYCLE CONSIDERATIONS

The stage of therapists' own psychological and professional life cycle has a great influence on their interactions with patients, and has been dealt with extensively elsewhere (Weiner, 1982b). There are positive aspects and pitfalls at every stage.

Therapists who are chronologically and professionally young often have the enthusiasm of youth and identify strongly with the presumed potency of their mentors. Enthusiasm helps to mobilize chronic mentally ill patients and leads to overestimating the ability of borderline patients to make use of insight-oriented therapy. Professionally young therapists have difficulty withholding their clinical observations and formulations from patients. To young therapists, withholding the information they possess is tantamount to withholding curative medication.

With great difficulty, supervisors finally succeed in having young therapists hold their tongues and listen long enough to hear what patients are trying to tell them.

There are, on the other hand, novice therapists who attempt to deal with their fear of patients and their own inadequacy by becoming withdrawn and mechanical. This group of therapists has been found to do poorly with schizophrenics (Whitehorn & Betz, 1954). Some therapists become so preoccupied with understanding patients' verbal productions that they fail to see contextual issues, such as patients' disinterest in psychological self-exploration, as detailed by Chessick (1971) in a description of his own encounter with an involuntarily hospitalized patient when he was a trainee.

Buckley, Karasu, and Charles (1979) asked supervisors to rate the most common mistakes in psychotherapy made by psychiatric residents. In order of descending frequency, they were (1) wanting to be liked by the patient, (2) inability to "tune in" to the patient's unconscious, (3) premature interpretations, (4) overuse of intellectualization, (5) inappropriate transference interpretations, (6) assuming a stereotyped analytic stance regardless of the actual treatment situation, (7) unawareness of countertransference feelings, and (equally common) (8) inability to tolerate patients' aggression, inability to tolerate silence, and avoiding setting fees.

By mid-career, therapists are able to balance careful attention to patients' productions with communicating observations and formulations to them. Many skillful mid-career therapists indicate that most of their learning has come from making mistakes in their clinical practice. Many professional therapists seek peer supervision or formal supervision as they encounter difficulties in their own practices, and find that supervision more helpful than the supervision received during training because they are better prepared for it.

Mid-career therapists tend to settle into one level of therapy and to exclude from their practice persons who require another level of therapy or who have personality constellations with whom they interact poorly. Some mid-career therapists become disillusioned or dissatisfied with their earlier training and seek training in other modalities. Therapists most frequently move from more intensive forms of therapy to therapies that involve less frequent contact and greater managerial skills. Mid-career psychiatrists have in the past tended to shun work with hospitalized patients, but that tendency is now reversing, and psychiatrists are continuing to work with more seriously ill patients throughout their professional careers.

Acting out of countertransference seems more common in mid-career therapists (Weiner, 1982b), often stemming from situations such as divorce that increase their interpersonal needs (Dahlberg, 1970). Therapists with poor object relations and few interests outside their profession tend to make their professional contacts the center of their social lives as well as their professional lives.

Late-career therapists tend to stick with what they already know and enjoy relative insulation from intense transference and countertransference involvement (Weiner, 1982b). They withdraw from treating patients such as adolescents and borderline individuals who generate intense transference-countertransference issues. They find with more stable patients that transferences are less highly eroticized and that, because of their age, countertransferences are also less highly eroticized. Older therapists seem more free to give advice, but generally are not concerned with assuming actual direction of their patients' lives. As a therapist in his late 70s put it, he now had an Olympian view of patients' emotional problems and enjoyed that sense of panorama and detachment.

Life Cycle Events

Events relating to the therapist's own life cycle frequently impinge on the therapeutic relationship. These include positive experiences such as personal and professional successes, and negative experiences such as illness or financial misfortune; both classes affect therapists' mood. The possible events are too numerous to mention, but include the formation of love relationships and the vicissitudes of those relationships, including divorce and loss of the loved one through illness or death. The birth, maturation, and departure from home of children are all important events, as are the loss of children through death, the reversal of roles with parents as parents age, and the eventual loss of parents.

Most of the life cycle events of their therapists go on outside of patients' specific awareness, other than their recognizing that their therapist is in a good or bad mood, is attentive or inattentive, is exceptionally tuned in or is having difficulty understanding. Granet and Kalman

(1982) have also called our attention to the fact that therapists are also subject to anniversary reactions – time-specific responses of an individual in whom previously successful repression of an intrapsychic conflict is undone by a meaningful event that serves as a temporal trigger. Granet and Kalman reported that therapists' recognition of their anniversary reactions facilitated therapy of their patients, as in the example that follows.

> The patient was a 60-year-old man with severe chronic obstructive pulmonary disease. He had begun treatment for an adjustment disorder and his therapy had progressed well for several months. Over that time, the therapist found himself becoming depressed during sessions. This was followed by the therapist's tardiness in starting sessions, something very much out of keeping for this well-organized, punctual physician. The therapist was thinking about this patient one night when he was unable to sleep and found his thoughts leading to a family member who had died of a chronic illness at the same time of year two years earlier. Recognizing his own anniversary reaction helped the therapist to work through his unresolved emotional conflicts and enabled the treatment to continue more positively. (after Granet & Kalman, 1982, p. 1599)

Life cycle events may pose greater problems for female mental health professionals than males. Scher, Benedek, Candy, Carey, Mules, & Sachs (1976) point out that women experience concern about combining marriage, child rearing, and career, while men take it for granted. One life cycle event unique to women that literally intrudes in the therapist–patient relationship is pregnancy.

At first, of course, a therapist's pregnancy is known only to herself, and she deals with concerns about expanding her role from wife-professional woman to wife-professional woman-mother. At some time during the second trimester, the fact of pregnancy usually can no longer be concealed by the therapist or denied by her patients. The therapist's physical discomfort during the latter part of pregnancy may interfere with sessions. Exaggerated mood swings during pregnancy can become a problem, too (Nadelson, Notman, & Feldman, 1974). Therapists who have difficulty dealing with their own limitations may have difficulty accepting their own need to reduce their activities. Patients have their own reactions, ranging from competition to fear of abandonment. It is the therapist's responsibility to deal with the effects of this normal life cycle event in the therapy, directing her interaction with the patient so as to maximize the therapeutic benefit of the event.

PROFESSIONAL BURNOUT

Substantial literature is developing on the special problems of psychotherapists in relation to their chosen profession (Edelwich, 1980). Groesbeck & Taylor (1977) suggest that psychotherapists are constantly exposed to psychological tensions that may emotionally poison them. Bermak (1977) finds that psychiatrists suffer a sense of isolation due to physical aloneness, unsatisfied intimacy needs, and inability to discuss their work because of confidentiality constraints. He also finds that psychiatrists confronted with patients' deep emotional issues become stirred up, but are unable to discharge the tension. In addition, they are humbled by frustration of their wish to be omnipotent.

Whether psychiatrists' high suicide and divorce rates (Rich & Pitts, 1980) indicate the unsettling effects of being a mental health professional has yet to be established. It is certainly clear that many mental health professionals' difficulties long antedate their professional status, even among candidates in psychoanalytic training (Shapiro, 1971).

Burnout, the experiencing of one's chosen profession as no longer personally rewarding, is probably most frequent among poorly trained paraprofessionals in understaffed institutional settings (Edelwich, 1980). The expectation that one is helping emotionally disturbed persons to alter their lives is soon crushed by massive service demands, inadequate professional backup, and institutional constraints. Disillusioned help providers then seek ways to avoid the frustrating aspects of their jobs, or quit to seek other employment.

Some psychiatrists seek refuge in drug treatment of mental disorders, in which results are at least quantifiable. Others seek refuge in administrative positions. We are reluctant to tell professional newcomers that psychotherapy is taxing and often tedious; that they must cultivate sufficient satisfaction in their personal lives to bring enthusiasm to the office; and that they must be continuously open to education so that they can bring fresh perspectives to bear on their practices.

New professionals should be thoroughly grounded in at least one theory of psychopathology and one theory of therapy, but as they mature they should expose themselves to other theories and other forms of practice, not in the hope of finding or becoming a messiah, but in the hope of broadening or refreshing themselves for their own sakes and for the sake of their patients.

Peer support through participation in professional organizations and informal socialization is invaluable. It relieves professional aloneness and allows sharing of frustrating professional problems. As suggested earlier, support groups led by peers or by outside professionals can be of value, and have been shown in groups of nurses to reduce turnover and to enhance job satisfaction (Weiner & Caldwell, 1981, 1983).

Inevitably, people become disillusioned by some aspect of their work, but burnout is by no means unavoidable for professionals who take care to balance their personal and professional lives, to remain open to further education and peer support, and to see a higher purpose in life than the gratification of their own or their patients' needs.

THE IDEAL THERAPIST

Ideal therapists are self-aware, recognize that they cannot be all things to all people, and recognize personality types or types of psychopathology that they deal with poorly. They also are self-aware enough to recognize situations that commonly lead them to be defensive or to overreact. While they are able on the one hand to control their impulses, they also have controlled spontaneity; the ability to make an association at the right time to catalyze an important intrapsychic or interpersonal process (Foulkes, 1968).

The ideal therapist has sublimated his or her aggression well and can use it to comfort, to defend the self, and also, through humor, to reframe patients' views of themselves in ways that enable them to see more clearly and cope more effectively (Schimel, 1980).

Ideal therapists enjoy being potent as a therapist, but also enjoy seeing patients deal effectively with themselves and with life for their own sake. Ideal therapists take responsibility for their own conduct and, instead of rationalizing or blaming others for their mistakes, use self-examination, supervision, or personal therapy to help change aspects of themselves that are counterproductive with patients.

The ideal therapist knows his or her level of expertise, and does not hesitate to consult with peers or with experts when in doubt as to a patient's diagnosis or treatment.

The ideal therapist attends professional meetings to help maintain his or her own sense of professional identity, to absorb new knowledge, and to maintain positive contacts with professional peers, who may be needed during times of illness or at vacation time to cover the therapist's practice.

New theories and their supporting data are examined critically in the light of the therapist's own experience treating patients and the therapist's knowledge of statistics and experimental design.

Like all other professionals, psychotherapists rapidly become technically obsolete. However, their mastery of the basic tools of human understanding and relatedness never become outdated, and may enable them to continue practicing effectively even if they fail to master the latest in psychotherapeutic technology. If, as Frank (1974) has suggested, psychotherapies mainly combat the demoralization that is secondary to and reinforcing of emotional disturbances, they may not need to learn any of the newer techniques.

SUMMARY

There are enormous technical and emotional complexities in doing psychotherapy. To be an effective therapist, one must develop an appreciation of normal behavior, and of levels of intervention as they relate to patients' ego strength and to their dynamic or descriptive diagnosis, in addition, one must also learn how to deal with events in therapy in such a way as to further the progress of patients at an appropriate psychological level.

Mature self-awareness is another important asset of the therapist, and includes awareness of strengths and liabilities, and willingness to seek consultation, supervision, or personal therapy when needed. The active cultivation of non-work-related interests is also of benefit to therapists and patients alike. It insures a balanced view of their patients and of life by therapists, and thereby promotes a balanced treatment in which the treatment needs of the patient and the personal needs of the therapist do not become confused.

CHAPTER 9

Preparations

Before beginning therapy, therapists select patients and prepare themselves, the physical setting, and their patients. Preparations also include contracts, fees, and record-keeping arrangements.

SELECTING PATIENTS

The evaluation of patients for psychotherapy requires that three interrelated questions be addressed. What kind of therapy is needed? For whom? And, conducted by whom? Unfortunately, no one question can be answered without addressing the other two. Even when these questions are answered as fully as possible, the only way to finally determine the issue of treatability is a trial period of therapy.

Evaluating the Therapy

Therapists begin by asking themselves if the treatment or treatments they have to offer will fit the patient. That, of course, means getting to know the patient as a person as well as making a diagnosis. The basic principles of ascertaining the best level and type of therapy are enumerated and described in Chapter 6. The general rule of thumb is that persons who operate at Vaillant's (1977) neurotic level can be dealt with in sensitively conducted evocative, ego-supportive, or repressive therapies. Persons who operate at an immature level (usually the diagnosis is character disorder) are best dealt with in ego-supportive or repressive therapies, and those who operate at a psychotic level can only tolerate a nonintrusive repressive approach.

155

In making these comments about patient selection in relation to type of treatment, we must also consider the therapist's style. A repressive therapy can be conducted so intrusively that it will disrupt a tenuous adaptation or will overwhelm a decompensated ego. Some evocative therapies are conducted in such a didactic way that ego defenses are rigidified, not altered.

Evaluating the Patient

The evaluation of candidates for psychotherapy involves assessment of patients' ego strength, ego structure, and their interaction with the therapist. The ability to assess overall ego strength is an important aspect of selecting patients for therapy. Ego strength is not a stable personality attribute. It varies in relation to social, psychological, and biological factors (see Figure 1, p. 20). Changes in patients' ego strength may call for different interventions by therapists or for transferring the patient from individual therapy to another type of therapy.

Ego strength is determined by evaluating a person's history and present behavior in life, by formal mental status examination, and by assessing the quality of the person's interaction with the therapist. The evaluation of ego strength was covered in Chapter 3.

Ego structure is another important consideration that bears on the therapist–patient interaction. Therapists may do well with poorly functioning obsessive-compulsive patients, but very poorly with histrionic personalities who have equally little ego strength. Some therapists cannot tolerate the aggression of borderline patients, but deal well with the self-recrimination of the decompensated depressive personality. To sum up in a few words: ego strength dictates the therapy; ego structure the therapist.

Evaluating the Therapist

In considering potential patients, therapists must ask themselves if they can establish sufficient rapport to work with particular patients and if they can tolerate the demands these patients are likely to make. Therapists who already have one borderline patient in therapy may be appropriately reluctant to take on another one because of the emotional storms such patients create. Therapists must also try to screen out those persons with whom they will interact poorly because of the therapist's personality or present life situation. A therapist who is struggling with his or her adolescent children's overassertion of their autonomy must respond with caution to the desire to have a certain adolescent in treatment with the object of teaching him or her a lesson. Other indications of potentially interfering emotional reactions are the offering of contracts that are much more liberal or stringent than the therapist's ordinary contracts, and intense emotional reactions to prospective patients that stimulate dreams and fantasies (Langs, 1973).

Generally speaking, therapists do well with patients they like and with whom they can identify. The danger here is overidentification with patients that may lead to promoting their acting out.

PREPARING THE THERAPIST

Therapists face many of the same concerns as prospective patients: that their personal and professional ineptness will be evident, and that they may be psychologically or physically attacked. Therapists actively evaluate their own suitability for treating each patient. If they have misgivings about how they react or may react to certain patients, it is wise for them to evaluate and clarify the situation by discussing it with a colleague or supervisor before beginning the therapy.

PREPARING THE PHYSICAL SETTING

The principal physical requirements for individual therapy are an adequately illuminated, well-ventilated, quiet, moderately soundproof room with comfortable furniture. If the sessions are to be videotaped, the chairs in the room may need to be specially arranged. There is probably little lost by allowing smoking and eating in the room unless those activities disrupt therapy.

PREPARING THE PATIENT

Prospective patients require different amounts and types of preparation to facilitate their entry into therapy and to keep their apprehension at tolerable levels. Prospective patients usually have reservations about entering therapy. They fear disclosure of their weaknesses, expecting that the therapist will be as unaccepting and judgmental as they are of themselves.

The way in which prospective patients are prepared depends on the setting in which therapy takes place, their life experiences, psychodynamics, and any previous experience they may have had with therapy. Therapists, after introducing the possibility of therapy, therefore need to ask prospective patients their knowledge or concerns about therapy, and to give prospective patients a chance to communicate that knowledge and their special concerns.

It is generally more desirable to lower than to raise prospective patients' concerns about entering therapy, unless the therapist is testing prospective patients' motivation or assessing the ability of a person with an ego-syntonic disorder to tolerate tension. If prospective patients' level of tension is allowed to rise too high, they may terminate therapy.

Therapists can allay the concerns of prospective regressive and ego-supportive therapy patients by emphasizing the positive aspects of the experience, or they can allow prospective evocative therapy patients to develop fantasies about and associations related to the idea of being in therapy.

Prospective patients often ask therapists what will happen if therapy is not a positive experience. After exploring prospective patients' concerns, therapists can reassure them that in the event of a negative outcome, they will both reassess the situation and attempt to work out a suitable alternative.

After explaining the potential benefits of therapy, the therapist indicates the place, frequency, and duration of meetings, the rules, the fee, and, at times, specifically discusses the legal limits of confidentiality. Therapists also deal with those persons in patients' environment who are involved in the treatment process, and finally deal with patients' own resistances.

Frequently, prospective patients' concerns about therapy are displaced onto issues such as confidentiality. It is important to recognize these issues as displacements, but it is also useful to give concrete answers in addition to dealing with the questions as expressions of concern about entering therapy.

Observing prospective patients' means of defense and adaptation related to the prospect of entering therapy also gives the therapist valuable insight into their overall coping and defense mechanisms, especially those related to being in new life situations. It is important that therapists not become so caught up in alleviating prospective patients' anxiety that they overlook this important opportunity to observe them.

CONTRACTS

Contracts between patient and therapist are important in themselves, but they also point to a deeper, more essential aspect of psychotherapy. Treatment is not merely a prescription by therapists for patients. Treatment involves negotiation of attitudes and viewpoints by patients and therapists alike. Patients bring their view of their troubles; their therapists have their own views. The treatment process is their joint effort to bring about the rapprochement of those views that will be the most effective and most satisfying in the situation (Muncie, 1956).

Eric Berne (1966) was the first therapist to strongly emphasize the importance of contract-making in psychotherapy. He recognized that persons begin therapy with no idea of what to expect from the therapist or themselves, and that contract-making is also psychologically important. It establishes a therapeutic direction, a mutual frame of reference, and a benchmark for progress.

A contract between psychotherapists and potential patients is an explicit, noncoercive, mutually agreed-upon statement of the tasks each is to perform, and the ends to which those tasks are a means (Weiner, 1981). The contract may be written, but is usually verbal, and is recorded in the therapist's notes. The therapist's record of the patient's agreement to the contract documents that the therapist has obtained the patient's informed consent to the treatment (Cohen, 1979). For many types of medical and surgical treatment, obtaining the patient's informed consent requires enumerating the dangers of the proposed treatment, but there are presently no informed consent requirements for any form of psychotherapy.

Contract-making can be a corrective emotional experience, as defined by Alexander and French (1946) and as described by Strupp (1977). Therapists do not oppress patients or impose values on them without reference to their wishes and needs. Through contract-making, patients learn cooperation and mutuality instead of negativism, passive aggression, or manipulation as means to deal with others. Contract-making acknowledges patients' influence in the therapeutic process, encourages patients to assume part of the responsibility for the treatment, and also allows for changes in methods and goals of treatment based on periodic reevaluation of its progress by therapist and patient alike. That affirmation of patients' potency and therapists' willingness to share the direction of the therapy help to consolidate patients' self-esteem and their sense of ability to deal with the world, paralleling the experiences of persons growing up in healthy families (Lewis, Beavers, Gossett, & Phillips, 1976).

Evaluation Contracts

Contract-making begins with an *evaluation contract*. An evaluation contract is an agreement that prospective patients will reveal enough about themselves to enable their prospective therapists to evaluate them for treatment.

Some institutions use a formal evaluation procedure performed by a designated diagnostic team. The evaluee is told in advance that the evaluation team may not be the eventual treatment team. The evaluee knows that evaluation is the sole purpose of his or her contract with this group of people, and enters into an evaluation contract (Schectman, De La Torre, & Garza, 1979).

An evaluation contract is a commitment to exchange information. It involves no commitment to action by either party. The evaluee contracts to supply enough information for the evaluator to formulate a diagnosis and a treatment plan.

Clearly, individual practitioners will have more difficulty (not only with their potential patients, but within themselves) establishing an evaluation contract than therapists practicing in an institution with a formal evaluation program. It is especially difficult if the evaluee is referred by another professional who has already provided a diagnosis and a recommendation for treatment. The individual practitioner is additionally handicapped by the fact that the referral source may not have ascertained the evaluee's capacity to work psychotherapeutically, although the referring person may have based the referral on an intuitive sense of fit between the person referred and the therapist.

When potential patients are referred without an evaluation, therapists can justifiably start at ground zero and give evaluees a chance to convert complaints into diagnostic and treatment issues (Schectman, De La Torre, & Garza, 1979).

Establishing an evaluation contract separate from the therapeutic contract can be of great value. It helps avoid premature closure owing to failure to explore the psychological and interpersonal context in which the difficulty arose and in which it currently operates. It also helps avoid focusing too sharply on the chief complaint and thereby avoids premature action based on an inappropriate therapeutic contract.

An evaluation contract is subject to abuse if taken too literally and if imposed under circumstances in which such an overt agreement is not in the evaluee's best interest. Talking about evaluation to a person who is preoccupied with possible desertion by important people in his or her life is tantamount to threatening desertion as the opening move of the therapeutic relationship. *Imposing* a contract negates the entire concept of a contractual relationship as a means to develop patients' potency in interactions with other people. Furthermore, viewing psychotherapy as a contractual relationship merely provides a conceptual framework for the therapist. It does not require rigorous application. It requires only thoughtful, judicious use when appropriate.

There are more reasons to hesitate in making evaluation contracts. Persons who seek help with emotional problems want concrete assistance, not just a description of their difficulties from the therapist's point of view. Therapists also wish to help, and not merely to label problems and make recommendations. However, failure to establish an evaluation contract that is separate from the treatment contract may be an unwitting agreement by the therapist to deal with the problem as the evaluee sees it, and on the evaluee's terms, which is frequently a setup for impasse. Sharply separating evaluation from treatment allows therapists acting as evaluators to define the problem in their terms, stating what they believe to be the primary problem, outlining secondary problems, and indicating the likelihood of ameliorating each. Following this, they make recommendations for treatment.

Therapeutic Contracts

Therapeutic contracts are commitments to helpful actions. They commit evaluees to the role of patient and evaluators to the role of therapist. A delay in offering a therapeutic contract can be useful. It can stimulate healthy reflection, self-awareness, and self-control on the part of patients. It can also frustrate patients excessively and undermine the eventual establishment of the therapeutic contract.

Let us examine several clinical problems in relation to therapeutic contracts.

A couple's primary complaint is difficulty managing their 11-year-old son. Evaluation of them as a couple suggests that their difficulties with their son are secondary to the way in which family roles are defined, and that individual treatment of their son is not presently indicated. Instead, the family is seen as a whole, and all agree to rework the process of family role assignment with the stipulation that the contract can be renegotiated if the difficulties with the child fail to clear as the family problems are worked on.

After indicating the problem toward which the therapy is to be directed, the therapist also specifies by what means the treatment will be carried out and who will be responsible for what aspect of the treatment.

Patients' responsibilities in one treatment approach may be to record certain thoughts and feelings, and how they deal with them (Beck, Rush, Shaw, & Emery, 1979). In another approach, patients may be asked to free associate without attempting to draw conclusions about their mental productions until their patterns become clear.

After explaining patients' responsibilities, therapists ask if they understand the method proposed, and if they are willing to cooperate. In paying meticulous attention to establishing the therapeutic contract, therapists begin educating patients in their theory of patients' problems and their treatment. In doing so, therapists also begin to work out the type of therapeutic alliance that best meets patients' treatment needs.

When dealing with crises and when patients' capacity for emotional maturation is limited, uncritical obedience to authority or acceptance of suggestion on the part of patients is the preferred relationship.

With stable patients who have greater capacity for emotional growth, therapists work toward an understanding cooperation with the treatment process that will serve as the nucleus for a mature therapeutic alliance.

Most patients initially view self-understanding as explanation by the therapist, a passive-receptive process in which therapists observe, interpret, integrate, and give patients a finished product to swallow. Therapists point out that there is more to therapy than attempting to figure out why, and, when appropriate, that therapy will involve facing the consequences of acts as well as their probable cause, and will involve implementing actions based on patients' new view of themselves and their world that is acquired through insight. Phobic individuals, for example, must be told that at some point they will need actively to confront situations that were initially too frightening, but only at a mutually agreed-upon time and place.

Commonly, therapists are seen as commentators on interpersonal difficulties that arise outside the therapeutic hour. Patients are occasionally aware that interpersonal difficulties they experience in their outside lives may arise during therapy sessions, but they tend to deny or to be unaware that they may bring their interpersonal set into the relationship with the therapist. It is therefore important for therapists preparing patients for ego-supportive or evocative therapies to suggest that unconsciously motivated behavior may develop in the therapeutic relationship. If therapists wish to establish an interpersonal, here-and-now focus for the therapy, they may state that they will supply feedback about the impact of the patient as a person with whom they have a relationship. If therapists wish to establish an intrapsychic focus, they may state that they will seek the origins of behavior in the patient's past relationships and in the unconscious mind.

Patients are usually unaware of the transference potential of the therapeutic relationship. To help orient patients, therapists can inform them that many people recapitulate some aspects of former relationships in therapy – relationships as patients felt they experienced them, or as they wished they had experienced them. Therapists can also tell patients that such occurrences are usually stimulated by some real aspect of the therapist or by some interaction that occurs between them.

Patients may be encouraged to report their perceptions of the therapist, especially if these perceptions change or if they lead to intense emotional reactions.

Without an orientation to the level at which therapy will operate and the means by which therapist and patient will work, the transference-developing aspect of therapy may flourish while the supportive aspect fails, leading to emotional decompensation. Or, the supportive aspect may succeed without the sufficient development of insight to prevent the recurrence of the same interpersonal situations.

Despite the sharp line I have drawn between evaluation and therapeutic contracts, there is usually no abrupt change in the therapist–patient interaction. The evaluation is carried out in a comfortable, conversational manner, not as an interrogation. Patients are also supported in the transition from highly focused questioning to a more open-ended approach. They are not suddenly left high and dry with no cues to guide them.

Contracts are not always needed, even with patients who are able to make them. In many cases, therapist and patient never come to an explicit goal for therapy. Patients seek treatment for vague, ill-defined unhappiness, discuss a number of issues in their lives, and leave feeling better. No explicit contract was established or required for them to reach the implicitly agreed-upon goal of feeling better.

Contract-making is at times contraindicated, especially for hospitalized persons who are unable to act rationally in their own behalf and who must be guided by others until they become better able to make decisions for themselves.

Most patients seek therapy to feel better. It is the therapist's job to ask, "Feel better about what?" Some patients would like to feel better about abusing others. A few would like to tolerate abuse better. Therapists ascertain which of patients' treatment goals are in their best interest, or in the best interest of the community at large. They must also ask if patients' goals for themselves are reasonable, and if not, must help set reasonable goals.

An explicit contract not only helps keep therapists and patients on the track toward reasonable goals, but also can facilitate progress. Goals that are made small enough can be readily reached, and patients's experience of success is encouraging. Each small goal reached also serves as a benchmark so that patients and therapists can assess progress.

Contracting for Therapeutic Level

The therapeutic contract establishes whether the therapeutic process will operate at a repressive, ego-supportive, or evocative level (Weiner, 1970). The therapeutic level can vary from time to time during therapy, as the following example shows.

A woman who had earlier successfully concluded several years of once-a-week therapy, returned because of difficulties in her marital relationship.

As therapy progressed, it became evident that there was a deepening gulf between her and her husband. When they eventually separated, she experienced a positive upsurge in her own development as a person. Being concerned that divorce might be unavoidable, she and her therapist agreed to temporarily shift from an evocative–ego-supportive therapy to a repressive mode that would focus on the practical demands of living alone.

Repressive therapies. In crises, when patients' ego strength has been acutely depleted, therapists do not engage in elaborate contract-making. They respond to patients' cry for help with direct interventions based on their professional judgment. Contract-making is, however, a useful exercise for persons with chronically low ego strength. It acknowledges them as people and provides a healthy interpersonal relationship in which there are no covert power moves and in which responsibility is shared as equally as possible. It also establishes that therapists do not think for patients, and that they cannot know what is good for any patient without knowing the particular patient and without taking that patient's goals and wishes into consideration. This helps establish patients' individuality and reinforces their ego boundaries.

Ego-supportive therapies. A contract for ego-supportive therapy stresses that the reactions of the patient to the therapist, and vice versa, are important elements in the therapeutic process. Patients are also helped to understand that the observations made about their interactions are only observations and not criticisms. However, they are encouraged to report feelings of criticism that they do experience. Thus, therapists come to understand the factors that mobilize the punitive aspects of patients' superegos.

A contract for ego-supportive therapy is generally worked out over time. It calls for a shift in the traditional doctor–patient relationship that might produce an adverse reaction were it spelled out at the beginning. Establishing initial therapeutic contracts is easier in repressive and evocative therapies because they involve generally accepted relationships, that of traditional doctor to patient and of analyst to analysand.

At the beginning of an ego-supportive therapy, the contract is for self-understanding at an interpersonal level, to help patients become aware of the self-defeating behavior that causes interpersonal difficulties that are responsible for the individual's emotional discomfort. As therapy progresses, therapists introduce themselves as part of patients' interpersonal world. They are observers, commentators, and participants. As the patient's interactions with the therapist become important in his or her emotional life, the therapist asks the patient to take note of them.

Evocative therapies. The therapeutic contract in an evocative therapy acknowledges the frustrating nature of the relationship and underscores the need for patients' active participation and reflection. In turn, it offers greater understanding of unconscious mental processes and the hope that this understanding, as experienced in the transference relationship, will lead to more adult patterns of thinking and behavior.

The negotiations involving the therapeutic contract should also involve the patient's expectations of the therapist. Patients may say, for example, that they expect the therapist to be completely passive and that they expect to shoulder the entire responsibility for the therapy themselves. Instead of contradicting patients, as they might in negotiating repressive or ego-supportive contracts, therapists need to ask, "Why?" The reply may give an important clue about patients' attitudes about parents and about designated helpers.

Establishing a therapeutic contract in an evocative therapy is far less important than observing and commenting on how patients make and enter contracts. In theory, the stably neurotic and mildly personality-disordered patients who are amenable to evocative methods require the experience of negotiating less than they do that of observing how they negotiate.

When therapists fail to negotiate an adequate contract for the optimal level of psychotherapy for their patients, there are two basic risks. Establishing a contract for an evocative therapy with a person who needs a repressive method may overwhelm the person's ego and also may stimulate unrealistic expectations that will make therapy interminable. Establishing a contract for a repressive therapy with a person who has the capacity for an ego-supportive or evocative approach may limit the patient's growth.

Renegotiation

Many therapeutic contracts require renegotiation as therapy progresses or fails to progress, or as patients see themselves in a different light.

> Mrs. A. U. first presented for therapy at age 29 because she was anorgasmic. As therapy progressed, there was evidence of a generalized anhedonia that seemed to stem from guilt that arose in her relationship with her mother. As she improved, she became involved with and married a man whom she enjoyed greatly, but was still unable to reach a climax.
>
> She later returned to therapy feeling very inadequate because her husband seemed totally self-absorbed. She had concluded it was her fault, and felt depressed and hopeless about herself. During this part of her therapy, it became evident that her experience with her husband was much like that with her mother, in which she was either abused psychologically or ignored. As she gradually felt better about herself, she focused on the marital relationship. She eventually tried marital therapy with her husband, but he was not willing to invest energy in changing their relationship.
>
> Finally, she separated from him and found that she felt much better about herself as a single woman. At that point, she became much more conscious of her intellectual and personal assets and began actively to explore and cultivate them in a manner that broadened and deepened her personal relationships.
>
> Over the 15 years during which this woman intermittently sought treatment, her therapeutic contract changed from eliminating a symptom to improving a relationship to becoming as fully a person as she could. Each change of focus was separately negotiated or was established during the course of working on one of the several complaints she presented.

Many persons whose initial goal was symptom relief become intrigued with the possibility of understanding themselves better. Persons whose initial goal was insight often find it of little help and opt for advice or behavioral measures. Ideally, therapists are flexible enough to renegotiate contracts when indicated.

Situations arise in which therapists and patients are unable to renegotiate a contract. These cases usually involve a strong transference-countertransference bind in which the therapist, the patient, or both cannot shift. The best approach to resolving the bind is to employ a consultant who works with patient, therapist, or both (Weiner, 1982a).

Contracts with Adolescents and Their Families

Becoming a person separate from one's family is one of the crucial tasks of adolescence. In the therapeutic situation this is manifested in teenagers wanting to have a relationship with the therapist that is uncontaminated by the presence of their parents. This developmental issue usually arises under the guise of confidentiality – will the relationship with the therapist be private, or will parents be involved?

With well-functioning, mildly neurotic older adolescents, therapists may be able to confine the therapeutic relationship to the teenager. Most often, an extreme concern that parents be excluded indicates that teenagers are trying to hide something from themselves.

Therapists can ordinarily agree that the content of sessions will not be discussed with the parents unless the adolescent is in danger. With teenagers who are close to losing control of their aggressive or suicidal impulses, therapists reserve the right to breach confidentiality specifically as it applies to impending actions that might endanger the patient or others.

The contract with adolescents includes ascertaining who will be responsible for transportation and informing the patient about fees for missed appointments. Older adolescents can be told the fee, and if they are seen without the therapist having been in touch with the parents, should be asked who will pay the bill.

Some therapists do not have direct contact with the parents of adolescents with whom they work unless the child is present. The rationale is to demonstrate an alliance with the child. By establishing such a contract, therapists may rob themselves of a positive alliance with the parents and a valuable source of information about the child. While the therapist must accept the adolescent's point of view as legitimate, it is often useful to have another point of view or to have background material the patient cannot provide.

Most parents understand the importance of a confidential therapist–patient relationship if it is adequately explained. Parents tend to object when they do not receive adequate explanation of the need for confidentiality or when the child's behavior is frightening. There is an occasional parent who is so intrusive that he or she will not allow therapy unless given a direct pipeline into the therapy sessions. Unless the adolescent is institutionalized, the therapist had best refrain from contracting with a parent who is that intrusive. If the parent cannot tolerate this minimal amount of individuation, psychotherapy alone is not likely to be of great value. The therapist must in a firm, but positive manner, hand the problem back to the family until they decide they can afford to let an outsider in, or one of the family out.

Therapists can, on the other hand, welcome input by the family, but can also indicate that they will pass along the information to the adolescent. This insures that the family will think twice before calling and that the information provided can be used by patients for self-understanding or for understanding their impact on the family.

Periodic progress reports from family to therapist and therapist to family are very useful. Their frequency usually depends on the degree of tension generated by the identified patient. The reports need not always be direct, but may be funneled through a colleague to whom the family turns for periodic advice or ongoing therapy.

Contracts with Spouses or Other Concerned Persons

Contracts can also be made with the spouses, other concerned relatives, and other persons concerned about adult patients. This is particularly important when the identified patient's judgment is poor and there is need for others to provide information and to be prepared to take action.

Brushing aside spouses or other concerned persons can complicate the treatment of any patient. It gives the concerned persons a real reason to be angry, and that anger is likely to be acted out against the patient in the form of derisive remarks or overt efforts to disrupt the therapeutic relationship.

Family members and other concerned persons can be told that direct contact with the therapist will not be frequent, is welcomed if there is considerable stress or distress in the family or with other concerned persons, but that it will be reported to the patient. The provision that contacts will be reported tends to minimize calls and keeps therapists from having to referee fights.

Therapists who deem direct contact with families or concerned others to be inadvisable need to offer an explanation and someone to whom they can turn to deal with their concerns about the patient.

Written Contracts

Written contracts have been employed in many situations. Ayllon and Skirban (1973) have written contracts with parents for the behavioral treatment of their children. In this situation, parents literally sign on as part of the treatment. Rutherford (1975) has created a behavioral contract for use with delinquent adolescents. Simons, Morris, Frank, Green, & Malin (1975) report the use of contracts in dealing with chronic pain patients. Consumer advocates Adams and Orgel (1975) recommend that patients have a written contract with therapists that includes the day, time, and length of the visits, the goals, the fee, the fee for missed sessions, the patient's option if dissatisfied, a provision for renegotiation, and an agreement by the therapist to maintain confidentiality unless given written consent by the patient.

The greatest merit of a written contract is that it helps ensure that the therapist and the potential patient review the important aspects of the therapeutic contract: what they will work on, how they will work on it, and what is expected of each in the process. Putting it in black and white makes it more real and prevents retrospective distortion by patient or therapist.

FEES

The fee is an important part of the contractual relationship between therapist and patient. Therapists are responsible for setting fees, for indicating how they may be paid, and with what frequency payment will be expected if treatment continues. When contracts for ongoing therapy are negotiated, therapists can deal with the issue of charging for missed appointments and the possibility of change in fee structure.

Discussion of fees by therapists early in the patient–therapist relationship allows patients to express and deal with their feelings, and also allows patients to deal realistically with the fee and to set the frequency and length of visits in relation to their ability to pay. Failing to allow patients to deal openly with the therapist about fees may diminish their expectation of being allowed a voice in other important issues, and may establish the therapist–patient relationship as arbitrary and one-sided.

Therapists omit or sidestep discussion of fees for many reasons. Trainees often feel they are not worth it. Therapists who are employed by institutions express their negative feelings toward the institution in this way. Private practitioners may wish to reinforce the illusion that the therapist is a priest-healer, above such banalities as money. That attitude of the therapist can intensify the transference expectation of nurturance and may lead to acting out of the therapist's anger toward the patient when the unmentioned fee is unpaid. To pretend, by avoiding the subject, that money is not a consideration affronts some patients' reality testing and reinforces others' denial of reality. The therapist's unconcern about fees pleases people who want special consideration in life but is an important behavioral contradiction when dealing with patients who must be told that no special concessions are available in life.

Failure to deal with fees also disturbs people who need to know the extent and nature of their indebtedness to others.

Charging for uncanceled appointments or for appointments canceled with inadequate notice is another important aspect of fee negotiations. Charging fees for unkept appointments underscores patients' responsibility to their therapists, where other aspects of the therapeutic contract deal largely with patients' responsibility to themselves. It emphasizes one of the real needs therapists have of patients and indicates the real consequences that will occur if therapists' needs are not met.

If, in discussing fees with their patients, therapists do not set up a contract, they set the stage for an impasse, as the next example shows.

A young woman was referred for continuation of her treatment by a hospital psychiatrist because she had reached an impasse with her former psychotherapist. In the first interview, she disclosed that she had not paid a large portion of her former therapist's bill. The therapist told her that he would not tolerate unpayment of his bill. She responded with a smile. Her unpaid bill eventually became the central issue in their relationship and resulted in the therapist temporarily interrupting their working relationship.

She had responded to the therapist's ultimatum by asserting her own power, A contract about fee had never been entered into. The therapist had, instead, triggered a struggle in which she proved herself as powerful as he.

It may be unwise to discuss fees with hospitalized persons. Discussing fees can intensify the anguish of a psychotically depressed person or a suicidal person. It is appropriately deferred until the severely decompensated person achieves a better psychological balance.

Therapists must also note their own willingness to negotiate their fees. Unwillingness or overwillingness to negotiate fees may point to important potential difficulties in the therapeutic relationship.

CONFIDENTIALITY

Confidentiality is an important consideration for many patients, and some persons will not enter therapy or disclose fully during therapy, fearing a breach of their confidence. In 48 of the 50 states, there are privilege statutes (West Virginia and South Carolina are the exceptions). Although privilege allows therapists to testify only with their patient's consent, none guarantees complete confidentiality of therapist–patient communication (Shuman & Weiner, 1982).

The question of confidentiality, especially if raised by patients, is more than a legal or ethical issue. After the realities of the situation are discussed (or even beforehand, providing the limits of confidentiality are eventually discussed), therapists need to ask their patients why confidentiality is an issue. This will ordinarily unmask thoughts or feelings of which patients are ashamed, or a history of past betrayal. It is tempting to guarantee complete confidentiality to persons who are ashamed, embarrassed, or victims of past betrayal, but the most that therapists can realistically promise is to maintain confidentiality within the limits of the law and with regard for the safety of the patient or others. With more disturbed patients, this type of statement will often lead to a discussion of how therapists will deal with patients' expressions of suicidal or homicidal intent. Here, it is well to indicate that the therapist is committed to sustaining life, whether that of the patient or an endangered third party, while being careful to avoid with borderline or histrionic patients gamelike interactions in which the therapist is supposed to anticipate and control the patient's behavior. In dealing with nonpsychotic acting-out patients, therapists may need to build a proviso into the therapeutic contract that patients' actions are their own responsibility — that therapists cannot be patients' guardians or wardens.

It has been argued that without a guarantee of complete confidentiality, patients will not disclose themselves fully because the prerequisite for full disclosure is absolute trust (Dubey, 1974; Freedman, 1980). Appelbaum (1978) argues that to grant absolute secrecy is to create a situation that will be untenable or life-threatening for those patients who are asking in a roundabout way for therapists to actively intercede if they become overwhelmed by their impulses. The most convincing argument against a need for absolute confidentiality is that patients are readily able to understand and accept both the legal limitations of confidentiality and therapists' duty to preserve life and physical safety (Weiner & Shuman, 1983). Furthermore, disclosure seems more a function of trusting the therapist as a person than trusting a declaration that all communications will be kept confidential; nearly half of patients surveyed indicated that they had withheld information, even from therapists they trusted (Weiner & Shuman, 1984).

RECORD-KEEPING

Therapists need to keep a written record for the benefit and protection of their patients and themselves. The written record guides the treatment as conducted by the therapist and documents patients' progress. The record should include evidence of psychological assessment sufficient to support the therapist's working diagnosis, including mental status examination and psychological testing, when they are indicated. A statement concerning potential dangerousness to self is important when treating depressed patients; one concerning potential dangerousness to self or others is appropriate when treating patients who have been violent or are threatening violence. The therapist's working diagnosis should be part of the record, as should be the treatment plan and a history of the patient's progress in treatment. If the therapist's treatment plan differs greatly from the standard treatment for patients with a particular diagnosis, the therapist should also include the rationale for the treatment, indicate that the treatment was explained to the patient as innovative or unusual, and also indicate that the patient gave consent to the treatment. If the treatment employed is experimental, the patient should sign an informed consent document that is placed in the record.

The treatment record is also part of the therapist's defense in the event that a malpractice action is initiated by the patient. Absence of a written record by itself can be construed as evidence of malpractice (Pope, Simpson, & Weiner, 1978).

Ideally, therapists record their observations about each session, and may include comments about their own reactions. The record contains sufficient information to orient the therapist at the next session, but not so much that it is a burden to read. Some therapists take notes during therapy sessions. Most prefer to record their observations and reflections afterward. Writing notes after the session is generally preferable because therapists can reflect on the session as a whole and are not distracted from interacting with patients by note-taking. However, note-taking during sessions can be a means to slow the therapist–patient interaction so that the therapist can better keep up with the action when dealing with difficult patients.

Audiotapes or videotapes are more useful for teaching and supervision than record-keeping because they do not compress the therapeutic interaction or extract themes, since they record therapy sessions verbatim. If therapists plan to audiotape or videotape therapy sessions, this stipulation should be part of the contract and should be explicitly documented.

VIDEOTAPING

Videotape recordings are far superior to audiotapes in capturing the important interactions occurring in psychotherapy sessions. Videotapes are useful for replay by the patient or for the therapist's reflection or supervision, and videotaping is readily accomplished in ordinary offices. One table model omnidirectional microphone or an overhead omnidirectional microphone is usually adequate for sound recording. Unfortunately, omnidirectional microphones pick up hall noises and other extraneous sounds, so the room and the outside hall need to be carpeted, and the treatment room should be adequately insulated from street noises. Individual lavalier microphones are the best means of obtaining audio input, but they require multiple audio leads into the recording equipment, and must be attached at the beginning and detached at the end of each session.

A single fixed camera with a wide-angle lens mounted near the ceiling in one corner of the room is the simplest and cheapest means of obtaining a visual record of the therapist–patient interaction. The best (and most expensive) arrangement is in a studio with two individually operated movable cameras, and a producer who blends the video input – an arrangement suitable only for producing teaching materials. Berger (1970) uses a camera that he directs himself.

McCarty (1975) finds videotapes useful in developing patients' capacity for self-observation and for stimulating them to further thoughts and fantasies concerning their verbal and nonverbal behavior. Viewing tapes of sessions afterward enables patients to be confronted by patterns of interaction and modes of self-presentation without the judgmental quality that often accompanies the therapist's confrontations.

Videotapes can be replayed during the course of a session, at its end, or afterward by patients alone. It is important, however, that therapists and patients do not become distracted from their own interaction by becoming overly involved in viewing tapes of the sessions.

SUMMARY

Making the arrangements for psychotherapy is important. Careful attention to this aspect of the treatment enables therapists and patients to function more effectively. Preparing themselves and the physical environment, and providing for recording of therapy helps insure that therapists will secure the best possible setting and helps to keep the therapy on course.

Preparation by therapist and patient of an evaluation contract and a therapeutic contract, education of patients by therapists about the therapeutic process, and working through patients' resistance to therapy enable patients to participate more fully in therapy.

CHAPTER 10

Repressive Therapies

As stated earlier, repressive techniques are the most widely useful of the three broad levels of psychotherapy, and can be used to treat patients with differing levels of ego strength.

After briefly expanding on some of the points in the outline of repressive therapy presented in Table 4 of Chapter 6 (pp. 115–119), I will discuss certain patient populations for whom repressive techniques seem particularly applicable, and will discuss the variations in repressive techniques that may best meet the needs of each of these populations.

The specific populations that will be discussed are persons with ego deficits, both reversible and irreversible, and persons who are cognitively impaired relative to their therapists. Under the heading of ego deficit fall psychotic patients, psychosis-prone patients, and patients with borderline personality disorders.

STRUCTURING REPRESSIVE PSYCHOTHERAPY

Repressive psychotherapeutic techniques enhance ego development and reintegration by promoting impulse control, avoidance of painful affects, the differentiation of internal stimuli from external stimuli, secondary process thinking, and accurate perception of external reality. Therapist interventions in repressive therapy develop or restore adequate suppression and repression and develop patients' coping skills through direct teaching, through stimulating identification with the therapist, and through other means to help patients experience and deal with the world more rationally.

Repressive interviews with psychotic and psychosis-prone patients

174

generally lead patients away from discussing their liabilities, their delusions, or their inability to control themselves. Therapists are not highly confronting with poorly integrated patients unless the patients are in a controlled environment, especially if they have impaired social judgment and impulse control. Even in controlled settings, injudicious confrontation can provoke physical violence or can permanently alienate patients and destroy their potential for eventual cooperation. Ego-impaired patients are frequently given antipsychotic or antidepressant medications to help them deal with their feelings, with reality, and with confrontation by their therapists.

Setting direct limits on patients' behavior during interviews may be done when there is some danger to the patient, the therapist, or the physical environment. With adolescents, it is appropriate to encourage families to set certain reasonable limits at home, but it is frequently unwise for therapists to directly set limits on patients' behavior outside of the therapeutic session when they are dealing with severely ego-impaired persons. Psychotherapists avoid setting limits on behavior outside the therapeutic hour to avoid setting themselves against patients, because in patients' struggles to win the battle for control, they may lose sight of the real battle for their emotional well-being. Where limits are needed for severely ego-impaired patients, they can best be supplied through a controlled environment.

Therapists also gently point out patients' positive aspects; gently, because they are trying to inform, not to coerce. Patients' assets may be their mathematical ability, their sense of humor, or their interest in helping other people. Therapists encourage patients to use the assets that are most readily available to them and ask patients to report on the use of these assets in their daily life.

Therapists also notice their patients as people, what interests them, what they dislike, and what pleases them. Therapists then communicate that awareness to help reduce patients' sense of alienation. At times it is useful for a therapist to indicate that he or she and a patient have something in common (Weiner, 1983a). It may be only the fact that each is a person struggling to cope with reality in his or her own way (Wolf, 1983).

Whitehorn and Betz (1954) found that schizophrenic outpatients responded best to therapists who were warm and personable. However, certain patients find warmth and personableness threatening, and see these qualities as potential intrusions into their protective isolation. The wish of some emotionally isolated people to keep their emotional distance must be respected by the therapist.

Repressive therapy focuses on patients' real life in the here-and-now. Therapists draw patients out of fantasy and out of their concerns stemming from the past except as these directly impinge on patients' present life situation. They are encouraged to seek practical answers to problems by weighing the objective advantages and disadvantages of different solutions. Without negating patients' intrapsychic lives, therapists encourage them to live in reality.

Because of the emphasis on dealing in a practical way with reality, repressive sessions often appear banal and plodding. Therapists encourage patients to take one step at a time and to face one issue at a time. While therapists give the appearance of being preoccupied with mundane issues, they stay alert for signs of increasing ego strength that may eventually allow them to move therapy from a repressive approach to a more reflective, ego-supportive approach. They look for the use of humor by patients. They note when patients become less self-preoccupied and more interested in others. They stay alert for normalization of sleeping and eating patterns. They note patients' increasing capacity for self-observation and concomitant diminution of self-criticism. They attempt to quantify patients' self-control, and, in addition, try to keep the transference positive without shutting off patients' verbalization of negative feelings.

There are times when therapists encourage patients to undertake tasks or encounters that they fear. At other times, therapists lag behind and allow patients to develop momentum. Whether or not therapists take the lead or wait for patients depends on the way patients deal with their regressed or immature psychological state. If they tend to cling to immature ways, therapists push. If they are eager to move forward and to cope, therapists allow themselves to be pulled along.

Finally, repressive therapies do not stress autonomy as a goal of treatment. They stress a life of productive interdependence, using homilies such as "no man is an island" to underscore the fact that all people need other people to depend on and interact with. The issue is not one of autonomy versus dependence, but rather of the quality of the dependence one has on others; whether it is nurturing or draining, painful or rewarding.

TRANSFERENCE MANAGEMENT

In psychoanalytic treatment, the transference neurosis enables patients to reconstruct and reexperience in the therapeutic hour residuals from their past that distort their present-day thinking and modes of interaction. The transference neurosis is a regressive process (Dewald, 1983) that develops slowly in persons with adequate coping skills and ego defenses. Because of the therapist's alliance with patients' observing ego and the slow, controlled development of the regressive process, the transference neurosis remains confined to the therapeutic hour and is dealt with by interpretation as patients become aware of the irrationality of their thoughts and feelings toward the analyst and seek to understand their origins.

The transference neurosis is based on the mechanism of projection, which exists in minor forms in all people, but assumes a major role in the psychological operations of persons with severe psychopathology. If the ego were conceived as the responsibility-assuming organ of the body, the ego's weakness can be seen as the inability of more psychologically ill persons to assume responsibility for their thoughts or actions, seeing themselves instead as helpless victims or as acting only in response to environmental threat. When intense transferences are allowed to develop in ego-impaired persons, there is no "as if" quality to them. The therapist becomes a lover or a persecutor; one who satisfies or one who frustrates. Thus, patients experience sudden, massive transference reactions depending on how they perceive therapists; these reactions impel patients to act toward therapists and others instead of reflecting on their own thinking and feelings.

When therapists respond to such transferences by interpreting them, ego-impaired persons do not acquire insight. Instead, they feel demeaned, criticized, and wounded for having been told in essence that they are crazy. Therapists are not who they seem to be; patients feel that they have been told they are "all mixed up."

There are many techniques for minimizing the development of transference, such as the use of brief, highly structured therapeutic interviews in which therapists maintain a high level of activity and allow patients to know exactly what to expect. In addition, therapists can discourage the discussion of fantasy, can avoid free association, and can act against the transference, as shown in the following examples.

Mrs. U. had been severely traumatized by her father's death, which occurred while he was on a business trip when she was a teenager. In her twenties, she became preoccupied that she might develop an undiagnosed illness and die; or that she might accidentally ingest a poison or overdose with a prescribed medication.

Her once-a-week treatment extended over many years and resulted in little change. The major turning point occurred in her forties, when she developed asthma. At first, she struggled against the need for regular inhalation treatments and the need to take several medications every six hours around the clock. Soon, however, she came to understand that her following the prescribed treatment made a substantial difference in her asthmatic symptoms, and as she did, her fears of poisoning or overdose faded. Furthermore, she began savoring what she could of her own life instead of being preoccupied with death.

Her gains were consolidated when her mother was diagnosed as having a leukemia-like illness. She responded, not with concern about herself, but with concern for the quality of her mother's life and with recognition of the need to live day by day.

Finally, her therapist announced that he was leaving the city for a year of special study; this constituted a potential reenactment of her father involuntarily vanishing from her life. The therapist distanced himself from her father by emphasizing that he really wanted the assignment, which allowed her to voice anger over him leaving her for something he deemed more important.

They agreed to weekly therapy over the telephone (in this way, asserting that the therapist was not dead). To the patient's surprise, she tolerated the separation well and used the separation to initiate a spacing out process after 14 years of therapy.

In the next example, a patient's impulsive behavior was brought under control.

An intensely narcissistic man sought help in coping with his frustration in trying to obtain the hand of the woman he loved. She felt deeply committed to him, but family obligations made it difficult for her to marry him. The patient was concerned that he was getting out of control emotionally; a concern that was underscored by an earlier suicide attempt when he had been similarly frustrated in the same relationship. The patient, who saw himself as a self-made success, had been strongly dominated by his mother and grandmother. The patient's conscious wish was for a means to capture his beloved. His transference wish was for a state of blissful satiety. His transference fear was of a smothering, maternal bond.

Early sessions involved the patient and therapist estimating the chances for the patient's success in becoming united with his beloved and allowing the development of an idealizing transference. Capitalizing on the idealizing transference, the therapist constantly reiterated that the patient could not control his lover's actions. Thus, the therapist countered the patient's transference wish for satiation by the therapist, who also indicated that the patient's attempts to provoke his lover to action only showed that he doubted her love. After months had gone by, the patient felt more stable within himself and began a series of maneuvers to force his lover to accept or reject him. The therapist kindly, but firmly, told the patient that he was acting crazy; that his attempts to force action by his lover would only embarrass and humiliate her; and in essence that he was a grown man who could stand on his own two feet instead of clinging to her.

The patient's transference wish to be satisfied by the therapist was never dealt with directly. The overt presumption that the patient could both tolerate frustration and nurture himself was maintained. While the patient clung to the therapist during times he felt deprivation deeply, the therapist avoided dominating him by reflecting back the idealizing transference through admiring the ingenuity of the patient's plan while assuring the patient that he could survive psychologically.

EGO DEFICIT

Ego deficit refers to a transient or stable defect in ego function. Ego deficit commonly manifests as lack of anxiety tolerance, poor impulse control, little ability to repress or to sublimate, and a tendency toward primary process or magical thinking. Ego deficit may be determined by biological or psychosocial factors or both. It may result from a genetic propensity to psychosis or from failure to stimulate the development of a function (such as speech or interpersonal relatedness) at a crucial point in development. It can also result from inadequate environmental support to maintain a function, or from intrapsychic conflict. In most instances, ego deficits result from interacting biopsychosocial factors. Ego deficits can appear early in life, but they also occur in adult life as the result of severe psychological traumas or brain injury.

Specific ego deficits that occur early in life may lead to developmental deficits in other ego functions. The failure, for example, to develop a capacity for relating to others impairs the later acquisition of social skills in persons with schizoid personalities. The inability of a person with an antisocial personality to adhere to ordinary moral precepts is probably also a developmental defect. Both the schizoid and antisocial personalities may also have a constitutional vulnerability to their disorders. In the case of the schizoid personality, it may be low toleration for interpersonal frustration. In the case of the antisocial personality, a biological component is suggested by a high familial incidence of alcoholism and depression. Combat-related posttraumatic stress disorders are examples of psychologically induced ego deficits of adulthood.

Brain injury is a good example of a traumatic structural ego deficit. A brain injury can interfere with the acquisition, processing, integration, or effective response to information received by the brain. While a structural ego deficit such as a brain injury may be recognized by the victim (I can't speak), many types of ego deficits (such as losses due to right hemisphere strokes [Benson, 1979] and Alzheimer's disease [Reisberg, 1983]) are unrecognized by the impaired ego. When neurologically based, such awareness is termed agnosognosia. When psychologically determined, it is termed denial, or it is said that a certain aspect of a person's behavior or thinking is ego-syntonic.

Generally speaking, persons with borderline personality disorder, persons prone to recurrent psychotic episodes, and persons who are psychotic all have major deficits of ego functioning. The deficits may result from excessive frustration of id drives in the case of persons with borderline personality disorder (Kernberg, 1975). They may be genetically determined or may result from damage to the nervous system in psychosis-prone or psychotic persons.

Persons with mild to moderate neurotic and personality disorders often do not have structural ego defects. On the other hand, it is impossible to tell from patients' symptoms or their descriptive diagnosis whether or not an ego deficit exists. Many persons develop neurotic symptoms because they are excessively vulnerable due to underlying deficits. Therefore, it is possible that a symptom of mild to moderate social anxiety may be less amenable to psychological change than more severe symptoms of a phobic nature that result primarily from intrapsychic conflict.

Some ego deficits can be overcome, given an intact nervous system and an environment that supports change. Information-processing skills can be learned, the ability to repress or modify id drives can be cultivated, and the ability to change one's cognitive set can be acquired through practice.

It is in dealing with ego-defective patients that the biopsychosocial approach to patient care becomes most relevant. Persons with mild psychological problems can be dealt with solely in terms of psychological conflict. Severe personality disorder and psychosis are better conceived of as disorders similar to diabetes and epilepsy; conditions in which the metabolic or physical flaw may not be amenable to resolution. The task of therapy is to help patients recognize and live with their specific vulnerabilities. That is not to deny the possibility that exceptionally talented or motivated patients may succeed in actually achieving a higher level of integration than they ever had prior to treatment. Indeed, many persons with physical deficits are able to transcend their limitations and live fuller lives than persons with no evident impairment. Unfortunately, there are very few Helen Kellers in the world to respond to the host of Ann Sullivans we might be able to train as psychotherapists.

Whether or not ego deficits are inherited or acquired, and whether acquired deficits result from psychosocial or physical factors, the treatment of persons with ego deficit differs considerably from the treatment of ego-intact persons who have mildly deviant patterns of behavior or mild symptom neuroses. The basic aim of treatment for ego-impairment persons is teaching them to cope with their deficits.

Considerations of Psychotherapy

Until the advent of electroconvulsive therapy in the 1930s and psychotropic drugs in the 1950s, psychosocial treatments were the mainstay in treating patients with severe ego deficit. Many psychoanalysts worked with psychotic patients. Some reported impressive successes with schizophrenics (Arieti, 1974) and in patients with major depressive disorder (Arieti, 1977). Such treatments were long, tedious, and frequently ineffective, but were marked by great therapeutic optimism, great faith in patients' ability to learn and to grow emotionally, and great willingness on the part of therapists to commit themselves to intense person-to-person involvement. The aim of the treatment was to correct the predisposing ego defects and thereby to help patients achieve a higher level of function than they enjoyed premorbidly. Such treatment was based on the assumption that psychotic decompensations result from premorbid cognitive style or style of conflict avoidance/conflict resolution. Unfortunately, no systematic study of the psychotherapy of schizophrenia has been published since Gunderson (1973) reviewed the controversies about which type of psychological therapy is optimal. Since that time, however, the trend has been clearly away from intensive psychotherapy as a primary treatment for schizophrenia (Mosher & Keith, 1979).

In a recent article, Cancro (1983) noted the limitations and dangers of antipsychotic drugs, and suggested a reassessment of treating schizophrenia psychotherapeutically. He returned to the earlier stand of Rogers, Gendlin, Kiester, & Truax (1967) that therapist-offered conditions are more important than technique in the psychotherapy of the chronic mentally ill. Cancro suggests that the key variable in successful outcome is the therapist being there during the patient's experience of madness without becoming frightened or rejecting.

Only one study of the intensive psychotherapy of manic-depressive psychosis has ever been reported (Cohen, Baker, Cohen, Fromm-Reichmann, & Weigert, 1954). Much work has been done on the psychological treatment of depression, with emphasis on directly altering cognitive style (Beck, Rush, Shaw, & Emery, 1979) instead of resolving intrapsychic conflict. However, the relationship between cognitive style and vulnerability to depression has still to be demonstrated convincingly.

As the role of intensive psychotherapy in the treatment of psychosis diminished, there arose an interest in applying psychoanalytic treatment methods to another group of persons with severe structural impairment—persons with severe personality disorders. This work is epitomized by Kernberg (1980), who suggests that an ego-supportive therapy offers more hope for achieving a higher level of function in patients with severe personality disorders than a repressive therapy. Kernberg, in a study of 42 patients treated at the Menninger Foundation, found that nonpsychotic ego-impaired patients improved more with ego-supportive therapy than with repressive techniques (Kernberg, Burnstein, Coyne, et al., 1972). However, 8 of the 16 patients treated with ego-supportive or combined ego-supportive/repressive techniques required hospitalization, while only 2 of the 8 patients treated by repressive means required hospitalization. The number of patients is too small for these data to be of statistical significance, but they do confirm the clinical observation that vigorously probing or confronting the ego-impaired person often leads to psychological decompensation. This course of action is too risky for therapists who do not have the backup of a tailor-made therapeutic environment, such as a hospital or a residential treatment center. Unfortunately, Kernberg essentially discounts the hospital treatment of these people, which may have been more useful in stabilizing them than their intensive individual psychotherapy.

The most important general considerations for psychotherapy in persons with ego deficiency are the means for dealing with the inadequate ego, for preventing further ego decompensation, and for stimulating ego maturation or reintegration. These goals are best accomplished by structuring psychotherapeutic interviews in a repressive manner, by structuring patients' environment, by capitalizing on the positive, idealizing transference without engulfing patients, and by minimizing the negative transference without ignoring the source, importance, or effects of patients' anger.

Structuring the Environment

The individual with borderline personality, the psychosis-prone person, and the psychotic person require ego-supportive and repressive techniques to help them with ego development and reintegration of ego function.

An important aspect of treating severe ego dysfunction is controlling the patient's environment and simplifying its demands. Environmental control includes tailoring the environment to meet patients' needs for predictability and limits. Simplifying the environment includes reducing conflicting demands and reducing patients' responsibility for themselves and others to a level that they can manage.

Generally speaking, one cannot easily structure an adult's environment. One cannot ordinarily prevail upon an individual's boss, spouse, and the people with whom the individual carpools to deal with the person in a consistent way. Therefore, if environmental structuring is necessary for an adult, psychiatric inpatient care is frequently suggested. A psychiatric inpatient facility supplies a controlled, simplified environment tailored to individual needs, but at the same time it raises certain issues and creates certain problems.

The involuntary patient. In theory, entering a hospital for treatment entails the relinquishment by the patient of a certain amount of self-regulation in exchange for a chance to improve psychological health. In practice, psychiatric inpatient treatment is perceived by patients as an unequal tradeoff.

Many hospitalized patients are in treatment against their will. Their involuntary admission is due to danger to themselves or others, not their own perceived discomfort or malfunction. Because many persons are confined to hospitals by judicial process, the initial treatment agreement is between the court and the therapist, not between the patient and the therapist. Patients are unwilling participants in a unilateral arrangement which deprives them of their freedom until others are satisfied with their thinking and behavior. The relationship can become an adversary relationship in which patients attempt to discover what is expected of them, hoping that they will sufficiently satisfy their captors so that they will be freed. Through a process that has come to be known as institutional insight, paranoid patients learn to keep their delusions to themselves, and alcoholics learn to feign interest in sobriety. A limited degree of social control is achieved, at least until termination of hospitalization. Even after winning their freedom, patients with institutional insight may continue to behave acceptably because of the threat of reinstitutionalization.

Ideally, involuntarily hospitalized patients come to agree that their captors are right and begin to invest energy into combating the symptoms that peers and therapists find so distressing. Viewed in this way, accepting treatment is a form of capitulation by persons whose psychosis has seemed to conquer a hostile world, or who believe that their drug use has alleviated their physical and emotional pain. It is not surprising, when seen from this perspective, that so many of these patients struggle against treatment. What helpers see as symptoms, patients delusionally see as creating their autonomy, or experience as a protective shield against overwhelming pain or anxiety. We hope to prove to delusional patients that the world is not so personally inimical and to addicted persons that physical or emotional discomfort can be tolerated. It is only after patients make these discoveries that they are capable of entering negotiated relationships. Delusional patients come to appreciate their real potency in negotiating with others, and addicted patients their ability to withstand uncomfortable feelings.

Some patients cannot be convinced of the correctness of their captor's views, and will not enter a therapeutic contract. Perhaps we can be more comfortable as professionals if we view this as the best choice they can make, rather than as recalcitrance or perversity. Acknowledging patients' unwillingness to interact on therapists' terms after efforts to convince them fail gives the patients enough power to enable them to return to treatment at a later date without experiencing a sense of giving in or giving up.

The voluntary patient. Many patients who agree to accept hospitalization are actually coerced, and the potential helper is again in an adversarial relationship. In some cases, patients' complaint of coercion is a bluff that can be countered by opening the hospital door. In other patients, complaints of coercion reflect the patients' life-style of perceived victimization that can only be cut through by therapists' persistent asking, "What do *you* want from this hospitalization?"

Many of the therapeutic agreements made with hospital patients are poorly disguised coercive maneuvers, such as telling emaciated anorectic patients they must gain a certain amount of weight before discharge, or telling school-avoidant adolescent patients that they must attend school in the hospital before they can be released. While coercion may not be directly growth-promoting for these persons, it helps to protect them against further regression. One may have to temporarily sacrifice growth to maintain function, because the more function is relinquished, the longer the path to appropriate levels of autonomy.

The role of administrative hospital physician must often be separated from that of psychotherapist. Administrative physicians are associated with a struggle for control that may so color their relationship with patients that it is impossible for them to reflect objectively on their own behavior. Administrative physicians deal with the regressed aspect of patients, and their presence may continually stimulate its emergence. Psychotherapists make an alliance with the self-observing part of patients and avoid struggling with them for control of their thinking or behavior, preparing them for a time when they will no longer require coercive measures to help maintain function, but will still need a therapeutic relationship.

The division into administrative and psychotherapeutic roles also takes into account the phenomenon of splitting: the inability of regressed patients to recognize that one person can both gratify and frustrate, making it necessary that psychotherapists initially be experienced as gratifying in order for patient and therapist to establish a relationship at all.

PSYCHOTIC PATIENTS

When the ego has no surplus energy after exerting the necessary intrapsychic repression and after coping with reality, there is constant danger that an additional demand for ego energy will render it unable to maintain repression of unconscious drives and unable to maintain its outer boundary, at which reality-testing takes place. As a means to preserve energy for coping, the ego allows repressed material to be discharged (see Figure 5, p. 52). The ego shapes the material from the unconscious just as it gives shape to the material from the unconscious that arises in dreams, but thereby relinquishes some of its reality-testing ability. The ego is sometimes so overwhelmed that it fails to be aware of common dangers such as the fact that one can be cut or burned.

The ego's shaping of material from the unconscious depends on the person's psychological makeup and biological predisposition. The immature ego of a child and the compromised ego of the elderly person, debilitated by sudden impairment of brain function, experience the same intolerable confusion as the ego of a person who becomes functionally psychotic before explanatory delusions and hallucinations begin. The organically impaired ego is even more compromised than the functionally impaired ego, and a disorganized state of delirium occurs, in which the ego attempts to organize its perception in a comprehensible, but frequently incorrect manner.

Because the development of a functional psychosis is usually insidious, the ego can systematize and integrate the stimuli it cannot grasp or must disown. It is also likely that the form of a functional psychosis is partly determined by the specific metabolic abnormalities that characterize a schizophrenia or a bipolar affective disorder.

The goal in treating acute ego disruptions is to restore continuity to the ego's internal and external boundaries. To minimize difficulties at the boundary between ego and reality, therapists simplify and clarify patients' environment, and require the patient to do little decision making. This frees ego energy for reality testing and for repression. Repression is aided by reducing stimulation of unconscious aggressive or sexual drives. As much as possible, therapists distract acutely psychotic patients from their troubling and troublesome sexual and aggressive fantasies and behavior and encourage them to involve themselves in the routine of daily living.

In a hospital environment, the behavior of the personnel and the structure of patients' activities can be constituted so as to pose the least possible threat. People who fear their own dependent needs can be helped to preserve a feeling of autonomy. People who are threatened by homosexual impulses can be kept from close personal contact with others of the same sex until their repression becomes more effective.

Contractual Issues

Psychotic patients are dealt with by attributing their thinking and behavior to illness. Patients are thus enabled to put distance between themselves and their symptoms, which allows them to accept treatment. Persons experiencing a first or second episode of psychosis rarely perceive themselves as ill, but they frequently feel great emotional distress. After several bouts of overt mental illness, many patients seek treatment when they begin to experience dysphoria accompanied by delusions, hallucinations, mania, or depression. Unfortunately, many are so severely impaired that they cannot cooperate with the treatment they seek and must be treated in a controlled environment.

The first level of contract-making with psychotic patients sets as a goal the achievement of control by patients over illness-produced thoughts, feelings, and behavior, along with the bringing of patients into better contact with the real world. This is augmented by antipsychotic or mood-altering drugs which are administered and taken in the same spirit that one takes antibiotics: as a means to help defend against invasion by foreign matter.

When there has been significant remission of psychotic symptoms or change of mood toward a reasonable baseline, therapist and patient can begin to consider whether or not to examine the relationship of life events and intrapsychic events to the onset of shaping of the patient's illness. Ordinarily, people who have been psychotic are interested in learning how to decrease interpersonal stresses and the unreasonable demands that they make of themselves. It is usually unwise to contract for insight-based therapy on exploration of the patient's unconscious. Few ex-psychotics are able to tolerate this type of treatment (Lambert, Bergin, & Collins, 1977). They can gain helpful self-awareness through accepting therapists' explanations of what happened and why. Therapists can teach their patients about the unconscious and can discuss with patients the life events and probable intrapsychic events that caused the failure of repression, the orgy of self-recrimination, or their dangerously elated mood.

Absolute confidentiality cannot be promised by the therapist of a hospitalized patient. Hospital treatment is a team effort, and the other members of the team need certain kinds of information, such as the danger patients pose to themselves or others. Therapists can reasonably promise that they will only disclose information relevant to patients' immediate management, and that patients' entire past and present life will not be disclosed to the other members of the staff.

Process Issues

Because of patients' greatly compromised ego function, therapists keep their psychological distance while still maintaining a personal and professional interest. Therapists' nonintrusiveness in the early stage of treatment helps patients to reestablish what is inside themselves and what is outside.

Some withdrawn autistic patients require active intrusion by the therapist into their psychological world as a means to draw them into the real world. This intrusion must be gentle, persistent, and neutral so as to avoid creating a transference storm by patients' mis-identification of therapists with psychologically devouring or persecuting parents.

If possible, therapists move away from being responsible for patients to being responsible along with them (Arieti, 1974), but, as noted earlier, a move away from a benevolent paternal or maternal stance may not be possible or even desirable for persons with chronic ego impairment.

PSYCHOSIS-PRONE PATIENTS

Psychosis-prone persons ordinarily have chronically impaired ego function. Because of an underdeveloped ego and other specific biological vulnerability, most people retain their vulnerability to severe decompensation (Bowers, Steidl, Rabinovitch, et al., 1980). There is no specific character structure associated with psychosis-proneness, but even between episodes of psychosis many of these people use Vaillant's (1977) first-level adaptive mechanisms to a significant degree. Few psychosis-prone people seek treatment before their first episode of psychosis. Some of those who do seek treatment with naive or unskilled therapists become psychotic as a result of their treatment.

The best technique for treating patients who have chronic ego inadequacy and little resistance to psychosis is the encouragement of authority dependence. It is the assumption of the traditional physician–patient role in which patients come to the physicians for advice, are told what to do, and stay under the physician's care until they are released.

This is a useful technique for dealing with many recompensated psychotics who visit mental health care professionals for follow-up as one might visit an internist after hospital treatment for heart failure or an orthopedic surgeon after hospital care of a fractured hip. Therapists help patients decide what stresses they can handle and what they cannot handle. Therapists give advice for dealing with patients' spouses and children. They are benevolent authorities, who are able to understand and respect patients' points of view, and who offer objective professional advice.

Patients are encouraged to rely on their therapists. Therapists do not object to patients drawing their own conclusions, but also do not frustrate patients when they are unable to come to a conclusion. The focus of the therapy is on daily living, but it also includes a great deal of material about the patient's interests and daily life that is purely conversational. Its aim is to keep the patient in contact with reality.

These people are not treated as if their attitudes toward themselves and toward life cause their difficulties. They are treated as people whose illness causes their difficulties, who come to the therapist for treatment of that illness.

Many patients who have recompensated from severe psychosis can be maintained for years by using this technique in addition to maintaining their medications. Without the relationship with the therapist, they will fail to take their medication and will relapse. Many patients resent long-term medication. They resent the dry mouth, postural hypotension, and constipation caused by some drugs, and the Parkinson-like effects of others. They may also fear the long-term toxicity of the medication prescribed, such as the tardive dyskinesias that occasionally result from prolonged use of antipsychotic drugs. Therapists can see that patients are kept on the lowest possible dose of medication, but they should also tell patients that the medication provides them with an important chemical insulation that helps keep them from becoming overly stimulated or overly distressed, and that this insulation is an important means to prevent a relapse of illness and hospitalization.

Visits with chronic, recompensated patients need not be frequent. They may be once a month or less, but they need to be regular. Therapists' discontinuance of regular visits may be taken by patients to mean that they are well and that they no longer need to take medication or to be reasonable in their demands on themselves. Likewise, discontinuing appointments can mean to patients that the therapist no longer cares. Many patients react to this feeling by saying to themselves, "If my therapist doesn't care, I don't care either," and discontinue their medications. This response may be due to patients' need for an external source of acceptance to counter their negative view of themselves. A positive introject of the therapist is used to displace or to nullify other negative introjects. The same response may also be due to patients' attempt to hurt the therapist-introject, which unfortunately cannot be separated from hurting themselves.

Contractual Issues

The therapeutic contract is usually quite simple: to stay out of the hospital. Some patients express interest in learning why they became mentally ill. Others want to work on their thinking or their patterns of interpersonal relationships.

When patients' discharge from the hospital is contingent upon agreeing to outpatient follow-up, patients often make a token visit or two and drop out of therapy. They usually lack awareness of their illness, and see themselves as having been unfairly confined. If there is a significant prospect of relapse and patients are under the legal control of the institution, therapists can use the threat of reinstitutionalization to help patients stay in treatment, usually with medication.

When patients see themselves as having been ill and are willing to enter a therapeutic contract, they and their therapists contract for a repressive therapy as described above. Patients are encouraged to see themselves as having a specific vulnerability to dealing with certain types of stress, and they are encouraged to find ways to compensate for it and to avoid the stresses that tend to trigger their illness. Patients who wish to be cured of their vulnerability to mental illness can be told that much can be done to reduce their vulnerability, but there are circumstances that will cause anyone to break down mentally, and that there is no guarantee that such a circumstance will not occur.

In some cases, the therapist who treated the patient in the hospital is the best person to continue the patient's care outside the hospital. In other cases, patients prefer to separate themselves from the hospital and its personnel, reasoning that if they are treated by the hospital personnel, they are still seriously ill. If they are treated by others, they are better.

Process Issues

As usual, therapists must pay attention to patients, and not merely to their diagnosis. In this way, they will not become too therapeutically ambitious for severely ego-compromised persons or too restrictive of persons who are capable of further emotional growth. And, they will stay alert to changes in patients' status.

As stated previously, negative transference needs to be kept at a minimum, but there is no harm in patients being angry with their therapists about real issues in the here and now, like therapists continually being late for appointments. However, therapists' attempts to escape real issues by labeling them as transference may do harm to patients by recalling relationships that they cannot deal with emotionally and by contradicting their valid perceptions.

The attitude of therapists toward persons who have been mentally ill plays an important role in the treatment (Rabkin, 1977). Therapists must be able to deal with patients both optimistically and realistically. They must appreciate patients' psychological assets while not losing sight of their liabilities, and they must not use medication as a way to avoid talking to patients about important issues.

Much of what therapists do with ex-psychotics is determined by their comfort with their own unconscious impulses. Therapists who are not entirely certain of their own ability to repress may become very uncomfortable with people whose repressive mechanism has failed. They may seek to protect their patients unnecessarily, or avoid as much contact with them as possible. Most therapists' ability to manage ex-psychotics will depend on the interplay of their personalities; the more reconstruction to be attempted, the greater need for mutual compatibility (Berzins, 1977).

TREATING THE BORDERLINE PERSONALITY

When persons with borderline personality disorder seek treatment, their character problems can be easily missed because their symptoms often suggest a neurotic diagnosis: free-floating anxiety, phobias, obsessive-compulsive symptoms, conversion symptoms, dissociative episodes, and hypochondriasis. If the evaluating/treating therapist looks beyond the presenting symptoms, the signs of ego deficit and developmental failure will be obvious. From a developmental standpoint, there is inadequate character formation; the failure to develop predictable, consistent means for handling environmental stress and internal conflict. There is failure of self-other differentiation, failure to recognize, tolerate, and master separation, loss, and loss of self-esteem, and failure to develop enough self-identity and self-esteem to allow a reasonable degree of autonomy and to enable maintenance of stable interpersonal relationships (Weiner, 1983a).

People with borderline personality disorder use the primitive defense mechanisms of splitting (actively separating introjections and identifications of opposite quality), primitive idealization, projection (including projective identification), denial, omnipotence, and devaluation. These primitive mechanisms manage to conserve enough ego energy to ward off psychosis except for episodes when environmental pressure is great, or when alcohol or other drugs are used (Kernberg, 1975). On the other hand, persons with borderline personality disorder tend to deal with ordinary events of daily living and with their own wishes and libidinal urges in a helter-skelter fashion. Unlike persons with other character disorders who have hit upon one predominant pattern for managing their psychological affairs, coping and defense mechanisms in borderline patients are fluid and unpredictable. Thus, a suicide attempt may follow a minor frustration, but primitive idealization may be used to defend against dealing with a destructive long-term relationship.

Given the above facts, it seems evident that an evocative therapy for borderline personality disorder as advocated by Kernberg (1968, 1975) will be less useful than the techniques of Zetzel (1971) and Friedman (1975) that take into account borderline patients' impaired reality testing and limited ability to tolerate painful feelings and directly augment ego function through repressive and ego-supportive techniques. Persons with borderline personalities who are treated by evocative techniques frequently require hospitalization, but the hospitalization is usually seen by the therapist as a result of the patient's psychopathology and not as an effect of the treatment. A severe regressive stalemate is no more therapeutic for borderline patients than for persons with any other type of emotional disorder. Borderline patients who worsen clinically are not improving; they are becoming overwhelmed and need to reintegrate. Hospitalization protects them from their actions in response to the psychic pummeling administered by their therapists, and the hospital staff helps to develop improved reality testing, frustration tolerance, and capacity to sublimate. The core pathology of the borderline personality cannot be corrected by exposing it through a regressive transference neurosis and reworking it in the transference relationship. It is instead adapted to and compensated for by the patient's ego under the therapist's guidance.

The focus of the borderline patient's treatment is quite different from the treatment focus with psychotic or psychosis-prone persons. The latter group are dealt with as ill persons, and their symptoms are attributed to illness. Borderline patients, to the contrary, are told that their problems are psychological, and that their symptoms are means to avoid facing reality or attempts to manipulate others. Their treatment calls for them to gradually become tolerant of unpleasant feelings, to distinguish fact from fantasy, to develop relationships that are reciprocal and not parasitic, and to assume responsibility for themselves. Thus, the here-and-now purpose of their behavior in the therapeutic hour is dealt with, instead of interpreting it in terms of its transference origins. For example, patients who continually come late for sessions are told in a businesslike but friendly way that their time will not be extended beyond the scheduled hour. When queried as to why such a concession cannot be made, therapists need only reply that it complicates their work day and inconveniences them and the other patients who are scheduled; that in some ways, they would like to make concessions such as extending the hour, but in the long run they work better if they stick to their schedule. No mention needs to be made of patients' motivation until a number of concessions have been asked for. At that time, therapists note the number of concessions that have been demanded and ask their patients how they might respond to such an array of requests, and ask why they think that anyone might make the concessions demanded.

Contractual Issues

Contractual issues arise often in the treatment of borderline patients. Common contractual problems involve the payment of fees, keeping appointments, and the patient's wish to be incorporated into the therapist's life.

In spite of their ability to manipulate others, borderline patients often live so chaotically that they have few financial resources. Or, if they have the financial resources, they frequently put paying the therapist low on their list of priorities. Therapists need to consider seriously the issue of reducing fees for borderline patients. Reducing fees can set the stage for the therapist developing negative feelings, especially when the therapist's generosity is unappreciated or denigrated. The issue of nonpayment also needs to be taken seriously and handled in a timely businesslike fashion instead of waiting until the bill is so large that the patient realistically cannot pay it.

Appointment-keeping is another important issue. Generally speaking, it is best not to offer makeup appointments when patients cancel. That tends to stimulate acting out. Borderline patients should be subject to the same penalties for missing uncanceled appointments that apply to other patients, whatever the therapist's general policy may be. While not stated explicitly as part of the contract, emergency sessions should generally be avoided. Otherwise, what will follow is a series of emergency visits with no ongoing therapy. Because one of the therapeutic goals is helping borderline patients to tolerate dysphoria, it is useful to emphasize that patients can bear the pain until the next session.

Borderline patients tend to ignore the line between professional and personal relationships. Neurotics have fantasies of social involvement with their therapists. Borderline patients insist on having their fantasies gratified and, in doing so, push the therapist toward an all-or-none relationship. Because of that, the calm, accepting attitude that is useful with the neurotic fails. Therapists need to actively bar the door with borderline patients; they must strenuously reject patients' sexual advances or requests for special favors, not only because these are not good for the patient, but because the therapist has no wish for the type of relationship for which the patient is striving. Therapists make it clear to borderline patients that they are not whom patients would like them to be.

Holding patients to their therapeutic contract requires that therapists be able to deal not only with seductive behavior, but with the direct aggression that will certainly follow their frustration of patients' wishes. Dealing with borderline patients' aggression also demands that therapists be comfortable with their own aggression so that when it is called forth by the borderline patient, it vigorously confronts the patient's out-of-bounds behavior instead of being acted out through increased passivity or through interpretive comments that are, in effect, sadistic attacks.

Process Issues

It is difficult to form a therapeutic alliance with a borderline patient (Adler, 1979) because these patients are busy attempting to incorporate therapists into their real interpersonal world or to spit them out. What patients agree upon at one moment, they negate the next. Therapists resist being drawn too much into the patient's world, but do not engage in defensive withdrawal. From the beginning, they make the personal relationship between themselves and the patient a part of the therapeutic inquiry, use their relationship to draw conclusions about the way the patient deals with people in general, and do not hesitate to tell the patient about it.

As noted previously, the therapy of borderline patients can become an antitherapeutic alliance in which therapists make their observations about patients' interactions a vehicle to discharge their own sadistic impulses. It is easy to engage borderline patients in sadomasochistic relationships because they projectively identify with a persecutor and cannot let go. They can only respond with counteraggression that becomes so destructive that hospitalization is required for limit-setting, or that requires the termination of treatment.

The most important process issues, by far, are transference and countertransference. Borderline patients quickly enter into transferences that are characterized by splitting, projective identification, negativistic merger, and serious acting out (Masterson, 1976; Boyer, 1977). Therapists frequently fall victim to these profound, primitive transferences, and there is often a stalemate (Saretsky, 1977). Therapists become anxious, angry, confused, or despairing, and begin to wonder if it is they or their patients who have the emotional problem. Patients usually work actively to convince their therapists that the therapist is the one who is really out of step with reality. The stirring up of intense transference and countertransference feelings is now regarded by many as a diagnostic criterion of borderline psychopathology (Gunderson, 1977), and Green (1977) contends that the ultimate criterion for the diagnosis of borderline personality disorder is the affective quality of the patient's communication and the therapist's response to it.

The positive transference feelings patients have for their therapists are expressed through enticing them to become real parents or sexual objects. When therapists refuse, patients attempt to coerce by suicide threats or by threats of blackmail. Negative transference feelings are handled in the same way. When feeling the threat of desertion, patients often disrupt treatment or make a suicide attempt. Reality-based positive and negative feelings are handled in the same way; act first and think later.

Therapists are strongly tempted to hospitalize borderline patients so that some degree of control may be exerted over their actions (Adler, 1975). Unfortunately, hospitalizing borderline patients tends to perpetuate a struggle for control, unless therapists can maintain separation between themselves and the staff responsible for the patient's daily management and unless the patient can be hospitalized for an extended period of time (Johansen, 1979). When borderline patients become suicidal, some reasonable person with whom they are involved should be told, but therapists need to emphasize that a decision about hospitalization must be made only by the patient, unless he or she has become psychotic. In this way, patients are pushed to accept responsibility for their own lives, and are made to face the fact that they are not so ill that they cannot think for themselves.

While most of the feelings of patients toward therapists are based on misidentification and projective identification, most of the therapist's feelings toward borderline patients are reality-based, not countertransference-based. These patients are annoying, frustrating, unpleasant, and unrewarding to therapists, and it is helpful if therapists tell patients this in a constructive way (Weiner, 1983a). A great deal can be gained from the therapists expressing their reactions if they can avoid a shift in the focus of therapy away from the patient's behavior onto their own inner feelings. Borderline patients often claim to be startled by their therapists' reactions, and attempt to shame therapists for the feelings they experience. If therapists are overly concerned about their own aggression, they may feel apologetic for having struck out at the patient. There is no need for therapists to apologize for having had an ordinary human response, although patients will tell them that they ought to be above such things. Therapists can remind their patients that they are not above having feelings, and that their job in this instance is to show patients the impact they have on others' feelings (Chessick, 1968).

When therapists become angry with borderline patients, the next step is to ask the patients what they may have done to trigger the therapist's anger. Patients will attempt to discount their own behavior, but they will know! This is quite different from therapists' management of the situation when they become overtly angry with neurotic patients in an evocative therapy. In the latter instance, therapists start off by asking themselves what has been triggered in their own unconscious, and then ask patients their reactions and associations to the therapist's behavior. In addition, an apology on the therapist's part may be in order, as it also would be if the therapist's response to the borderline patient were unreasonable in degree or manner of expression, or if it originated in the therapist's specific vulnerability instead of the patient's provocative behavior.

COGNITIVELY IMPAIRED PATIENTS

Another group of patients for whom repressive techniques are indicated is the cognitively impaired. Whether as a result of a particular defensive style, cultural deprivation, inadequate schooling, brain trauma, stroke, or loss of cognitive function due to aging, there is a large group of patients who cannot understand communications at an abstract level.

Psychotherapists rarely assess their patients' ability to reason abstractly as a means of evaluating their ability to cooperate in psychotherapy. Since they fail to do so, it is assumed by therapists that patients' varying psychological resources require no changes in traditional psychotherapeutic techniques and interventions.

Weiner and Lovitt (1984) found, in a sample population of hospitalized medical-surgical patients at a city–county hospital, that the average full-scale intelligence quotient as measured by the revised Wechsler Adult Intelligence Scale (WAIS-R) was in the low 80s. In addition, commonly used nonmedical words such as tranquil, domestic, and obstruct were often not understood by the patient population.

On routine mental status examination, few of the patients examined by Weiner and Lovitt could understand abstract similarities or proverbs. A later study by Weiner and Crowder (in press) confirmed this finding. Because many traditional psychotherapeutic interventions depend on the patients' ability to understand and to perform mental operations involving complex abstract reasoning, these observations raise questions about the effectiveness of such traditional techniques in cognitively impaired patients.

Psychotherapists reason by analogy and frequently communicate their thoughts to patients through simile and metaphor, with the expectation that their patients understand abstract contingent relationships and the "as if" that is explicit in similes and implicit in metaphors.

A typical insight-oriented therapeutic analogy compares one authoritarian relationship with another. In dealing with passive aggression, for example, the therapist may say: "Just as you feared striking out at your father directly, you are now striking back indirectly at your boss by not carrying out his orders." The analogy is followed by a simile: "You seem to fear your boss, as if he were in some way like your cruel father." And the simile by a metaphor: "Perhaps [in your own unconscious mind] your boss is your feared father."

The therapist hopes that by understanding the displacement of feelings from father to boss and by later working through the feelings of anger originally directed toward the internalized father, the patient will no longer antagonize the boss for reasons unrelated to their real work relationship.

The type of reasoning and communication described above comprises what many consider the mutative element in psychotherapy: the therapist's interpretation that one aspect of a patient's life is *like* another, and the patient acts *as if* they were the same (Brenner, 1982). Thus, generalization and the "as if" contingency are at the heart of traditional psychotherapeutic interventions.

A difficulty arises in that cognitively impaired patients often do not grasp abstract analogy, simile, and metaphor. Under this circumstance, it is difficult, if not impossible, to help patients achieve self-awareness and to change unconscious attitudes that are assumed to be the causative and aggravating factors in neuroses and personality disorders.

Some therapists acknowledge this but seem to apprehend the patient's concreteness as a defense to be interpreted and worked through (Oberman, Wood, & Clifton, 1969; Lager & Zwerling, 1983). Dealing with the concrete problems with which these patients often present is viewed as merely a dreary step toward real work.

The latter view, however, regards concrete cognitive styles too lightly. If, for example, concrete thinking results from genetic and sociocultural factors, we put ourselves in the naive position of attempting to perform genetic engineering and/or massive sociocultural rehabilitation in one hour a week of psychotherapy!

Alternatively, a concrete cognitive style may not be just a troublesome resistance-abetting defense in a constellation of defenses, but an entity that serves a larger function. Persons who can think abstractly, and who have good ego strength, are well served by a matrix of repression that contains most conflicts but allows a circumscribed few to rise to consciousness to be examined and modified directly. Because repression serves as a reserve of defensive energy, other defenses can be interpreted and exchanged for more mature ones. As long as such a repressive matrix is intact, no single conflict threatens to overwhelm the patient's entire defensive structure.

Such is not the case with the patients under discussion. Many cognitively impaired patients seem not to possess such a repressive reserve. Lager & Zwerling (1983), referring to their experience with lower-socio-economic-class patients, indicate that in many instances repression has never developed adequately. Generally, repression allows active forgetting of conflicts that cannot be immediately dealt with and allows focusing on problems that are within patients' capacity to solve. Concreteness may function in a similar manner for those unable to use repression. It reduces all time to the present, and its exclusively external, tangible orientation reduces all problems to concrete manipulations of objects and people instead of struggles with motives and emotions whose outcome is vague and uncertain.

As an example, many lower-socioeconomic-class patients become demanding when they feel their emotional needs or discomforts are neglected by their therapists. When patients demand specific gratifications by their therapists, their needs for a perfect mother, future, and past are concretized into "can I get this one thing from my therapist now?" If the behavior is dealt with through interpretation, patients may regress severely, not because they are resistant to change, but because they have no other defensive options. Lager & Zwerling (1983) note that the alternative to demandingness in many lower-socioeconomic-class patients is psychosis. Thus, "resistance" to dropping demandingness may be a strength that helps avoid regression in a patient whose concrete understanding of the situation is a substitute for other patients' ability to repress.

It is therefore questionable that concreteness, even if it is defensive, must be transcended before patients can receive substantial help. In patients who need their concreteness, therapists cannot recreate thought patterns based on their own abstract cognitive style. Nevertheless, new coping mechanisms/defenses must be learned because patients' presence in our clinics signifies some degree of adaptive/defensive failure. How is the learning process to be approached if conscious abstract learning is impossible or contraindicated because of concrete patients' lack of repression?

One possible answer is that conscious abstract learning may not be necessary. Much learning in psychotherapy is unconscious (Freud, 1914/1958). Bandura (1974) has presented evidence that behavioral conditioning, while not promoting conscious cognitive change directly, nevertheless produces cognitive alterations. Experimentation by M. L. Weiner (1975) provides evidence for a "cognitive unconscious" capable of acquiring skills and altering conscious perceptions without direct formal educational experiences. French (1958) proposed much the same idea when he stated that insight could be therapeutic without being conscious. Sternlicht (1965) found several therapeutic techniques useful with mentally retarded patients, who for obvious reasons did not rely on conscious insight.

Thus, patients whose mindsets cause them to be labeled uncongenial or unsuitable to therapy may actually be unsuited for working in the abstract cognitive style with which therapists are more comfortable.

Techniques ordinarily eschewed by abstract insight-oriented therapists might be useful for patients who must operate concretely. Such techniques include using paradoxical intervention (Weeks & L'Abate, 1982), assigning tasks (Puryear, 1979), nurturing an identification with the therapist (Weiner, 1982a), using operant conditioning principles of reinforcement, and giving concrete advice and education. These methods tend to repress conflict. They may not have been appreciated for their true value because they run counter to the approach of working through repression. On the other hand, repressed conflict is universal, present in the psychiatrically healthy as well as the ill. Furthermore, the most mature defenses make people *less* directly aware of their conflicts and drives, sublimating these into productive expression which is simultaneously drive-gratifying.

It follows, then, that the best interventions for cognitively impaired patients may be those producing behavioral and intrapsychic responses that parallel defense mechanisms. For example, consider the passive-aggressive employee dealt with earlier (pp. 196–197). An alternative interpretation would be:

Therapist: It sounds as if you don't like your boss.
Patient: I don't. He's a real S.O.B.
Therapist: Do you want to continue working where you are?
Patient: Yes. Jobs are hard to find.
Therapist: Then let me make some suggestions. They won't change your boss, but they may make it easier to work for him. Let's do some play-acting together. You say what your boss would say and I'll be you, trying to find a better way to handle him. Go ahead. Try it.
Patient (as his boss): Paul, I want those boxes moved.
Therapist (as Paul): I can't. It's lunch time.
Therapist (as himself): How do you think your boss would react to that?
Patient: He'd get mad at me.
Therapist: Then how about, Yes, Mr. Jones. It'll be the first thing I do when I get back from lunch.
Patient: That would probably go over better.
Therapist: Sure, because you've told him "yes" and told him when you'll do it instead of saying "no."

This intervention channels the patient's aggression into productive activity (moving the boxes and negotiating for a more agreeable time frame) and gratifies ambivalently felt needs for independence (timing is now more suitable to the patient) and allowing dependency on and obtaining approval of authority figures (the therapist has told him what to do and praises him for accepting the advice). Focusing on a concrete task, expressing the drive, and receiving gratification all serve to defuse the conflict and repress awareness of it. The intervention performs all these functions at once and is therefore very time-efficient. It avoids a long series of complicated interventions. This is important because of patients' present-time orientation (Lager & Zwerling, 1983). Patients also learn new coping/defense mechanisms without anxiety-provoking abstract interpretations they might not comprehend.

Although repressive techniques foster dependency on the therapist's expertise and authority, such dependency can be in the service of the ego. When patients enter a hospital for treatment of a physical illness, they regress in a positive way, becoming dependent on doctors and nurses to give what they cannot supply for themselves. In the same way, a positive dependence on the therapist is generally of far less concern than the ego deficits and acting out common to cognitively impaired patients. They are initially unable to overcome these problems on their own, and their dependence is acting in the service of the ego.

It might also be argued that the therapist is "doing too much work for the patient," and that by lending his or her own ego the therapist prevents permanent change. However, in M. L. Weiner's (1975) experiments, subjects learned new perceptual skills and interpretive sets which they applied automatically and unconsciously to new situations similar to, yet different from, the conditions under which the skills were originally learned. Therefore, patients do not have to possess conscious insight to generalize the application of a skill learned in one situation to another. Because generalization is an integral part of abstraction, Weiner & Crowder (in press) suggest that humans may have the capacity for an unconscious abstracting process or "para-abstraction." If that is the case, teaching patients how to deal with specific problems *can* produce lasting changes in their cognition and behavior, even when conscious abstract insight does not occur.

Further evidence of para-abstraction comes from the observation that all patients develop transferences. For example, patients traumatized by maternal abandonment in childhood often experience a therapist's vacation as another abandonment. That is, the patient reacts as if the therapist were the patient's mother; there is generalization from one situation to another. Moreover, developmental theory holds that the conflict becomes embedded in the patient's unconscious long before the formal operations phase of cognitive development makes conscious abstraction possible. Once again, it seems that conscious abstract insight is not necessary for the application of learning from one situation to another.

It seems reasonable to test what patients can and cannot understand, and to invest time helping patients learn abstract cognitive skills they may not already possess if they seem capable of acquiring them. However, patients whose native ability or defensive needs preclude abstract thinking can benefit from therapeutic techniques other than abstract clarification, reflection, confrontation, and interpretation.

The notion that some persons may defend against using abstracting ability they actually possess raises intriguing questions as to the developmental origin of this need. Do culturally deprived persons subvert the development of conscious abstract reasoning altogether? Or do they begin to emerge from concrete thinking into a more abstract mode only to find the realities of poverty and physical danger too painful to bear when abstractly interpreted and understood? The avoidance of pain that concreteness offers might be ample incentive for patients to repress not only individual cognitions and emotions, but the entire cognitive process of abstraction. The alterations of cognitive style occurring in hypnotic age regression in which abstract thinkers return to the concrete style of thinking typical of their youth suggest this as a real defensive possibility (Crasilneck & Hall, 1975), as does the work of Piaget, who actually refers to a process of cognitive repression (M. L. Weiner, 1975).

There is also a large group of people whose cognitive impairment results from compromise of brain function, not to mention those with early profound deafness, who also tend to think quite concretely.

The inability to grasp abstract concepts can be detected with short-length diagnostic instruments that are presently in wide use. The similarities subtest of the Wechsler Adult Intelligence Scale (Wechsler, 1955) is an easy test. Persons who can abstract no more than the first two items are probably not suitable for other than repressive therapy. The Mini-Mental State Examination (Folstein, Folstein, & McHugh, 1975) is a useful short test for dementia (see Appendix). High-school educated persons scoring less than 23 points in this scale (maximum of 30 points) are probably experiencing impairment of brain function. Estimating level of cognitive function in well-educated persons by the richness of their vocabulary or their fund of information is often misleading. These are the last functions to show decline.

SUMMARY

Because psychotic persons, psychosis-prone persons, and persons with borderline personalities all have structural ego deficits, they cannot repress adequately. In order for them to function, their ability to repress must be reinforced and those conflicts that have remained unconscious need to be kept in the unconscious. Each of these three groups of patients requires different repressive techniques because of the differences in their respective ego structures.

The psychotic person's environment is made understandable and predictable through hospitalization and often through family therapy sessions. Psychosis-prone individuals need help to understand that they have been ill and, often, that they need to take maintenance medication. Borderline patients need to be confronted with the effects of their behavior on themselves and others. Involuntary hospitalization often helps psychotic persons, but it is probably unwise to coerce borderline patients into hospitals because it turns their attention away from themselves and onto the struggle for control with the institution. The therapist's relationship to psychotic persons and persons whose psychosis is in remission is that of professional healer to patient. With borderline patients, therapists strive for a person-to-person (Chessick, 1968) relationship in which, when necessary, they confront patients with the effects of their behavior on the therapist and on others. To borderline patients, a neutral response or a lack of response is approval of their behavior.

Cognitively impaired persons present an important challenge to public sector psychotherapists who need to teach them concrete means of dealing in a positive way with difficult reality situations.

CHAPTER 11

Ego-Supportive Therapies

In this brief chapter, what has been said about ego-supportive therapies in other chapters will not be repeated. Instead, this chapter will fill in the gaps in areas that are not elsewhere fleshed out adequately.

Ego-supportive techniques are probably the most popular ones in use today. They are useful as short-term and long-term treatment modalities. Patients and therapists enjoy the lively, interactive quality possible in this treatment modality, along with the sense of having a real relationship with one another. Usually operating on a once-a-week basis, the therapy focuses on problems in present-day living that are caused or intensified by patients' style of interpersonal interaction. The therapist–patient relationship becomes an experiential laboratory in which patients come to know themselves at an interpersonal level, in part through reflecting on the quality of their relationship with the therapist, and on the changes that occur in that relationship.

In ego-supportive therapies, the therapist is neither the all-knowing authority required by the repressive treatment technique nor the blank screen required by the evocative modality. Instead, the therapist is an active partner in the patient's self-exploration. The therapist's role vis-à-vis the patient is not one of mentor or neutral reflector, but rather that of an expert guide who allows the person being guided to use as much as possible of his or her own resources.

ELEMENTS

Ego-supportive therapies use the elements described in Table 3 on p. 114. The most-used elements are feedback, identification with the healthy aspects of the therapist, education, reframing, and focusing. Feedback, identification, and education need no further elaboration. Reframing, which was briefly described in Chapter 4, requires further discussion.

Reframing

In the author's view, reframing (within the context of a positive therapist–patient relationship) is probably the single most potent psychotherapeutic intervention. As mentioned earlier, reframing enables the ego to circumvent or better defend against the superego, freeing energy for constructive activity. The psychological mechanism underlying the therapeutic effectiveness of reframing is that of the patient substituting a nurturing superego attitude for a punitive one. It results from the patient's projection of punitive superego introjects onto the therapist, with modification of the superego resulting from reintrojecting a modified attitude toward a particular act or situation.

The most classic type of reframing is done with patients who are ashamed of being in therapy because of the weakness implied in needing and asking for help. Therapists characteristically reframe the situation into one of taking the courageous step of facing one's self – a sign of strength instead of weakness. Patients who are inadequately allied with the therapist to accept reframing statements characteristically respond by saying, "You're only trying to make me feel better." Thus having been tipped off that such patients feel as if they are being seduced into dropping their guard and being made more vulnerable to their own projected introjects, therapists may respond by asking, "And why shouldn't I try to make you feel better?" Or, the therapist can ask, "Does it seem as if I'm trying to put something over on you?"

Another classical use of reframing in ego-supportive and evocative therapy is in redefining symptoms. Anxiety is not an unpleasant state to be avoided, according to the therapist's reframing, but rather the signal of intrapsychic conflict. Increased anxiety is therefore reframed by the therapist as a sign that the treatment is getting closer to the underlying conflict, and increased anxiety is a signal for further exploration instead of prescribing medication or changing the subject to ease the tension.

The following vignette was reported from a psychoanalytic treatment.

A sexually inhibited, frightened man developed the transference expectation of being criticized and beaten by his analyst; this was an intense superego transference. As he began telling of his masturbation when an adolescent, he did so with enormous guilt and sweat trickling down his face.

The patient described having found some paraffin among his mother's canning supplies, which he fashioned into a vagina and used for masturbation. After confessing this, he paused fearfully, awaiting punishment by his analyst. The analyst instead replied, "That was ingenious." The patient then burst into tears and experienced a flood of emotion. It was the first time he had been able to cry during his analysis, and much good work flowed from the analyst separating himself from the patient's introjects by this reframing remark (Aruffo, 1984).

Reframing statements differ from manipulation in that they require a positive alliance with patients. They differ from education in that they are presented as a different point of view, not as assertions of fact. Their potency is in diminishing the harshness of the superego. In contrast to interpretations, which often intensify anxiety and require numerous repetitions, reframing statements usually give prompt relief of anxiety or guilt, and the energy of defending against the id or superego, thus freed, contributes further to a sense of well-being and potency. Like interpretations, reframing statements must be used sparingly. Interpretations much too frequently become rationalizations. Reframing used too frequently gives patients excuses to avoid responsibility. Both, when used too freely, promote excessive dependence on therapists as the ones who really understand everything, and who, if properly manipulated, will give forth the answers.

Focusing

Focusing was mentioned in Chapter 4 under the heading of education. Focusing is a concentration of attention. Most candidates for ego-supportive therapy have the capacity to focus, but tend to use their focusing ability defensively – as a means to distract them from issues that are painful for the ego. Focusing on emotional issues in ego-supportive therapy stands in contrast to distracting patients in repressive therapy from emotional issues and helping them focus on daily coping. Focusing at an ego-supportive level requires that there be surplus ego energy over and above what is needed for day-to-day coping. Indeed, the signal to therapists that patients' attention is being focused too strongly on emotional issues is when daily coping becomes impaired during the course of therapy. Gustafson (1984) describes the process of focusing as relentless interference with defenses, and gives the following example.

> After an adventuresome summer, a young man's spirits dropped suddenly in the first week of school. Focusing revealed that the drop occurred when a professor was outlining the semester's work. The patient felt his professor was going to spend the semester dealing with trivia, which provoked a flood of feelings. As the patient resisted the flood of feelings, he felt as if the therapist's focusing indicated that he was doing things all wrong and that the therapist had lost patience with him. Asked when he had felt similarly before, he sobbed, telling about trying to explain to his father the year before about taking off a semester from school. His father replied, "I knew you could never finish anything."

Focusing in this instance led to catharsis, and eventually led to understanding the student's trying overly hard to be loved by his entire world.

All of the elements in ego-supportive therapy enable therapists and patients to focus on external reality and its reflections in the therapeutic relationship, with emphasis being placed throughout on developing patients' basic self-sufficiency and judgment.

TRANSFERENCE

The lively interactive style of ego-supportive therapy is a form of transference gratification. Therapists helping patients to actively focus on areas of concern that they have found difficult to explore on their own is generally appreciated and stimulates positive feelings toward therapists as helpers. This optimal degree of transference gratification helps limit both erotized transferences and transference anger. Both arise in the course of ego-supportive therapy, but not with the strength that they would in a fully developed transference neurosis. Because these transferences are experienced in diluted form, they do not interfere with the main thrust of therapy—focusing on interpersonal relationships in the here-and-now.

Enough is exposed of the therapist as a real person to limit the transference potential of the relationship, but enough of a personal barrier is maintained so that the relationship does not become a social friendship and so that anxiety is not diminished to the point that patients lose their motivation to work in therapy.

As in repressive therapies, working with transferences is not the primary therapeutic medium. Transferences are dealt with as they interfere with focusing on attitudes and interpersonal behavior. As long as patients' positive transferences keep them on track, they are allowed to stand. When patients' admiration or anger begin to stall the process of mutual inquiry, therapists call them to patients' attention as interferences and distractions, and unfinished business that colors all relationships, including the relationship with the therapist.

In order to detect transference-based behavior, it is best to assume that all behavior in the session not otherwise explainable is transference-based. Therapists take the point of view that they are, at that moment, the center of the patient's interpersonal world. The same is true when unexplainable behavior occurs in other relationships. The first question therapists raise (to themselves) is, "Does that have anything to do with our relationship?" In that way, therapists are on the alert for acting out and have a good basis for decreasing emotional pressure on patients during sessions if acting out becomes too severe, or for increasing pressure on patients to face what is going on in the therapeutic relationship.

Knowing when and how to gratify the transference calls for therapists' use of empathy, with the concomitant danger that therapists may be responding to their own needs. Sometimes the transference gratification is the therapist believing or believing in the patient. Aruffo (1984) presented a vignette in which he finally came to believe and express his belief in his patient's account of her mother being nearly psychotic and very nonnurturing. As he suspended his analytic neutrality, the patient became better able to work in therapy. His empathy allowed him to be accepting in a way that neither her mother nor father had been, and thus provided a basis of trust on which she could build more stable self-esteem.

The patient said, in effect, "My mother was crazy." The therapist initially responded, "You only believed your mother was crazy because you were viewing her from the vantage point of a four-year-old." The patient's reply, in effect, was "If you can't see how crazy my mother was, you repeat the traumas I experienced with my father and I can't trust you enough to proceed in the analysis. I had a right to be protected from my mother by my father and now I have the right to expect you to believe me."

Said in still another way, actions speak louder than words, and through use of empathy, therapists come to understand which traumas can be dealt with by words, and which require siding with the patient. By failure to participate in the transference in this way, therapists may lead to the repetition of traumas suffered with a silent, unempathic, uninvolved, or skeptical parent.

Feedback is also a form of participating in the transference. Therapists reporting their feeling responses to patients' behavior as a means to help them become self-aware at an interpersonal level and also can help to limit the behavior. Thus, provocative patients can be confronted with the effects of their behavior and can be pushed to examine their motivations for behaving as they do when they do.

Active focusing by therapists on the real interactions in the therapeutic relationship also limits the transference and limits the emergence of primary process material. Instead of encouraging patients to fantasize during the hour, therapists press for communication about real events, except when the communication is blocked. When a block does occur, therapists can make use of guided imagery (see Chapter 13 on dreams and imagery) to help patients delineate and work through the block.

MANAGEMENT OF DYSPHORIA

The aim of ego-supportive therapy is to increase tolerance for dysphoria. As mentioned earlier, increasing anxiety is reframed as an indication of getting close to the basic conflicts. The same is true of depressive affect. Dysphoria serves as a cue to investigate more deeply the interpersonal events surrounding the dysphoric episode. Patients are usually aware that their therapists' goal is to help them bear unpleasant affect. Many patients come to take pride in their ability to tolerate dysphoria and see this as an important means to please the therapist. This can lead to situations in which patients' wish to please their therapists leads them into overwhelming anxiety or depression, and their esteem is further compromised by their inability to bear it. Therapists need to make it clear to their patients that nothing is gained by excessive suffering. Should dysphoria compromise patients' daily functioning, antianxiety and antidepressant drugs may be useful adjuncts to therapy.

The following vignette illustrates "boring in" at the point patients become dysphoric.

In trying to find out why a young woman experienced no sexual feelings for men, the patient described a boy she dated as "flabby." In saying the word flabby, she became very rattled. As the therapist persisted in following her dysphoria, she became more upset, and began crying. In the next therapeutic hour, she was flooded with memories of how her aggression had led to losing people, how her parents divorced after much fighting, how she lost her best childhood friend from fighting back, and how she couldn't object to her roommates keeping her waiting. In short, she didn't know how she could defend herself without losing love. (after Gustafson, 1984, p. 938)

This case also illustrates how therapists strive to make patients aware of the feelings that determine their behavior. Doing so enables therapists to challenge dysfunctional interpersonal defenses and styles of relatedness.

The therapeutic contract usually specifies which interpersonal operations therapist and patient see as the problems to be resolved. This also helps confine patient and therapist to working on a specific part of the ego instead of trying to undo all ego defenses at the same time. Confining the therapeutic attack (and that is the way it is often construed by patient and therapist alike) to one facet of the patient's personality enables patients to maintain their psychological equilibrium. It also ensures that dealing with one issue will not be defended against by creating another one.

When patients experience therapists' interventions as a hostile attack instead of a neutral or caring uncovering of sensitive areas, there may be transference and countertransference forces at work; patients' wish to be attacked, and therapists' failure to deal adequately with their own sadistic urges.

DEALING WITH REALITY

Patients all live in a real world, some of which they actively shape, and some of which they do not. Ego-supportive therapy is best conducted from the point of view that patients create their own interpersonal world. While not entirely true, adopting this viewpoint keeps therapists from missing neurotic or characterologically based behavior or distortions of reality. As in relation to transference, therapists keep their view of patients as shaping their own world as a private point of reference, thereby not burdening patients with the absolute sense of creating their own world. But therapists are always ready with the question, "Is there anything you did to contribute to what happened to you?"

This question is asked judiciously, because it is dangerously close to the primitive notions of an animistic world – that illness or natural disasters occur in retribution for individuals' acts. This primitive level of thinking is so commonplace that it is heard in connection with almost any illness of great severity. "What did I do to deserve (or cause) my heart attack? I've been good, I don't (or do) deserve this!" The notion of a talion principle in the universe still exists, and there is always present the fear that one must be careful lest the gods be offended. The question is also close to asserting infantile omnipotence; children's view that what happens in their world is somehow caused by them.

While therapists operate from the point of view that patients frequently contribute to what happens to them, they are often in the position of asserting the opposite; that patients did not cause, or could not have caused, disasters such as their parents' divorce or mental illness. The tension is often broken by the therapist asserting smilingly, "Gee, you must have been a very powerful six-year-old to have caused your parents to divorce." By phrasing a comment in that way, therapists separate themselves from parental superego introjects that assert it was the child's fault; an assertion that originally helped the parents escape responsibility as adults for maintaining their marital relationship.

In addition, there is occasional need for therapists to take an active role in the lives of relatively healthy persons who are basically self-reliant. A parent, for example, may be concerned about an operation suggested for her child and unsure about following a consultant's advice. The therapist can reasonably suggest a second opinion and, if sufficiently knowledgeable, can suggest names of persons from whom further consultation might be obtained. Therapists do not take it on themselves to make diagnoses of medical or other problems without firsthand knowledge, but patients are frequently helped with difficult decisions by being reminded that they often have alternative courses of action.

Taking such a step also has consequences for the therapy. Patients can use therapists' advice-giving to keep from facing their responsibilities, they can feel protected by an omniscient parent, and they may strive harder to incorporate the therapist into their lives as a source of real nurturance. On the other hand, failure to respond with what expertise therapists have at hand is a dereliction of ordinary professional and human caring.

Whatever transference consequences occur can be worked out. Should therapists enjoy giving advice and receiving patients' admiration of their wide knowledge, they have the option of finding other means of satisfaction or of doing primarily repressive therapy, in which a therapist's wish to be a benevolent authority can be readily gratified without harm to patients.

Unless therapists are unempathically intrusive, there is more to be lost by abstinence at times of crisis than from offering advice or suggestions. It is better to be seen as a little foolish, but caring, than as technically expert but uncaring.

DURATION OF THERAPY

It is not possible to make definitive statements about how long an ego-supportive therapy should last. Repressive therapies can be conducted on a short-term basis or can reasonably go for a lifetime if patients' egos have need of continued augmentation. Psychoanalyses usually last a minimum of four years and frequently run to six or seven years without being regarded as excessively long.

Ego-supportive therapies are well-suited to dealing with life tasks and life-cycle stages in that they encourage growth instead of retaining the status quo. Therapists who prescribe and carry out ego-supportive therapies for particular patients often view those patients' problems in terms of life tasks and life cycle stages; separating from parents in the case of late adolescents, establishing a personal identity in the case of mothers whose children have grown up.

It would therefore be difficult to conceive of an ego-supportive therapy that needed to last a lifetime and, in the author's experience, ego-supportive therapies generally last from a few months to a few years. In rare cases, such therapies have lasted more than ten years.

In reviewing the literature on short-term dynamic therapy, I have been impressed that most of the technical operations correspond to ego-supportive therapy in which a designated term of therapy is used to compress and intensify therapist–patient interactions (Mann, 1973; Malan, 1976; Sifneos, 1979). The reader is referred to Gustafson (1984) for an excellent overview and integration of the workings of short-term therapies, but it will be useful to consider here the rationale for establishing a time limit for an ego-supportive therapy.

Time-limited therapies are proposed largely because they represent a particular therapist's point of view, because of externally imposed time constraints, or because of limitations imposed by third-party payors.

Some therapists are concerned that therapy, like work, expands to fill the amount of time allotted to do it, and that prolonged therapy stimulates overdependence. It certainly behooves all therapists to think in terms of helping their patients as quickly as possible, but there is little need on the other hand to set an arbitrary length of therapy. Most patients are eager to get about the business of living, and instances of prolonged clinging are relatively infrequent unless actively promoted by therapists.

Therapy is often limited in duration because it is tied to a school year, as in student health services. Students who seek help in September frequently terminate their therapy at Christmas break; those who start at the first of the year terminate at the end of May. Terminations of this sort are often fitting. Freshmen college students are helped in the fall semester to make the transition from home. Seniors are helped in the spring of their last year to ease their transition into the adult world. Others are seen throughout the college years as they deal with issues of competition, intimacy, and career choice.

Limitations of mental health benefits to payment for 20 or less sessions per year (as a means of cost-containment for insurance companies) has also contributed to the development of short-term therapies. Therapists in health maintenance organizations frequently indicate at the beginning of treatment that so many sessions per year are covered by their contract, and in this way encourage dealing with well-defined issues during a stated period of time.

I believe that ego-supportive therapy is possible under these conditions, given patients with adequate coping abilities whose emotional problems are confined to a relatively small area of their personality, and who can enjoy vigorous interaction with the therapist. I also believe that agreeing to focus on a particular issue has the advantage of educating patients in constructive means of dealing with their emotions and then giving them the responsibility for using what they have learned in other spheres of their personalities.

SPOUSES AND CONCERNED OTHERS

Meeting with persons who are important in patients' lives is almost always useful, especially at the beginning of therapy. It is most helpful to meet those important others (usually spouses) in the course of therapy as a routine matter. This meeting can serve a number of important functions. It can add to the history already given by the patient, can allow therapists to see their patients' spouses undistorted by the patient, and can make an ally of the spouse, especially if the therapist does not charge for the spouse's visit.

Such meetings are set up with patients' permission and with the assurance of the confidentiality of their relationship with the therapist. Resistances of patients to these meetings are explored and are, in themselves, valuables sources of information. At times, it may be best to interact with the third party in the patient's presence. That, too, can be a source of valuable information.

When patients propose meetings of the therapist with others, patients' motivations for the proposal are first explored. At times, patients, will attempt to set up an alliance between therapist and concerned others as a way of feeling victimized. It can also be a means to set up the therapist and the concerned others as surrogate parents. Or, it can be the only means patients have to communicate information they are unwilling to reveal directly.

Therapists, of course, need to be sensitive to their patients' needs for privacy. They need also to be aware they may be setting up an alliance that will undermine the therapist–patient relationship by encouraging phone calls to the therapist to report about the patient, which may reflect in certain patients' inability to establish a secure-enough link with their parents. Should a spouse call and ask to visit with the therapist, such a wish can be granted after securing the approval of the patient, inviting the patient to join the session, or telling the patient that whatever is communicated in the visit with the spouse will be passed back to the patient. Thus, there will be no reenactment of times when the patients were unreasonably excluded from family business of which they could have had knowledge.

It is often best to refer spouses who wish personal therapy to another therapist, unless both spouses are interested in therapy as a couple, or unless therapy has not proceeded beyond evaluation. After the evaluation stage, the elements of rivalry and concerns about displacement that arise affect the spouse who first entered therapy in a negative way. Referring the couple as a couple while maintaining a relationship with the original spouse helps to insure that one spouse does not lose out in relationship to the therapist because of displacement by the other. Or, the second spouse can be referred for individual therapy.

SUMMARY

Ego-supportive therapy is a lively, fulfilling therapeutic medium for therapist and patient. As such, it has the potential pitfall of becoming more of a social relationship than a therapeutic one, but a reasonably alert therapist can keep it on track.

Generally speaking, transferences are managed rather than interpreted, and therapists do participate in the transference and also attempt to separate themselves from patients' harsh introjects. Therapists' participation as real persons in their patients' lives limits the transference, but the human dimension added by such participation far outweighs the dangers of disturbing the transference or failing to work through negative transferences. People usually need more help with establishing positive forms of dependence than they do with ventilating pent-up angry feelings. The angry feelings usually subside as their relationships outside therapy improve.

CHAPTER 12

The Therapist–Patient Relationship

The outcome of therapy is related to therapists' skill, their interest in helping patients, and their personal adjustment (Luborsky, McLellan, Woody, et al., 1985). Once therapists have mastered the technical operations of their techniques and can tailor their treatment to patients' ego strength and ego structure, they are faced with an issue even more complex and more difficult to define – the therapist–patient relationship. There are three main aspects of the therapist–patient relationship. They are the matching of personalities or value systems and dealing with transference and countertransference.

MATCHING

A certain match of therapist and patient personalities and values is an important part of the therapeutic process, regardless of the level at which therapy is conducted. Matching may be based on similarities or dissimilarities that result in complementarity. Some persons will only discuss their personal lives with those who share the same religious convictions, and will ask their therapists at the outset whether they believe in God, or whether they have more specific religious beliefs, such as salvation through divine grace. On the other hand, there are persons who value certain differences. For example, some female patients feel more comfortable with male therapists. Certain male patients find themselves more compatible with female therapists.

Matching is important from a dynamic standpoint because patients learn new views of themselves and their world through partial identification with their therapists. Therapists' empathic understanding of their patients is also based on partial identification with their patients. It is also important that therapists have a sense of their patients' worth — that they find something they can admire in their patients. Thus, the predilection of therapists for young, physically attractive, well-educated, verbal, upper-middle-class patients (Rabkin, 1977) may be partially related to the real potential of these individuals for successful treatment, but part of the reason for their success in treatment may be that their therapists admire them and see in them capacities they are less likely to see in others. Or, therapists may seek to match themselves with patients who they can help overcome obstacles or develop attributes that the therapists themselves were blocked in developing. Finally, therapists may do well in attempting to help their patients through difficulties that their own family members were unable to surmount.

In most cases, personality-related matching difficulties arise from specific therapist–patient interactions, and not solely from the personality of the patient or the therapist (Strupp, 1980). There are, however, therapists who cannot tolerate certain personality types or who react judgmentally to certain patient behaviors, such as child abuse or exhibitionism.

During their training, psychotherapists need exposure to persons of varied personality types, coping and defense mechanisms, and value systems. They attempt, through supervision and through personal therapy, to work out their difficulties in relation to the patients they encounter. In doing so, they broaden their ability to deal with patients and find those aspects of their personalities and value systems that compromise their ability to function effectively with certain types of problems or certain types of persons. They also become self-aware enough to predict the kinds of transference reactions certain patients will have toward them and to predict some of the countertransference problems they are likely to have.

Value systems are also important in therapists' evaluation of patients for therapy. For example, a therapist's inability to see a person as a candidate for psychotherapy may be based on that person's socially undesirable behavior instead of his or her ability to cooperate with treatment.

The type of psychological adaptation toward which therapists urge their patients and the value they attach to the means by which they achieve it are also important variables. For example, therapists who see autonomy as the sine qua non of mental health may have difficulty accepting patients' unwillingness to leave their parents' home. Therapists for whom a successful heterosexual love relationship is the hallmark of mental health may undermine the treatment of homosexual persons or of schizoid persons who fear engulfment in intimate relationships.

At times, therapists' enthusiasm for their techniques blinds them to their limitations and causes a mismatch of technique to patient. It is also easy to value the means of treatment over the results of treatment and to insist, for example, that insight is the only truly mutative process. Resolution of symptoms through insight is not feasible for all patients. Other means of treatment are no less potent, although less highly valued.

Few therapists can treat all types of patients. Therapists usually develop conscious and unconscious means to screen from their practices the people whom they cannot help or with whom they cannot cope. Therapists need to recognize their limitations and to avoid situations with which they deal poorly. It is, however, important that therapists do not damage patients' self-esteem while protecting them from therapists' shortcomings. Therapists may need to tell patients that they can be better treated by another therapist and to specify the therapist instead of saying, "I can't help you," or "I can't treat someone like you." Part of the evaluation contract is to help patients find the best possible help commensurate with the values and exigencies of their own lives and with their expectations of treatment (Wilkins, 1977).

Racial and sociocultural factors are potential sources of difficulty and must be considered when there are obvious differences between therapists and patients (Sattler, 1977). The cultural stereotypes Hispanic and black patients have of "Anglos" or "whitey" may make it difficult for them to form productive therapeutic relationships with white therapists. The reverse may also be true. Class differences may make it difficult for therapists to understand the effects of grinding poverty or homelessness, or the ready acceptability of drug-taking as a way of life.

When there are obvious differences between therapists and their patients, therapists may be more likely to examine their relationships with patients for misunderstandings. Many times, patients take the lead, and are met with bland reassurances that further increase their concerns that they will be misunderstood. Misunderstandings can be averted by therapists dealing openly with the issue of the apparent differences, whether they be skin color or religion.

TRANSFERENCE

Transference is a form of resistance. In psychoanalysis, resistance originally referred to everything that prevents analysands from producing material derived from the unconscious (Fenichel, 1945). Nowadays, the term resistance encompasses everything that obstructs the course of psychotherapy.

Fenichel (1945) held that managing the transference is analysts' most difficult task. Instead of remembering their childhood, for example, analysands strive unwittingly to relive it and to make it more satisfactory than when they actually lived it. In this way, they transfer past wishes and attitudes to the present.

Endlessly repeating aspects of one's past in order to master them (and one's past wishes in order to gratify them) is called the repetition compulsion (Freud 1914/1958). Another goal of the repetition compulsion is to capture and maintain those aspects of the past that were most satisfying and were therefore most reluctantly abandoned, whether these were real or fantasied. The fact or fantasy of having been a favored child can stimulate as much transference behavior as the fact or fantasy of having been unloved.

Transference is also a regressive process. In the portion of their mental operations affected by the transference, patients may think and behave in terms of their cognitive and emotional processes at the stage of development from which the transference derives. For example, a patient experiencing jealousy of another patient just leaving the therapist's office may react angrily to the therapist and resort to the same negativism that he employed when he was two years old and a sibling was born.

Although transferences are a resistance to remembering, they often help to maintain the therapeutic relationship during its early stages. The therapist's calm, reflective attitude gratifies the patient's transference wish for a calm, understanding parent and stimulates fantasies of the therapist's omnipotence. The patient cooperates by giving personal information at the beginning of therapy in the transference expectation of receiving loving and caring and acquiring strength and wisdom.

When therapists wish to establish a more equal, cooperative relationship, transferences that were useful in creating the patient–therapist bond become obstacles. In repressive therapies, these transference wishes are not disturbed. Therapists allow themselves to be seen as wise and caring so that patients will accept their ideas and follow their suggestions.

Therapists must be prepared to recognize and deal with transferences when they obstruct the therapeutic process. Insight-oriented therapies that focus on the unconscious deal with transferences by bringing their unconscious meaning to light. In therapies that focus on here-and-now thinking and behavior such as cognitive therapy (Beck, 1976), transactional analysis (Berne, 1964), or behavior therapy (Wolpe, 1969), transferences may be labeled as irrational negative cognitions, as games, or as maladaptive learned behavior. These cognitions, games, and learned behaviors are dealt with by correcting negative cognitions, by abandoning interpersonally destructive games, and by learning new, more adaptive behaviors.

Transferences can be partially avoided by not fostering a climate in which they can easily flourish. Brief, highly structured interviews, short-term therapy, or infrequent sessions enhance a benevolent parental transference and lessen other transferences. Even under these circumstances, transference-based difficulties can arise.

Transference development is stimulated in psychoanalysis by free association and by the quietness and anonymity of the analyst in a relatively stimulus-free environment. People who seek out analysis expect to free associate and to be frustrated. People who come for psychological help in dealing with specific symptoms usually do not know what to expect. Extreme passivity and uncommunicativeness with unprepared patients can cause therapeutic stalemates based partly on a transference reaction to the therapist as a depriving parent. In this circumstance, however, the patient's hostility is partly reality-based. Without adequate preparation for the deprivations to be endured in therapy, patients tend to act out their negative transference reactions, and therapy may be disrupted.

To reduce the nontransference sources of patients' anger or frustration, it is useful if therapists describe the therapeutic technique they intend to employ and make certain that patients understand its rationale. Providing such explanations helps the therapist as well as the patient. Both of them know where they are supposed to be going and how they are supposed to get there.

Therapeutic neutrality is another transference-related issue. No psychotherapy goes on without a palpable human relationship (Stone, 1961), but active attempts to draw patients into a relationship with the therapist and to create a climate of mutual, intimate exchange can also lead to difficulty (Weiner, 1982b). This type of transference mismanagement results from therapists joining with patients in acting out aspects of the transference. The therapist fails to take into account that an apparent short-term gain in the patient–therapist relationship may eventually obstruct therapy. The therapist creates a channel for the discharge of impulses that is difficult to close because it is reinforced by the patient's pathologic ego defenses and is acceptable to the patient's superego.

Mismanagement of the transference may result from the interaction of the therapist's personality with that of the patient, from situational factors in the therapist's life, from the therapist's incompetence, from a miscalculation or oversight, or from a conscious or unconscious exploitation of the patient.

Every therapist is vulnerable to certain kinds of transference behavior. At times, they are due to similarities between a patient and an important person in the therapist's life, as we will see in the treatment of the patient in the following example.

A 30-year-old female therapist was seeing a 60-year-old depressed man who had prostate cancer. She had difficulty with his statements about liking younger women and was confused by his mild but persistent sexual advances toward her. She was afraid to confront him about his sexual interest in her, fearing that he would leave treatment. On the other hand, she knew she needed to confront him to keep therapy moving. She was paralyzed by these contradictory feelings until the patient left therapy. In discussing this case with a colleague, she realized that although she knew this man resembled her deceased father who was seductive toward her and had died of prostate cancer, she had not realized how much her feelings had inhibited her. (after Beitmann, 1983, p. 85)

Transference mismanagement also results in malpractice suits based on sexual exploitation of patients. Most suits arise when patients are spurned after having been sexually stimulated (Brownfain, 1971) or physically involved (Roy v. Hartogs, 1975). In one case of sexual exploitation, the judge stated that the therapist had "mishandled the transference phenomenon, which is a reaction the psychiatrists anticipate and which must be handled properly" (Zipkin v. Freeman, 1968).

Many cases in which therapists exploited the erotic transference have not stimulated malpractice suits; they have only left patients feeling bewildered, frustrated, and guilty. It is clear that not all of patients' erotic feelings toward therapists are transference-based. Many therapists are sexually attractive. However, Robertiello (1975) suggests that the evidence for strong transference elements in the attraction of patients to therapists is that many patients who have entered such relationships show very good judgment in their extratherapeutic relationships, and he cites cases in which well-functioning people allowed themselves to be swayed by the specialness of the psychotherapist–patient relationship. Confirming the role of irrational elements is Chesler's (1971) finding that women who were actively seduced by their therapists held themselves to blame and did not feel entitled to redress despite the fact that the sexual exploitation was falsely presented as therapy. These women preferred to see themselves as uniquely tempting instead of viewing themselves as victims of therapists who engaged indiscriminately in sexual liaisons with patients.

In the cases the author has seen, many transference wishes and ordinary social wishes were being gratified; the wish to be attractive to or loved by a powerful or attractive person; the wish to please; the wish to continue using sexual means to discharge emotional tensions and to avoid interpersonal and intrapsychic conflict; and the wish for a substitute relationship after an important loss.

Sexual contact between therapist and patient undermines patients' ability to establish a trusting relationship (Dahlberg, 1970; Barnhouse, 1978). A therapist and a patient who has been sexually exploited must sort out the original presenting problem from the therapist-engendered problem. They also need to determine how and why sexuality intervened and therapy stopped in the former treatment (Ulanov, 1979). Often, the point at which the patient's (and therapist's) sexual fantasy became real is when transference was acted upon and not dealt with by the therapist. The new therapist seeks to establish the reason for the patient's vulnerability and uses this information to prevent further abuse of the patient.

Less dramatic instances of transference mismanagement include the fostering of dependency and the stimulation of transference guilt. The main factor in fostering overdependence is not the length of treatment, but the quality of the relationship, the frequency of visits, and the goal of treatment. Many patients with major psychiatric disorders benefit from periodic contact with a benevolent parent-substitute. Such a relationship can be easily maintained with short visits once a month, or less often. It can also be maintained without the therapist presenting himself as an authority on all problems, emotional, financial, legal, and so forth. The rational part of all patients recognizes the impossibility of the therapist's omniscience, and it is the rational part of the patient that we seek to enhance.

Cultivation of transference guilt typically occurs when patient and therapist contract for a type of therapy that is beyond the patient's conceptual and emotional means and the therapist's skill. The contract, often made without an adequate assessment of a patient's assets and liabilities, offers to fulfill the transference wish to be transformed from a limited person to a socially graceful and intellectually stimulating person like all those (including the therapist) whom the patient idealizes. Patients may thus overextend their stay in an inappropriate insight-oriented treatment because they assume that something they are doing (or not doing) is impeding their treatment. This transference guilt is based on guilty memories from childhood when, because of failure to follow parents' instructions to the letter, some calamity occurred. The unconscious formula that makes these people continue with a nonhelpful therapy is the idea that if authority is followed, all will be well, and that all not being well is prima facie evidence of not conforming adequately. These patients deal with this transference guilt by trying harder to examine themselves; which compounds the problem.

COUNTERTRANSFERENCE

Countertransference is exactly equivalent to transference in the patient (Greenson, 1967). It is a reaction to some aspect of the patient as a person or to the patient's transference to the therapist. Countertransference usually develops over time, but it can develop in the first session with patients as a reaction to their personality, or as a reaction to the presenting complaint.

Important countertransference is probably present when the therapist's feelings and behavior toward a patient vary considerably from what the therapist would expect another therapist to feel and to do with a similar patient under similar circumstances, or when therapists' feelings and behavior differ from what they usually feel and do in the same situation. Countertransference feelings can include anger, guilt, fear, overconcern for patients, and many other feelings. They may be defended against by anger, indifference, restlessness, boredom, or sexual attraction to patients.

Fenichel (1953) conceptualized therapists' boredom as a defense against unconscious fantasy stirred up by patients. Therapists attempt to maintain repression by becoming bored and sleepy. Altshul (1977) suggests that it can also be a reaction to narcissistic depletion by patients to whom one gives and gives without any emotional return. By fostering withdrawal from the patient, boredom blocks further narcissistic depletion, and also indicates that the therapist is being drained excessively or is being depleted by being ignored.

When therapists experience intense emotional reactions toward patients, they tend to assume that countertransference is at work, but such is often not the case. There are many noncountertransference emotional reactions of therapists to patients, which I have enumerated elsewhere (Weiner, 1982b). In particular, patients with borderline personality disorders stimulate intense feelings in their therapists that are commensurate with the nature and intensity of their provocation. Because of the strength of their feelings, therapists often think that their reactions are countertransference-based (Nadelson, 1977) and need to be suppressed or dealt with in supervision or personal therapy. It therefore seems reasonable that when therapists experience intense feelings toward patients, it is best to first reflect on what the patients are doing to them and to next ask themselves if their response is in fact out of proportion to the stimulus.

Like the appropriate emotional reactions experienced by the therapist, countertransferences can be important diagnostic clues. It is important, however, not to confuse countertransferences with therapists' inappropriate defense against feelings such as anger which are fitting reactions to certain patients (Chrzanowski, 1977). This inappropriate defensiveness may stem from overzealous self-control; a sense that therapists owe their patients calmness under all circumstances. Each emotional reaction of therapists must be dealt with in the context of their real relationship with patients at that moment, as well as in the context of the therapist's unconscious mental life.

The following is an example of treatment complicated by counter-transference-based gratification of transference wishes.

Mrs. M. was a 36-year-old woman initially seen in marital therapy. She had filed for divorce from her husband, and he had filed a countersuit. She countered with the suggestion that if he would seek help for himself she could consider continuing the marriage. Each spouse felt the other was inconsiderate. Both had sought marriage counseling three years earlier, but no headway had been made. After four months of marital therapy, the husband was able to compromise better and show his wife more respect and tenderness. She responded well, and they discontinued their sessions. A few months later she returned, complaining that her husband was slipping back to his old inconsiderate ways, and was no longer as kind, considerate, and outwardly affectionate as he had been. At that point, the therapist tried to supply some of the considerateness her husband did not. The therapist told her in kind, friendly ways that he liked her, but following each positive expression on his part, the patient became more depressed. After seven months of psychotherapy, she required hospitalization because of weight loss, sleeplessness, increasing depression, and increasing hostility toward her husband.

The patient was one of four siblings. She intensely disliked all of her siblings and her parents. She felt that her older brothers and sisters had been given privileges she should have had. When her parents divorced when she was twelve, she lived with her father, whom she felt placed her in a mothering role. She tried to get along by being "good mother," but felt she had been robbed of her childhood. She saw her father as a person who had little feeling for her, but took advantage of her by making promises and then failing to keep them. After graduation from high school, she married a young man whom she supported and then divorced because she thought he was taking advantage of her. She had a short affair with a married man afterward, and married her husband when she was 23, a time when she felt relatively weak and helpless. She didn't love him at the time, but they got along fairly well and had three children. Then, she started to care about him. As soon as she started caring about him, she began feeling that he was trying to suppress her and that he didn't show her enough respect.

Based on the history, it should have been possible for the therapist to predict the nature and outcome of the transference relationship. She would demand affection and then resent and complain about what she received.

Her hospitalization, as also might have been predicted, was very stormy. Over her seven months in the hospital, she separated herself from her husband, began working, but dealt with the therapist as a frustrating object to be punished as her negative feelings developed. Although this woman's initial prognosis for treatment was not good, it was greatly complicated by the therapist's attempted transference gratification which provoked her regression to the point of requiring hospitalization.

A patient who has reached a transference-countertransference impasse with one therapist will not always reach an impasse with every therapist, as shown in the next case example.

A therapist became anxious during her first session with a 28-year-old, dark-haired, depressed, obsessive man. She realized that he strongly resembled a patient of hers who had committed suicide after 15 sessions. She became afraid that this new patient would also commit suicide. Believing she was unable to help him, she negotiated a transfer. The next therapist was able to disconfirm her fears, suggesting a neurotic countertransference reaction based partly upon a previous clinical experience. (Beitman, 1983, p. 85)

Countertransference is difficult to recognize until therapists have had prolonged experience with many patient types, and have had many types of interaction with patients. In addition to being aware of their personality traits, such as generosity, therapists must also know generous with whom, generous under what circumstances, and generous in what way. Having an awareness of themselves interpersonally and as individuals, therapists can compare their feelings and behavior with similar patients, or can ask themselves with whom else and under what circumstances in the past they have felt, thought, or behaved in the same way. Having made these comparisons, they are able to ask themselves the cardinal question that differentiates countertransference from an appropriate reaction to the patient: Do I behave, think, or feel substantially differently with this patient than I do with similar patients under similar circumstances? If the answer is yes, the therapist must ask if anything in his or her relationship has stirred something in the unconscious and, if so, determine its nature. However, even a countertransference-based act toward a patient can be useful in the proper context. It can demonstrate that therapists, too, have unconscious processes to which they are responsive and with which they must deal in their own daily lives. In situations where the therapist's countertransference thoughts and feelings are transparent, patients can be asked if others have ever reacted to them in the same way. Many patients are aware that they stimulate competitiveness, envy, or rescue fantasies in others. Therapists are not impervious to their own repressed urges and conflicts, but they accept the responsibility for them and for their reaction to them. In this way, therapists indicate to patients that all people have irrational aspects to their personalities, but that one need not be totally governed by them.

Therapists' best defense against countertransference interfering with therapy is adopting a neutral professional attitude toward their patients. Therapists' real concern for, and interest in their patients is best tempered (except in times of crisis) by a period of calm reflection before any action is undertaken toward the patient.

Working with the Elderly

It may seem peculiar that a discussion of working with the elderly is included in a section on countertransference instead of in a section on special populations. The fact of the matter is that the elderly are not a homogeneous population. In spite of facing many life tasks in common, the elderly are more dissimilar from one another psychologically and physiologically than persons in any other era of life. In a discussion of treating the elderly, one must ask which elderly person, and under what circumstances?

The chief barriers to effective psychotherapeutic work with cognitively intact elderly persons are not their short remaining span of years, the multiple losses or hardships they have suffered, their lack of environmental support, or the chronicity of their symptoms. Instead, they are therapists' stereotypes of elders and their transference reactions to these older persons.

The common cultural stereotype is that elders cannot change. You can't teach an old dog new tricks. Even Freud (1904/1953) thought so. Elder persons have been considered to have less by way of emotional resources and fewer brain cells than younger persons; their withdrawal from interests and activities has been viewed as a normal part of aging. Butler (1975) regards these attitudes as a form of bigotry that does great harm.

In addition to cultural stereotypes, unconscious dynamics in therapists contribute to their stereotyping. Partly this has to do with feelings about being parents to our own parents. Many of us resent having to relinquish our dependence on our parents, wanting to maintain the illusion that they will always be available for our nurturance and support. When this is compounded by elders' need for support, it may become doubly burdensome. Therapists who have not dealt with feelings about potential or actual role reversal with their own parents may avoid dealing with their feelings by avoiding treating elderly people. Others act out their resentment in the same way, or by medicating older patients instead of encouraging them to talk about the issues in their lives.

Therapists who have difficulty dealing with the fact of their parents and grandparents' sexuality will have difficulty recognizing and accepting the sexual wishes and activities of the elderly (Hiatt, 1971). They may also not want to lose their illusions about old age as a golden period of life, and may be very reluctant to face disability and death through the eyes of their patients. Indeed, fear of death is less of an issue, even for enfeebled elderly persons (Roberts, Kimsey, Logan, & Shaw, 1970) than it is for younger persons.

In deciding whether or at what level to treat elderly persons, therapists often need to review their feelings toward elderly persons and toward growing old, in addition to reviewing their feelings toward each potential candidate for therapy. Having dealt with these issues, decisions about treatment are made on the same basis as treatment decisions concerning persons at any age. Treatments ranging from brief contacts of 15 minutes once or twice a week for nursing home residents (Goldfarb & Turner, 1953) to modified psychoanalytic therapy with elderly outpatients (Wayne, 1953) have been employed with good results.

Vigorous treatment of depression in the elderly has been advocated because of the high incidence of suicide, especially in depressed elderly men (Bennett, 1973). Antidepressant drugs should therefore be started sooner, rather than later, if the vegetative signs of major depression are present. If patients do not improve rapidly, hospitalization and electroconvulsive therapy may be the safest course of action, especially in the case of frail elderly persons. It cannot be too strongly stressed, however, that drug treatment is not a substitute for dealing with issues in patients' lives, as the following example illustrates.

Mrs. A. A. D. was a 68-year-old widow who became depressed after the death of her husband. She had also experienced an episode of prolonged depression 15 years previously, which had responded poorly to drug treatment and electroconvulsive therapy, and responded best to her becoming more actively involved in her husband's business.

Brief treatment as an outpatient with antidepressant medication and psychotherapy was ineffective. She was therefore hospitalized and treated in group therapy and an activity program, in addition to repressive psychotherapy aimed at remobilizing her interest in creative writing.

Her depression began to clear in the hospital, but at the mention of eventual discharge she began to become upset. Instead of changing her antidepressant or suggesting ECT (which she would have refused), she and her therapist discussed the recurrence of her childhood fear of being left alone. He and she concluded that her depression was not worsening—rather, her problem was having to live alone. Having thus clarified the issue, Mrs. A. A. D. set about to obtain a housekeeper until such time as she could deal with the residuals of her childhood neurosis.

SUMMARY

Problems of matching, transference, and countertransference can impede therapy, but all can be dealt with effectively.

Adequate matching calls for mature self-awareness by therapists. Transference problems may be dealt with by interpretation, avoidance, or explanation. The frequent occurrence of certain kinds of transference toward a particular therapist may point to a characteristic behavior or attitude of the therapist. Acting on countertransference should be reduced to a level at which the patient and therapist can deal with it in the context of the therapeutic relationship after careful determination that the therapist's reactions to the patient are, in fact, inappropriate.

CHAPTER 13

Dreams and Imagery

While psychotherapy is primarily an interchange of verbal symbols, other types of symbols play an important role in psychotherapy, including the visual and kinesthetic symbols of dreams and fantasies, and of spontaneous or directed imagery. The fundamental difference between dreams, fantasies, and imagery is that dreams take place when conscious thought and will are partially suspended during the biological process of sleep, while fantasies and imagery occur during full consciousness and may be products of conscious will. We do not know the exact meaning of dreams, and we do not know how the human imagination works. We do know that since ancient times, the direction of the lives of many people has been strongly influenced by the interpretation placed on dreams (Dodds, 1971).

DREAMS

Dreaming results from the spontaneous activation of nuclei in the portions of the brain that trigger activity in specific neural circuits (Hartmann, 1980). Dreaming has a role in the human body's protective, defensive, and regulatory apparatus. It is associated with rapid eye movement (REM) sleep, which occupies approximately 20 percent of adult sleeping time. REM sleep is important in preserving psychological integrity, and deprivation of REM sleep leads to an increased biological pressure for REM sleep and dreaming.

This chapter is a revised version of Chapter 10, Dreams and Imagery, in Weiner, M. F. (1984), *Techniques of group psychotherapy*, Washington, D.C.: American Psychiatric Press, pp. 161–174.

Sigmund Freud viewed dreaming as the ego's means of preserving sleep (Freud, 1900/1960). According to Freud, dreams result from the sleep-weakened ego's attempts to blend the residue of the experiences of the previous day, nocturnal sensations, and material repressed during childhood in a way that avoids threatening the ego enough to cause awakening. At times, the ego's dream work fails, and the dreamer awakens in a state of fright or tension.

According to Freud, the remembered part of a dream makes up its manifest content; the disguised underlying motives and conflicts of which the dreamer is unaware constitute the dream's latent content. The structure of a dream is identical to the structure of a neurotic symptom. Its symbolic expression of forbidden id drives allows their partial gratification and partial symbolic expression (Brenner, 1973). The dream work of the ego involves displacement, symbolization, and condensation, as we can see in the following example.

A middle-aged white woman dreamed that she had engaged a young black woman as a sitter for her children. Suddenly, she saw the young woman swinging an ax at a black man, and became aware that this woman was an ax-murderer wanted by the police. She telephoned the police, who did not enter the house, but stayed outside and waited. While the police were outside waiting, she held her head in her hand and exclaimed, "How could I have made such a horrible mistake in hiring this woman and leaving my children with her!" She was surprised to notice that the police were wearing the tan uniforms of highway patrolmen instead of the blue uniforms of city police.

At the time of the dream, the dreamer had been on a trip away from her children (who were adults) for several months, and was very uncomfortable about being away. Her concern about her children in the dream was a displacement of her fear for her own emotional well-being in a strange community. The highway patrol uniforms symbolized her great distance from home. Her fear in the dream was a condensation of fear of losing her children's love and fear of losing her own mother (who was ill).

There are other psychological theories of dreaming. Alfred Adler (Ansbacher & Ansbacher, 1956) suggested that dreams express the dreamer's total life-style and personality and are attempts, during sleep, to resolve problems of living. Adler's view is similar to that of Carl Jung (1964) who theorized that there is no latent content to dreams. Jung viewed dreams as creative symbolic expressions of images that reflect the dreamer's mental life or some aspect of his or her life to which insufficient attention is being paid. For example, a psychotherapy patient dreamed she was becoming blind. She was referred to an ophthalmologist whose findings confirmed the dream. She had been aware of her failing eyesight, there were serious psychological problems she literally did not wish to see, and she was also having psychological problems as the result of her dimming vision (Wilmer, 1982).

Frederick (Fritz) Perls (1969), the founder of Gestalt therapy, suggested that each part of a dream represents a projected, disowned aspect of the dreamer. He emphasized a here-and-now orientation to dreams, tying their content to the dreamer's relationships with the therapist and others in the dreamer's life.

Repeated redreaming of a traumatic event is the hallmark of the posttraumatic stress disorder (American Psychiatric Association, 1980). Observations of posttraumatic stress disorders suggest that dreams lessen the impact of experiences that have traumatized the ego by exceeding its capacity for absorbing affect-arousing stimuli (Krystal, 1978). Repeated dreaming of traumatic events such as the horror of combat gradually reduces their impact (Freud, 1920/1955), perhaps through a process similar to desensitization.

Therapeutic Uses of Dreams

The accuracy of a particular dream interpretation is less important than its aptness. The true meaning (if there is one) of a dream is less relevant than what the ascribed meaning contributes to the dreamer's progress in therapy. In a different way, the same is true of fantasy and imagery. Because they can be consciously controlled, they impart a sense of potency and control over one's own destiny. The fantasies or images conjured up by patients are probably less important than their sense of being in charge of themselves and not helpless victims of fate.

The therapeutic use of dreams in psychotherapy depends on the level at which the therapy is conducted and the level at which therapists wish to intervene when the dream is introduced. When therapists are presented a dream by a patient in repressive therapy, they use it to teach a practical lesson in living. In an ego-supportive therapy, therapists use dreams to explore interpersonal relationships in and outside of the treatment relationship. In an evocative therapy, therapists employ dreams to explore the unconscious wishes, defenses, and conflicts of the dreamer. The Adlerian, Jungian, and Gestalt approaches are applicable to repressive and ego-supportive therapies. Investigating dreams for latent content is reserved for evocative therapies.

Patients in psychotherapy produce dreams and discuss them to the extent that therapists invite their introduction and discussion. Reports of dreams can be stimulated by therapists. They can ask if patients have repetitive dreams or have dreamed since the last session. They can also ask about daydreams or fantasies concerning the therapy situation. Like any other sort of activity, telling and discussing dreams can become a resistance, and therapists need to actively direct the discussion toward implementing the overall therapeutic goals for the therapy.

The dream that precedes the first therapeutic session may often foretell the transference that will develop. The quality and nature of dreams brought to the therapeutic session often gives clues to the dreamer's perception of the therapist as receptive or rejecting, friendly or hostile, and also gives important clues about the nature of the patient-therapist interaction. For example, when a patient reported a dream of driving his car into a lake, it was evident to the therapist that the patient was aware of the hostile response he was getting in his therapy (equivalent to "go jump in a lake") and his own role in stimulating that hostility.

From dreams, therapists may obtain valuable information concerning the patient's psychodynamics, defenses, ego strength, self-concept, and transferences. What therapists do with dreams depends on their impression of the information they contain and the stage of the individual's treatment at the time the dream is reported. Therapists must decide how deeply patients are ready to explore the unconscious content of a dream. The involvement of patients with the symbolic language of dreams or their attempts to disregard them may provide important information on their level of involvement in therapy.

The appearance of the therapist in a dream can have many kinds of significance. It may indicate acceptance of the therapist as a real person and the development of meaningful relationships with him or her. For example:

Mrs. A. S. dreamed that she and her therapist were in a bus together. They jostled each other in a friendly way while descending from the bus and walking along the street together, but soon parted ways, each going to his or her own church. The dream reminded Mrs. A. S. of the therapist's earlier statement that although their professional paths crossed, she would in the long run gain more from their professional relationship than from initiating a social friendship.

The therapist's presence in a dream can also mark the therapist's beginning role as a transference object and as a dream symbol (Whitman, 1973). For example, the therapist may appear as a police officer symbolizing a harsh father or a punitive superego introject.

Dreams in repressive therapies. In repressive therapies, therapists usually assume sole responsibility for dealing with a patient's dreams. They focus on the aspects of the dream that reflect everyday concerns, conscious feelings and attitudes, and the dreamer's characteristic patterns of behavior. Whenever possible, they point to the positive aspects of dreams, indicating that they reflect the dreamer's active attempts at mastery of his or her life situation. Therapists ordinarily suppress elements in the dream that stimulate emergence of further material from the unconscious. The dream is used to aid in problem-solving, as seen in the following example.

A woman with a borderline personality disorder told of a dream in which she turned her car over and went to a hospital, covered with blood. She found herself going to work from the hospital. The therapist dealt with her dream as her wish for and fear of psychiatric hospitalization instead of suggesting her probable unconscious wish for fusion with the therapist and her fear of being torn apart by him.

In a repressive therapy, therapists use dream material to tie dreamers to their present life situation. Unconscious elements are noted by therapists, but not explored with the patient.

Therapists usually do not ask for dream material in a repressive therapy, but it may be offered spontaneously. The manifest dream content is linked with the patient's real world and its latent content used for the therapist's guidance of the therapy. The manifest content is used to reduce anxiety while strengthening the ego through better coping with reality and life's demands. The repressive therapist explains dreams instead of exploring them.

Dreams in ego-supportive therapies. In ego-supportive therapies, therapists share with patients the responsibility for dealing with dreams. Dreams are tied to the dreamer's relationship with the therapist and with others in the dreamer's life outside therapy. Therapists avoid intrapsychic issues and use the dreams to break through denial and rationalization of patients' self-defeating interpersonal behavior. Patients' are asked if the dream indicates some aspect of themselves that they have hitherto disowned.

In the following example, the therapist avoided an intrapsychic issue and dealt with an interpersonal issue.

A man with claustrophobic symptoms reported a dream in which he was unable to board an airplane – a crippling symptom that had interfered with his work for many years. Instead of dealing with the castration anxiety that was suggested by the patient's history, the therapist tied the dream to the man's guilt over aspects of his relationship with his wife. The therapist selected that topic because the patient had in many ways accepted a castrated status in his work, and the area in which he seemed to have the greatest opportunity for change was in his marital relationship. It also allowed discussion of his behavior toward women, whose attention he actively sought.

Dreams in evocative therapies. In evocative therapies, therapists do not supply interpretations of patients' dreams. Dreams are used to elicit patients' unconscious conflicts and wishes. In that regard, it is important to ascertain the context in which dreams occur, including the events of the day and the significant tensions the dreamer was undergoing at the time. Then, the dreamer is asked to associate to the elements of the dream, whether they be names, places, or objects. At times, therapists can reveal their own associations (Weiner, 1983a). Those associations frequently enable the dreamers to make new associations to their own dream material.

At first, therapists take the initiative in dealing with dreams. As patients become more sophisticated, therapists become less active in dealing with dreams and allow patients to deal with their own dreams and resistances to dealing with their dreams.

Therapists need not explore all of the dream material they are presented, and need only deal with dreams at the depth that patients can productively integrate, as illustrated by the following sequence of dreams.

Mrs. A. Y. and her husband wanted to have a child. Early in her therapy, she noted that although she was warm in dealing with children at work, it was difficult for her to warm up to her husband as a sexual partner and as a person. She frequently distracted herself while having sexual relations with her husband, and in one session said that she might attempt to fantasize having sexual relations with another man as a means to understand what was so threatening to her. At her next session, she reported a dream in which she was nude and was on top of her husband. The therapist merely nodded, and they discussed the ways in which she pushed her husband away. It was the therapist's private observation that Mrs. A. Y. feared her own aggressive sexuality, but that it was too soon to deal with this issue openly. Despite the fact that the dream had not been discussed, she felt more relaxed at their next session, and reported that the chronic knot in her abdomen had eased a bit. The therapist had, in effect, accepted her sexuality without having had to comment on it.

A year later, as she was dealing with her aggression more effectively, and would frequently become irritated with her husband, she dreamed of having an opening in her abdomen through which she gave birth to a hideous deformed creature with bugs crawling out of it. At this point, she and the therapist explored her sense of being damaged (not being able to conceive), her anger over that, and began to explore her angry feelings in general.

Six months later, toward the end of therapy, she dreamed about being pregnant, losing the baby, and finding her parents unsupportive. She explored the dream herself, and came to the conclusion that she was no longer a person who would take whatever others handed out; that she was trying to stand up for herself. It was difficult to do in some ways, and was most troublesome with people who were not aware of the transition she was making, especially her family.

The series of dreams described above shows a change from the patient experiencing and reporting dreams, which are then left to the therapist to manage, to the patient assuming responsibility for understanding herself and actively exploring her dreams' meaning in the context of her life situation.

The way in which a dream is presented, or the dream itself, may be a resistance. Many patients do not recall dreams. Some relate only dream fragments, while others minimize the importance of dreams. Therapists can deal with this resistance by indicating the usefulness of dreams in the therapeutic process; by telling patients that dreams express emotions that a person cannot ordinarily express while awake; and that when we are asleep, the mind's censoring mechanisms relax and allow those emotions to be expressed in a disguised way so that sleep will be undisturbed. Patients are then encouraged to examine dreams so as to better understand the unconscious conflicts and feelings that create psychological problems.

The way and the time at which patients introduce and relate dreams are important. The dream may be a gift to the therapist, a means to postpone leaving the therapeutic session, or a resistance to dealing with some aspect of reality. At times, therapists can point out the circumstances under which a patient brings up dreams; at the very end of sessions, or at times when tension is building.

Dreams can elicit associations by the dreamer that help to overcome the dreamer's initial reluctance to "own" the dream and help work with it on many levels.

Dreams can be related to universal problems and conflicts, such as birth, death, aggression, and sexuality. The multiplicity of associations to a single dream helps to reveal many aspects of the dreamer's problems and the therapeutic situation.

Patients may avoid discussing dreams they have presented to the therapist; they may try to change the subject by bringing up a personal crisis, asking advice, or discounting the dream. The therapist must decide whether or not to continue focusing on the dream or to allow temporary sidetracking to diminish the patient's anxiety. Later, therapists can call patient's attention to his ignoring the dream.

Postural or behavioral changes from the moment the patient enters the room or starts to tell a dream can also be noticed and brought up in relation to the dream (Berger, 1958).

THE GESTALT APPROACH

Gestalt therapy has contributed to the use of dreams in psychotherapy. The Gestalt approach treats the elements of the dream as disowned parts of the dreamer.

Polster and Polster (1973) find that patients who experience frightening dreams are relieved when they identify themselves as the terrifying forces as well as the victims in their dreams. In a dream of a thunderstorm or a flood, the dreamers can be encouraged to see themselves as both the victims of forces in and around themselves and the source of power. This reinforces a sense of potency. To make dreams into a vivid here-and-now experience, therapists may ask patients to speak for a person or object in one of their dreams. They may be asked to talk to the object or person as if it were really present, by imagining it to be in an empty chair, and addressing themselves to the imaginary object or person. They can then be asked to change chairs, take the role of the imaginary object, and talk back to themselves. This can result in an animated, emotional dialogue.

As dreamers begin to experience the elements of their dream with immediacy and emotional intensity, their physical behavior may change. They may clench their teeth, stiffen, or relax. Therapists can point out this behavior and ask what patients wish to say, from whom they are withdrawing, or with whom they would like to relax. If they reply, for example, that they wish to express angry feelings toward their mother, they are encouraged to experience the feeling as deeply as they can. They are encouraged to say over and over again, "I am angry with you, mother!" until they experience the feeling fully and become able to penetrate to the next emotional level, which may be a wish for closeness. To help make the dream more real, the therapist or patient may role-play parts of the dream, again giving the dreamer a chance to work through feelings in a here-and-now situation.

Gestalt dream work emphasizes bringing patients into better contact with therapists and themselves, and staying out of their private, idiosyncratic world. This goal is no different from those of other ego-supportive modalities, but the action techniques of Gestalt therapy that actively assert the dreamer's ownership and ability to control the elements of the dream are a useful technical innovation.

THERAPEUTIC IMAGERY AND GUIDED FANTASY

Fantasies and visual images or kinesthetic sensations suggested by the therapist can be used therapeutically (Korn & Johnson, 1983). Imagery has been used in desensitization and implosive techniques that reduce the power of feared objects or situations by introducing them in fantasy in graduated intensity (Stampfl & Levis, 1967). It is used in psychodrama to initiate the interaction between protagonists and in Gestalt therapy to unite preconscious and conscious feelings, attitudes, and desires. Singer and Pope (1978) have reported the use of positive imagery and a variety of fantasies in direct interventions with neurotic patients. Singer (1974) has suggested that imagery may be a more effective means for uncovering intrapsychic material than free association.

Visual imagery and guided fantasy can be used therapeutically in many ways. They can serve as a rehearsal for anticipated life situations or can help shed light on intrapsychic conflicts (Leuner, 1969). A fantasy can be constructed by the patient alone, or with the aid of the therapist role-playing significant persons in the patient's life. As in psychodrama or Gestalt therapy, patients can enact significant aspects of themselves. A person seeking a job can be asked to role play an interview to help discover self-defeating behaviors and attitudes, and to reinforce useful attitudes and behaviors. A person who has difficulty becoming aware of his self-critical aspect can have the therapist role-play his conscience, and then reverse roles and play the therapist's conscience.

Schorr (1974) suggests a number of imagery techniques. Therapists can assign an imagery task to patients, such as the fantasy of being held by an important person in their life, and imagining that person's responses. Patients can be asked to create a fantasy about the therapist, or to respond to the therapist's fantasy with a fantasy of their own. Fantasies can concern the past, present, or future. For example, patients can be asked to imagine themselves as they were as children, as they are in relation to their spouse, or as they will be in 10 years.

By suggesting specific types of imagery, therapists help to overcome resistances that are part of supposedly free or spontaneous communication, which is always inhibited by unconscious defense mechanisms (Horowitz, 1983). The therapist's use of a nonthreatening imagery assignment may allow patients to approach a previously avoided topic.

Finally, it must be said that imagery, too, can be used as a defense against dealing with feelings or events that arise in therapy, and the use of imagery must be carefully balanced with direct questioning and confrontation.

DREAMS VERSUS GUIDED FANTASIES

Certain negative aspects of using dreams are circumvented by guided fantasy. Interpretation of dreams by therapists is often experienced by patients as therapists' special power to read minds. That can create a troublesome situation for patients who strongly wish and fear fusion with other persons, or who have difficulty establishing firm ego boundaries. When the therapist supplies a "correct" interpretation, this also helps create or foster the patient's dependence on outside authority. "Having" a dream also suggests that dreamers are the victims of forces in their unconscious mind that are beyond their control, thus reinforcing a sense of helplessness.

The use of fantasy, on the other hand, places patients in active control of their own mind, following the suggestions of the therapist. Patients are free to discontinue or change the fantasy at any time and can clearly see that therapists do not control their mind. The use of dreams or guided fantasy can stimulate either regression or a sense of greater self-control. Therapists then guide the use of the dream or fantasy in the most helpful direction for their patients.

SUMMARY

Dreams and imagery enable therapists and patients to express and deal with highly complex emotionally charged issues that are sometimes not accessible through ordinary verbal interchanges. Therapists' use of dreams and guided fantasy depends on their goals for their patients.

In repressive therapies, therapists can use dreams and imagery to assert their authority and to facilitate patients dealing constructively with day-to-day reality. Dreams and imagery can be used in ego-supportive therapies to highlight patients' patterns of interpersonal interactions, both with the therapist and in daily life, while patients in evocative therapies can be helped by the use of dreams and imagery to uncover unconscious material. Guided imagery and fantasy allow patients to confront aspects of themselves that may be unconscious or merely avoided.

The strong emotions attached to dream symbols and the amount of emotion that can be provoked through guided imagery enable catharsis, but also pose the danger of overwhelming an inadequately defended ego. Therefore, the ego strength of patients and the availability of external support are important factors when therapists considering delving into dreams or promoting guided imagery as a means of intrapsychic exploration. On the other hand, dreams and guided imagery can be used as repressive or ego-supportive techniques when modified appropriately.

The most important functions of dreams and imagery are introducing symbolic thinking into the therapeutic process, stimulating the interest of patients in their psychological and interpersonal lives, helping patients feel that they can be understood, and helping them feel and become more potent, or more accepting of guidance when needed.

CHAPTER 14

Patients with
Physical Complaints

This chapter deals with patients whose primary complaints are physical. They may be referred for psychological treatment because their difficulties seem psychological in origin or because psychological factors are thought to aggravate their difficulties. Many of these patients will not be seen in psychotherapists' offices, but in hospitals, where their attending physicians seek help in managing them or in dealing with their complaints.

Because there has been so much change in the psychiatric nomenclature, this chapter will begin with a review of diagnostic categories. The terms psychophysiologic disorder and psychosomatic disorder have been dropped from the psychiatric nomenclature because they are misleading; they suggest that certain physical conditions are actually caused by emotional factors. At present, very few physical conditions can be clearly designated as psychogenic, i.e., initiated by purely emotional factors. Examples are air swallowing, belching, tension headaches, frequency of urination, and functional diarrhea, all of which may occur in anxiety-producing situations without underlying change in the organs affected.

The disorders now classified under the heading "Psychological factors affecting physical condition" in the *Diagnostic and statistical manual of mental disorders, 3rd ed.* (DSM-III) (American Psychiatric Association, 1980) include, but are not limited to, obesity, tension headache, migraine headache, angina pectoris, painful menstruation, low back pain, neurodermatitis, acne, rheumatoid arthritis, asthma, tachycardia, other cardiac arrhythmias, peptic ulcer, cardiospasm, pylorospasm, nausea and vomiting, regional enteritis, ulcerative colitis, and frequency of urination. Other symptom complexes that fall under this heading are

240

spastic colon or mucous colitis, myositis, and itching stemming from various skin conditions.

Overeating and anorexia nervosa are classified as specific developmental disorders under the category of "Disorders usually first evident in infancy, childhood, or adolescence." Inhibitions in the normal sexual response cycle such as impotence and frigidity are diagnosed as "Psychosexual disorders."

Many physical disorders are influenced by thoughts and feelings and fit the model of health and illness presented earlier in Figure 1 (p. 20). Psychological factors also determine when people seek help to alleviate physical symptoms, whether they follow medical advice or cooperate with treatment, and how much disability they suffer as a result of physical illness. The diagnosis "psychological factors affecting physical condition" depends on establishing a link in time between psychologically meaningful emotional stimuli and the beginning or flareup of a physical disorder. Furthermore, the physical condition must have demonstrable organic pathology, as in peptic ulcer, or involve a known pathophysiologic process, as in the case of migraine or asthma.

The following example demonstrates a complex interaction of mind and body in which psychological factors exacerbated a physical disorder.

Mrs. A. Z. was a 29-year-old woman who had been hospitalized several times in several months for flareups of her chronic asthma. She had two children and was separated from her husband. She was unemployed and depended on her nearby mother-in-law for financial help and help with managing her children. She reported that her primary emotional stress was her husband's unpredictable returning to their home, and his physical abuse of her at those times.

Interviews with her mother-in-law and siblings indicated that Mrs. A. Z. was a very volatile, impulsive woman with extremely poor judgment who had relied heavily on others all of her life, and whose family had found her so frustrating that they no longer wished to be involved with her.

On direct interview, Mrs. A. Z. had great difficulty understanding simple ideas and responded with angry outbursts when she did not understand. She could read and write a few words, but did not know how to make a long distance telephone call to her sister in California, and could not understand the nature or the dosage of her asthma medication. She said that when she became upset, she could not think at all, and at those times often threw away her medications.

Psychological testing revealed that she was functioning in the moderately retarded range (full-scale I.Q. of 49), and had little capacity to control or deal with her feelings.

The psychological factors which triggered Mrs. A. Z.'s asthma were loss of family support, an unstable relationship with her physically abusive husband, inability to function adequately under stress, and inability to understand how and when to take her medication.

PSYCHOLOGICAL FACTORS AND PHYSICAL SYMPTOMS

Sigmund Freud (Breuer & Freud, 1895/1957) thought that functional paralyses (later termed *conversion symptoms*) were bodily expressions of thoughts and feelings that had been repressed from consciousness and normal expression. The price paid for repressing emotions is that a dynamic substitute, the psychogenic symptom, arises in their place; hence the expression *conversion disorder* (formerly, conversion hysteria), i.e., the conversion of an idea into a symptom. This formulation only applies to muscles under voluntary control and the sense organs. Autonomically innervated organs cannot express ideas (e.g., "I'm helpless" or "I won't") as do voluntary muscles and the organs of special sense. The reactions of autonomically innervated organs are concomitants of emotions such as anger and sadness. They do not ease emotional tensions or bind anxiety like conversion symptoms. The elevation of blood pressure in rage does not relieve the rage, but is sustained by it. Anxiety, on the other hand, is reduced by conversion symptoms.

Personality, Conflict, and Disease

Franz Alexander (1950) and Flanders Dunbar (1948) uncovered striking psychological similarities in patients suffering from the same organic diseases. Dunbar formulated these similarities into personality profiles; the ulcer personality, the coronary personality, and others.

Alexander identified common unconscious conflict patterns in persons with thyrotoxicosis, neurodermatitis, essential hypertension, ulcerative colitis, rheumatoid arthritis, bronchial asthma, and peptic ulcer. Thyrotoxic patients, for example, had often experienced the loss of a loved one early in life. They handled their dependent yearnings by early attempts at achieving maturity, and often by taking care of others. Neurodermatitis patients' longing for physical contact had been frustrated in early life, and they also showed conspicuous exhibitionistic tendencies. For each psychodynamic constellation, Alexander postulated a triggering situation that reactivated the underlying conflict, and an X factor; this latter term referred to a constitutional vulnerability of a specific tissue, organ, or system.

More recent investigators find that Alexander was only partially correct. A chronic illness seriously affecting an organ system has subtle, pervasive somatopsychic effects. For example, severe bronchial asthma in childhood probably alters personality development. Hofer (1975) offers an interesting learning theory model for asthma.

A tendency toward respiratory hyperactivity may be set in motion by an early experience, such as maternal separation, which provokes repeated and prolonged crying and the emotional state of "separation anxiety." Subsequent exposure to pollens precipitates asthma in association with environmental cues that afterward are able to produce bronchial constriction by autonomic pathways. Parents respond to the mild wheezing induced by environmental cues with increased attention and permission to avoid unpleasant situations, especially separations. This reinforcement heightens the likelihood of future episodes; the child learns to get what he wants by asthmatic breathing. At this point, an emotional state elicited by separation has become associated through classical and instrumental learning processes with a highly specific autonomic response pattern. (p. 548)

Friedman and Rosenman (1974) have formulated a "type A" personality (this designates a person with much free-floating anger who tries to do and to accumulate more and more in less and less time) that they associate with coronary artery disease. They have worked out a chain of physiologic events that connect the personality type to the pathogenesis of the disease. They found evidence suggesting that the chronic state of alarm of the coronary-prone personality stimulates the body's production of cholesterol, enhancing arterial plaque formation. This, together with the increased blood coagulability produced by the chronic adrenergic state attributed to the type A personality, predisposes to occlusion of the coronary arteries.

With the exception of the type A personality, the focus of treatment in psychosomatic disorders has shifted from dealing with specific conflicts and personality types to dealing with nonspecific psychological factors. There is impressive evidence that stresses and life changes of all types substantially increase the likelihood of falling ill from any cause. A significant correlation has been found between the number of changes in a person's life and the likelihood that he or she will fall ill from any cause (Petrich & Holmes, 1977). The greater the number of life changes in a short period of time, the greater the likelihood that the person will fall ill.

THE NEURAL MECHANISMS OF
THE PSYCHOSOMATIC PATHWAY

Emotion is the consciously experienced aspect of the processes that facilitate and coordinate the adaptive and mastery activities of the organism as a whole concerned with maintaining life and preserving the species. These adaptive responses have three parts: the conscious experience of emotion, a pattern of externally directed behavior, and visceral changes such as vasodilatation or vasoconstriction. Each aspect of an adaptive response may vary in amount. Any one may manifest without significant evidence of the other two. Of the three, the visceral changes are the most difficult to suppress or extinguish. The degree of association or dissociation of the three elements of an adaptive response depends on many factors, some of which are genetically determined, while others are related to level of biological, emotional, or social maturity. Still another factor is the conditioning effect of life experiences, operating at a conscious or unconscious level.

The autonomic changes that accompany all adaptive responses are mediated by the hypothalamus. With fear or anger, the sympathetic nervous system causes the pupils to dilate, splanchic vessels to constrict, and blood pressure and pulse rate to rise. The feeling of satiety that follows a good meal in good company is accompanied by decreased gastric motility, increased gastric secretion of hydrochloric acid, splanchic vessel dilation, and decreased pulse rate and blood pressure. These effects are due to a relative decrease in sympathetic tone and a relative increase in parasympathetic tone.

Autonomic responses can be altered by learning (biofeedback) or by conditioning, as shown by the work of Pavlov (1941) and Masserman. Masserman (1959) repeatedly frightened cats while they were eating and finally produced "neurotic" cats that experienced the autonomic responses related to fear instead of hunger when they attempted to eat.

In speaking of psychological factors affecting physical conditions, we must keep in mind that all illness results from physical and psychological adaptation to threats to one's biopsychosocial equilibrium, the final symptoms depending on the most vulnerable organ system.

STAGES OF ILLNESS

Considering all illness as having three stages – pre-illness, precipitation, and established disease (Sachar, 1975) – will help us understand how to deal with psychological factors affecting physical conditions.

Pre-Illness

This is the phase in which the susceptibility to specific types of malfunction is established. It begins with one's genetic heritage. Developmental physiology suggests that there are crucial stages in maturation when the systems responsible for the neural regulation of important visceral functions such as heart rate may be particularly amenable to conditioning. Autonomic learning occurring during these periods may shape a predisposition stored in brain circuits for specific visceral innervative patterns that could be activated under certain conditions later in life.

As mentioned earlier in connection with asthma, a genetic predisposition, if expressed in behavior, may partly shape the environment of a developing person. Gastric hypersecretion, for example, might manifest as an excessive need for nurturing, influencing a mother's behavior toward her infant and the subsequent behavior of the child. Reactive defenses might develop about a core conflict over nurturance generated between mother and child and determine the type of psychosocial stress that would later overwhelm defenses and activate conflict.

Conceivably, it would be possible to alter the course of an emotionally triggered disorder by psychological means if such incipient disorders could be detected at this stage.

Precipitation

Certain stresses of universal significance lower resistance to a variety of pathogenic factors. This is especially true of real, threatened, or symbolic object loss engendering feelings of helplessness and hopelessness (Engel, 1972). An individual's psychological makeup also renders that person more vulnerable to certain types of stress than others.

A patient with regional enteritis was able to relate two out of three episodes of bleeding to anger. One episode occurred the day after an argument in a restaurant. The patient had refused a steak because it was too tough. He also refused a second for the same reason. He went to the manager, who made a disparaging remark about his religion.

"For the first time in my adult life I wanted to hit somebody, but I just felt angry and refrained from doing anything. I did tell him what I thought about him. I suggested that if he were having a hard time in business, it might be the fact that he serves poor food rather than lack of patronage by Jews."

Physical factors can trigger a chronic illness. A case of viral or bacterial dysentery can be the last link in a chain of events culminating in ulcerative colitis. Use of detergents can trigger neurodermatitis in a person with an allergic diathesis.

Physiologic factors may contribute symbolically (a girl becomes frightened by her development into womanhood and experiences painful menses) or by their actual metabolic influence. Women's changes in emotional state in relation to their menstrual cycle probably have an endocrine component.

Psychosocial factors can be important. For example, a young woman developed hyperthyroidism after losing her mother; a change from a carefree to a restrained, responsible life-style occurred immediately before a young man developed regional enteritis.

Treatment at this stage might require only avoiding circumstances that typically trigger a disorder, or modifying attitudes toward typically precipitating events. Let us use competition as an example. If the physical disorder is acute and remits quickly, such as episodes of diarrhea produced by the stress of competition, reshaping of attitudes toward competition might be effective. In the case of life-threatening disorders, such as bleeding due to regional enteritis, it may be necessary to remove patients from competitive situations while acutely ill, and to discourage future involvement in competition.

Illness Phase

In the phase of established illness, specific and nonspecific mechanisms may continue to perpetuate physical disorders. With progression of the disease and decrease in organ reserve, nonspecific changes may also come to play a very large part, because the homeostatic capacity of the organism has been compromised. With time, the disease process also becomes incorporated into individuals' mental life. Symbolic meanings can be attributed to times of activated disease, and observers might conclude that the disease originated as a symbolic conversion symptom. Many people, for example, regard illness as a punishment for wrong-doing. In most cases, that is how people explain their illnesses, but it is not what causes them. In the case of accidents, however, an unconscious expectation of punishment may lead persons into dangerous situations to get the anticipated punishment over with.

In the established phase of illness, attention to psychological factors can mitigate the effects of illness and reduce the severity of exacerbations, but does not usually alter the underlying physiologic process. It may be possible to encourage dependency or illness-denying hypertensive persons to take their antihypertensive medications, or to encourage persons with rheumatoid arthritis to decrease physical activity during flareups of the disorder by helping them to see that physical inactivity is not lapsing into passivity, but is an active assertion of self-control.

There are many physically symptomatic disorders with no demonstrable physical alteration of structure or physiology. Tension headaches are a good example. Where there is no structural change or altered physiology, a permanent remission of symptoms can theoretically be brought about in the illness phase, but experience teaches us that some residuals nearly always persist.

TREATING THE EMOTIONAL COMPONENT OF PHYSICAL DISORDERS

Because multiple factors trigger, sustain, and aggravate physical disorders, and because of the complicated processes involved, treatment can be directed in many ways. Physical and chemical treatments are usually combined with some form of psychological treatment by all medical practitioners. Physical or chemical methods are usually the primary treatment, but on occasion, psychotherapy can be the primary means of treatment, as we see in the next example.

Mrs. A. A. A., a 33-year-old woman, was referred for evaluation of severe chronic cough. Her cough had begun six months earlier, and she had been hospitalized for bronchoscopy and a complete medical workup five months before she was seen by the psychiatric consultant. She had been examined by a family practitioner, a pulmonologist, and an otorhinolaryngologist. Her symptoms abated for a few months on antihistamines, and she had started allergy shots, but several weeks prior to her consultation with the psychiatrist her cough returned.

The patient was an ambitious, aggressive woman who was living with a man whom she experienced as less aggressive and ambitious than herself. The psychiatrist noted that the only time she coughed during their 45-minute interview was when she was discussing her wish to be rid of her live-in man friend, and when she talked about her two brothers.

Her symptoms of coughing subsided rapidly the next few sessions, in which she expressed anger with her man friend and her sense of helplessness in dealing with him and in making changes in her career. As her cough subsided, she noted a tendency to overeat, but that quickly passed. She continued psychotherapy for several months after her symptoms subsided and continued to explore her feelings of helplessness in dealing with others. When she terminated her weekly psychotherapy seven months later, she and her man friend had become more comfortable and open with each other, and she was much more comfortable with her own aggression.

In the above case, catharsis was followed by this woman's evaluation of her relationships with others and the decision that she could afford to be more aggressive without harming herself or others.

Additionally, the social environment can be manipulated to reduce specific and nonspecific psychosocial stresses. Competition, as mentioned above, may be a specific stress for certain persons. An appropriate psychosocial treatment for those persons might be placement in a less competitive environment. Nonspecific stresses that can be dealt with to some degree are uncertainty, noise, and crowding. Inactivity may be very stressful for people with type A personalities. They find that staying in bed after a myocardial infarction threatens their sense of potency and reduces their sense of being able to control their own lives. In this situation, sedation may be needed to reduce tensions generated by inactivity, or activities such as conversation or reading may be substituted for the steady stream of accomplishment necessary to maintain the type A person's self-esteem.

BIOPSYCHOLOGICAL TREATMENT

Physicians deal daily with psychological factors that directly affect patients' physical condition, but the factors with which physicians deal usually stem from the interaction of patients' personalities and the treatment environment. The therapeutic process also includes interacting with patients' friends and families, through which therapists gather important information about patients' support systems and coping skills, interpret patients' illnesses to concerned others, and help them deal with the impact of illness on their world. Therapists have the opportunity to help change destructive patterns of living and relating to other people that reinforce the sick role and that magnify the stress of daily living (Karasu, 1979). The following case of an uncooperative diabetic shows the ways in which attention to psychosocial factors can have a positive impact on the psychological factors that undermine physical health.

Mr. Y. was an 18-year-old diabetic who had been hospitalized three times in two months, largely because he failed to follow his diet or to take his insulin. His life pattern had been one of retreat and negativistic behavior in the face of stress. He quit school between the fifth and the eight grades, and had only a few jobs since then. The longest job lasted three months. He would not describe how he came to terminate at these jobs. When not working, he would "hang around" and watch television. He made several unsuccessful attempts to leave home. The last (about a year prior to admission) was marrying a woman whom he insisted was pregnant by another man. He lived with his in-laws, who eventually tired of him and demanded that he leave. His losing control of his diabetes seemed related to moving away from home and being out on his own with his wife. Each time the threat of independent living arose, he became ill after forgetting his insulin or not adhering to his diet. He used his diabetes to control his environment and maintain himself in a helpless, dependent position while saying that he really would like to work were it not for his diabetes.

To treat such a person psychologically in a general hospital setting, staff members must first swallow their anger and realize that this man cannot be forced to help himself or to see the long-term consequences of his behavior. He can only be guided in that direction. The staff needs to agree on an overall plan of action. They agree to firmly indicate to patients what they must do. For example, they must check their urine four times a day while in the hospital. A nurse is asked to stay with the patient at first to be certain this is done, and to be sure the patient actually knows how to do it. Patients are allowed to record the results themselves, again under initial supervision. A reward and punishment system is established to help patients maintain their diet, i.e., they may leave the ward only if their urine sugar is 2+ or less and there is no acetone in the urine. These limits must be firm, and the staff must be certain that patients will test their blood sugar level and adhere to the regulations. Initially, nurses inject the patient's subcutaneous insulin, but this is soon taken over by the patient under a nurse's supervision. The staff initially accepts a certain amount of helplessness on the patients' part, but as time goes by they place more and more of a demand on them to look out for themselves, or else pay the penalty of loss of freedom. This life pattern of retreat cannot be altered in a few short weeks, but a patient who has a brief experience of being treated like a grownup may decide to move in that direction.

Somatization Disorders

Persons with somatization disorders are often seen in consultation by general hospital psychiatrists, but are rarely seen by mental health practitioners who deal primarily with outpatients. These patients usually dedicate a large portion of their lives to the unconscious manufacture of physical symptoms which, when vigorously pursued by physicians, give rise to complications that produce physical symptoms that add to the wealth of functional symptoms.

A fairly typical course for a somatization disorder is an appendectomy during teenage years, oophorectomy during early adulthood, hysterectomy and cholecystectomy before middle adulthood, and complications of those surgeries thereafter. In the male, the course of a somatization disorder frequently begins with a trivial back injury that is followed by lumbar laminectomy and, later, a spinal fusion.

The basic principle of treatment is not to threaten the patient with a cure. Somatization is a way of life, and is usually heavily rewarded by the designated patient's family or by a disability pension. The therapist suggests only the possibility of moderately relieving symptoms after a long period of time, emphasizing the power of the body to heal *itself* over time. Thus, there is no need to struggle actively against the therapist.

Useful techniques in treating patients with somatization disorders are helping them avoid those aspects of their environment they find most stressful, whether it is child care, a dictatorial employer, or having to take initiative. Medications are an important part of the treatment of somatoform disorders, but they should be non-habit-forming. Visits need not be frequent, but should be regularly scheduled to monitor the patient's doctor shopping and to warn newly consulted physicians about patients' past histories. Each new physical complaint warrants medical investigation, but invasive diagnostic procedures such as exploratory surgery are generally to be avoided.

Conversion Disorder

Psychotherapists usually see only the mild conversion disorders, such as the cough presented by Mrs. A. A. A. The more severe conversion disorders, such as functional paralysis, are most frequently seen and treated by neurologists.

The first principle of treating a conversion paralysis in a hospital is to accept patients' symptoms as an illness over which they have no control, but from which rehabilitation is possible. Patients are allowed to partially regress by entering the hospital. Ordinary physical therapy and encouragement to use the affected limbs will usually cure the patient. Patients are also urged to begin moving the affected extremities, while being told that function is gradually returning. In order to minimize secondary gain, patients are not usually kept in the hospital until they are completely cured. Rather, patients are discharged to continue physical therapy as outpatients.

Patients with conversion disorders can be told that their symptoms are nervous in origin. Those who can accept the term "nervous" as meaning functional will do so. Those who cannot will experience themselves as having had a transient affliction of the nervous system.

Hypnosis can be used to treat conversion disorders (Crasilneck & Hall, 1975), but such dramatic measures are rarely necessary. Hypnosis can help therapists understand the emotional conflict engendering patients' symptoms, but most persons who develop conversion symptoms are not psychologically minded and are not interested in understanding how their difficulty developed.

Hypochondriasis

Hypochondriacs are rarely seen by mental health professionals for more than one visit. That single visit can be used to help the treating physician cope more effectively with the problem (Altman, 1975).

The principles of treatment are the same as for somatization disorder, and the treatment is best carried out by the patient's regular physician, who must be helped to be comfortable in changing the patient's medication from time to time and in scheduling regular appointments to prevent doctor shopping.

Hypochondriasis is only treatable from the psychological standpoint if it is one symptom of another disorder such as a major depressive disorder.

Dealing with Pain

The influence of emotional factors on physical symptoms is very obvious in dealing with pain. There is very little correlation between the amount of tissue injury and the amount of pain reported by an injured person, whether the pain is due to a crush injury of a limb or a myocardial infarction. Pain is clearly a psychosomatic process in which the amount of pain perceived or reported depends on a complex interaction of physical and psychological factors.

Beecher (1946) noted, for example, that men severely injured in battle experienced less pain and required lower dosage of analgesics than civilians undergoing major surgery. The injured soldier was relieved and thankful to escape alive from the battlefield, while civilians experienced surgery as a depressing, calamitous event. Cultural influences also influence reactions to pain, including the anticipation and experiences of pain. Some cultures insist on a stoic, noncomplaining attitude, and others encourage venting feelings and physical complaints (Zborowski, 1969).

Pain has special emotional significance to some persons; frequently, it is a deserved punishment (Engel, 1959). For others, it is a way to communicate distress and to indirectly ask for help.

In dealing with pain, therapists must be sensitive to all of these issues, including the issue of secondary gain which begins to arise when a painful condition becomes chronic. There are individual differences in pain threshold, and, as indicated by the work of Beecher and Zborowski, pain thresholds vary, depending on circumstance.

Generally speaking, people in acute pain (acute refers to duration, not intensity) are encouraged to regress, to be dependent, and to rely on analgesics. In situations where acute pain is experienced, it is useful to anticipate patients' pain complaints and to offer regular doses of analgesics instead of allowing unnecessary suffering by stoic persons or by persons who are reluctant to make demands of others. During this time, physicians can ask friends and family members about the patient's usual reactions to pain and patients' reactions to their present circumstances.

When a painful condition that should have resolved in a week drags on for months, there should be suspicion that the underlying process has not been corrected, that there is considerable secondary gain, or that habituation to analgesics has occurred. The likelihood of producing habituation can be reduced by substituting oral for parenteral analgesics as quickly as possible and by encouraging patients to communicate emotional distress through words such as, "I'm scared," instead of, "I hurt."

Managing patients with chronic pain is a far different situation than dealing with persons in acute pain. There is a high incidence of personality disorder, hypochondriasis, depression, addiction, and secondary gain in persons with chronic pain, regardless of etiology (Sternbach, 1974). Psychological and social factors form a much more prominent aspect of these disorders.

Persons in chronic pain need to be given the lowest possible dose of habit-forming analgesics, but they should receive their medication at regular intervals instead of receiving them when their pain gets worse, because the latter pattern of medication-taking promotes habituation (Black, 1975). Persons in chronic pain are encouraged not to regress, but to be as independent as possible, as means to reduce secondary gain and raise self-esteem (Hendler, 1984). Persons suffering the pain of a recently herniated disc are praised for staying in bed and resting. Persons with chronic low back pain are praised for being up and around and engaging in out-of-bed activities such as playing cards which distract them from preoccupation with their symptoms.

SUMMARY

Therapists need skills in dealing with psychological issues that are expressed as physical complaints and in dealing with the psychological aspects of physical illness. This often involves therapists leaving their offices to visit patients in hospitals, and requires therapists to interact directly with family members, hospital staff members, and patients' primary physicians instead of working directly with the designated patients, who often do not see themselves as in need of psychological help.

Dealing with the skills of acting as a psychiatric consultant is beyond the scope of this book, but many useful suggestions will be found in the author's *Manual of psychiatric consultation and emergency care* (Guggenheim & Weiner, 1984).

CHAPTER 15

Resolving Impasses

Psychotherapists sometimes fail to help people become more comfortable with themselves or act more constructively. Their treatment failures may manifest abruptly when patients terminate therapy prematurely. Potential failures may present as prolonged stalemates or impasses in which there is still a possibility for a positive action if the impasse is recognized and dealt with.

Dynamically, impasses result from investing more energy in sustaining resistance and from valuing opposition more highly than its resolution (Liff, 1970). Because impasses are the products of interactions, altering one or more elements of those interactions can relieve impasses. It is important to look for the antitherapeutic aspects of therapist–patient interactions instead of branding certain patients as untreatable or their therapists as incompetent.

Impasses stem from therapists' inability to receive and understand necessary information from patients, therapists' inability to respond appropriately to patients on the basis of information received, patients' inability to receive and integrate information from their therapists, and patients' inability to respond appropriately to therapists based on that information.

Impasses may arise from any or all of the above factors during the contract-making phase of therapy, or in the process of therapy.

CONTRACTUAL IMPASSES

Contract-related impasses are generally due to interfering reality factors, an unclear therapeutic contract, inappropriate enforcement of rules, an invalid therapeutic contract, or a poor fit between therapist and patient.

Reality Factors

Therapists must consider realistic aspects of their patients' lives, such as their ability to obtain regular transportation, to be regularly absent from the job, or to pay the bill. Patients' inability to be involved in treatment at regular intervals has the potential for stalemating treatment. Another type of stalemate occurs with patients who are given substantial discounts. Therapists must be aware that additional sessions may be required to deal with issues that cannot be dealt with in the time originally allotted. That in turn raises the question of doing without needed sessions, i. e., inadequate treatment, or raises the problem of lowering the fee for the session even more. Doing so may establish the transference expectation of therapists as all-giving parents and may place patients in the position of exceptional children, which may in turn feed their narcissism or enhance their guilt and block therapeutic progress.

Unclear Therapeutic Contract

The therapeutic contract includes the goals for therapy and the rules of the therapeutic situation. Ideally, patients and therapists agree on long-term and short-term goals. If no progress is made toward the short-term goals, therapists and patients examine those goals. An impasse may occur because therapists and patients have different conscious goals for treatment. For example, a therapist's goal may be to help the patient discharge anger, based on the notion that the patient's symptoms are due to suppression of angry feelings. The patient's goal may be to avoid the anger, and thereby to stay comfortable. If therapist and patient cannot agree that expressing feelings such as anger is an important part of the treatment, they may be forced to reassess the type of psychological treatment prescribed and to substitute a repressive treatment for an expressive modality.

Patients' unconscious goals for treatment often differ from therapists' goals. For example, the wish for an all-knowing parent often underlies patients' expressed desire to understand themselves. Such a wish can undermine a contract to work toward self-understanding by causing uncritical acceptance of therapists' formulations instead of the patients' thoughtful consideration and integration of them. Catharsis can be equated by patients to absolution. Therapists may need to explain that patients' giving vent to feelings is not the same as patients being given license to do whatever they please. In fact, the treatment of borderline or histrionic patients may consist largely of encouraging them to contain their feelings and to use rational processes instead. Patients can also attempt to use therapy to support their already established means of alleviating psychological tension, as the next example illustrates.

A middle-aged man, who had been married and divorced twice, sought treatment because he wanted to enter a third marriage, but feared that certain aspects of his personality might undermine a marital relationship. In particular, he was concerned that his means of sexual satisfaction would alienate the woman whom he wished to marry. She was repelled by his wish for her to act the role of stern governess while he acted out the role of a penitent boy during their sexual relations. His expressed wish was to reduce his drive for that type of satisfaction, but his expressed wish was a thin disguise for his stronger urge to have his spouse and the therapist accept his continued acting out of sadomasochistic fantasies.

Therapists attempt to determine patients' unconscious wishes, and then decide to gratify them, sidestep them, or bring them to consciousness and partial or full resolution. The differences between patients' unconscious wishes and therapists' treatment goals are always dealt with at some level, and their resolution is often the heart of the therapeutic process.

Failure to establish explicit goals for therapy often stems from therapists' unwillingness to tell patients that they cannot get what they want from therapy and from patients wanting to avoid knowing the limitations of therapy. Patients want therapy to be the path to happiness, not merely relief of self-engendered misery. Therapists want to believe that they can confer happiness, not merely the tools for their patients to use in coping with themselves and others.

If therapists fail to obtain an agreement to abide by the rules of therapy, that seeming oversight may point to characterologic or countertransference problems on the part of therapists that will significantly affect the course of patients' therapy.

Enforcement of Rules

The enforcement of rules or the failure of a therapist to enforce rules or to deal with infringements of rules can be an important source of impasse.

Rules facilitate therapy. When they are eventually violated by patients, they become important subjects for discussion. Rules are ordinarily implicit in individual psychotherapy. The rules depend on the type of psychotherapy, but the fundamental rules for all forms of therapy are the same: patients are to attend scheduled sessions, to cooperate with the treatment, and to pay the bill. At times, therapists prescribe certain behaviors. Some therapists ask their patients not to smoke in the office. With certain patients, it may be necessary to indicate the therapists' awareness that repeating certain behaviors (such as exhibitionism) may cause therapy to be terminated and the patient to be imprisoned. The therapist who is performing such treatment, which is usually court-ordered, needs to tell the patient that the therapist's only role is treatment; that the therapist will not disclose to the court whether or not the patient engages in exhibitionism again, but on the other hand can do nothing to avert imprisonment should the patient be apprehended.

A therapist who deals legalistically with violations of rules often produces an impasse. A threat of termination is appropriate, however, if patients' behavior literally endangers their therapists or others (Weiner, 1973b). Ordinarily, the best approach to violations of rules is neutral exploration of the circumstances surrounding the violation, of the possible motives of the violators, and of the reactions of the therapist. On the basis of that exploration, therapists and patients can determine if the violation demands action or if discussion alone is sufficient. In the rare instance of repeated absences, prolonged disruptive behavior, or recurrent misuse of therapy as a rationalization for acting out, a patient may be asked to leave treatment.

Invalid Therapeutic Contract

Psychotherapy calls for patients to share information about themselves and to implement actively what they learn as a consequence of sharing. Unmotivated patients frequently do not acknowledge that they share the responsibility for the work of therapy.

Patients may be taken into psychotherapy because they will not accept more appropriate therapy. Therapists make such compromises because their patients will not accept medication or hospitalization, and they wish to offer some treatment instead of no treatment. Therapists fail to let patients suffer the consequences of their decision to avoid or postpone appropriate treatment because of their unconscious reactions to their patients or the patients' appeal to their fantasies of omnipotence.

It may be reasonable, in attempting to establish rapport and a working relationship, to agree to a trial of psychotherapy as the sole means of treatment, leaving room for consideration of medication or hospitalization, as shown in the following example.

> Mrs. A. A. D. (see also p. 227) lost weight, was sleeping poorly, and had thoughts of suicide, but said that she didn't like the idea of medication and would prefer to resolve her problem with psychotherapy, if that were possible. She and her therapist agreed on twice-weekly visits.
>
> After a few visits, it was evident that the patient's mental state was worsening, and she agreed to a trial of an antidepressant. This seemed to stabilize her briefly, but she found herself less and less able to tolerate living alone. Each time the therapist gently mentioned the possibility of hospitalization, she reacted with agitation, but she finally conceded to hospitalization based on her therapist's underscoring that he could not prescribe an adequate dose of antidepressant for her unless she was under full-time medical supervision. She finally acceded, and underwent two months of hospital treatment, including higher doses of antidepressant, group therapy, milieu therapy, and individual psychotherapy.

In this case, the therapist's negotiation with the patient established her as in control of her life and allowed her to cooperate with the needed therapy, which was the temporary relinquishment of control.

An invalid therapeutic contract also results from misdiagnosis — usually an overestimation of coping ability or impulse control. A misdiagnosis is less likely to occur if therapists evaluate patients in more than one interview and over a period of time, carefully noting the quality of the interaction while taking a detailed history with emphasis on coping ability and impulse control, as reflected in the patient's ability to complete schooling, hold jobs, and maintain stable, positive relationships. If therapists are in a hurry to obtain treatment cases or perform hasty evaluations for reduced fees, they may miss their prospective patients' concrete thinking, their acting out, or their primary concern with direct alleviation of symptoms.

Inappropriate Treatment

Psychotherapy may be the treatment of choice for certain persons, but they may be selected for an inappropriate technique. Sometimes, an inappropriate technique may be used because of a misdiagnosis. Other times, it is due to therapists' inflexibility or commitment to a particular technique. Of the three varieties of treatment, evocative, ego-supportive, and repressive, evocative treatment is the most often mis-prescribed.

Evocative treatment may be misprescribed for patients who have not reached Piaget's (Elkind, 1980) stage of formal operations: children, adolescents, and adults with dull normal intelligence or with few coping skills. It is also misprescribed for people who conceive of their problems as environmental or interpersonal (Weiner, 1982b), and "alexithymic" persons who lack the capacity to put their feelings into words (Sifneos, 1975).

Ego-supportive treatment is occasionally wrongly prescribed to provide a helpful interpersonal experience for persons with rigid avoidant, obsessive, or paranoid defenses who cannot tolerate direct confrontation.

Repressive therapies are rarely misprescribed in the sense of doing damage. They can be viewed as misprescribed when patients' capacity or need for a treatment with an interpersonal or intrapsychic focus is missed.

Inappropriate Therapist (See Also
Section on Matching in Chapter 12)

Therapists need to be treated in certain ways by patients in order to treat them (Saretsky, 1980). Certain patients deny therapists the gratification that they need to do effective psychotherapy. It is up to therapists to ascertain quickly that their personal limitations make it impossible to work with particular patients and to arrange for transfer to someone with whom those patients can work.

Many patients who have had positive experiences in psychotherapy seek treatment again during other periods of emotional distress. Although a previous successful experience with psychotherapy is usually a positive predictor for later therapy (Malan, 1976), there are times when a carryover from the former therapy blocks further treatment.

The author has briefly treated several patients who were intent on recreating their earlier, positive therapeutic experiences, including the personal interaction between themselves and the therapist. In particular, three passive men sought to recreate the nurturing relationships they had with their earlier therapists. Unfortunately, the author's personality was not similar enough to that of the successful former therapists, and all three patients terminated their treatment with the author. In all three men, the gratification provided by the earlier therapists made it impossible for the patients to tolerate the frustration of self-examination and caused the author to be the object of hostility displaced away from the now-idealized former therapists. In the first two of the three cases, the patient simply dropped out of treatment. In the third case, the author was congratulating himself on having avoided the temptation to prescribe a minor tranquilizer when the patient announced that he was terminating therapy. In this case, the therapist was able to agree with the patient that there was not a good fit of personalities, that it was not the patient's fault, and that other psychiatrists who might work out better were available (the therapist named one).

It is better to treat these situations as personality mismatches than as intrapsychic resistances. Dealing with them as resistances heightens patients' self-blame because there is usually insufficient alliance for patients to deal with the impasse as a transference issue. The mismatch needs to be treated as a limitation of the therapist's personality. It is often not a professional shortcoming. It is just that no therapist has the right combination of personality ingredients for every patient.

On occasion, a therapist–patient encounter at the outset of therapy in which each agrees to modify some aspect of himself in order to establish a therapeutic relationship can herald a positive change for both. Sometimes, the change for the therapist can be an agreement to not take notes or to provide prompt feedback when the patient is acting destructively. For the patient, the change may be relinquishing certain behaviors, such as coming to sessions late, discontinuing self-administered drugs or prescribed medications, or noting and expressing feelings in reaction to the therapist.

PROCESS IMPASSES

Process-related impasses are stalemates that result from errors in the conduct of therapy in which the initial contractual agreement was sound. The principal process-related impasses are due to ordinary human error, an inadequate therapeutic alliance, an antitherapeutic alliance, adverse transference reactions, countertransference, and inappropriate transference gratification.

Human Error

Human error is readily corrected once therapists become aware that they failed to understand, failed to act when needed, or acted destructively. It is best dealt with by the therapists' admission of their error.

Profuse apologies or protracted explanations are not called for (Weiner, 1983a). Rather, therapists and patients attempt to reach agreement on the facts, with therapists encouraging the expression of patients' feelings and thoughts in response to the error. Following this, therapy continues, with therapists alert to changes in patients that may result from the error. If errors occur repeatedly with one patient or a particular group of patients, therapists must determine if one or more of the factors discussed below is operative.

Inadequate Therapeutic Alliance

The positive working relationship between the rational, mature, health-seeking aspect of patient and therapist does not develop immediately. It requires a period of interaction, during which the relationship is maintained by patients' positive expectations. Those expectations are partly based on the therapist's expertise, partly on the patient's hope of finding an accepting, powerful parent, and partly on the unconscious longing on the patient's part for a satisfying parent–child relationship.

At times, it is not possible to establish rapport. Failure to develop rapport may be due to patients' psychological makeup, transference factors, therapists' feelings or attitudes toward patients, or a poor match of personalities. If a positive relationship cannot be developed in the diagnostic interviews with the therapist, the first stage of treatment consists of uncovering and eliminating obstacles to rapport. Otherwise, patients' negative feelings may be acted on or expressed directly, and will be unmanageable because dealing with them by direct suggestion or by interpretation depends on the therapeutic alliance for its effectiveness. Without the therapeutic alliance, therapists' suggestions or comments are seen as hostile, critical, and demeaning. They reinforce patients' negative feelings and make change impossible.

Antitherapeutic Alliance

Antitherapeutic alliances take many forms, depending on patients' intrapsychic and interpersonal difficulties. If the therapist forms an alliance with the harsh superego of a severely depressed person this can deepen the depression. The first stage of working with severely depressed persons is offering them hope of relief while stating that patients' search for what is wrong with them needs to be postponed until more is going right psychologically.

When therapists encourage persons with little impulse control to express themselves more fully, this stimulates acting out by siding with patients' id impulses. This type of antitherapeutic alliance occurs, for example, when borderline patients who are transiently depressed are encouraged to externalize their aggression.

The middle ground between stimulating self-recrimination and promoting acting out is particularly hard to find in adolescents and other persons with immature personalities or profound ego weakness.

Adverse Transference Reactions

Many adverse transference reactions stem from inadequate appraisal of patients' ego strength or a failure to appreciate their dynamics, coping mechanisms, and defense mechanisms. The author has seen a number of patients in whom adverse transference reactions greatly complicated the course of psychotherapy (Weiner, 1974; Weiner, 1982a, b; Weiner, 1983a, b; Weiner, 1984b).

In the most dramatic examples, women with acutely or chronically decompensated egos developed overwhelming eroticized transferences, resulting in clinging to the therapist which obscured their need for hospital treatment. In less ego-compromised women, development of an eroticized transference stimulated an angry suicide attempt and increased dependence on alcohol. Other women, who functioned well, displaced their eroticized transferences and acted them out in the form of extramarital affairs. The author has also witnessed the results of dependent transferences in men and women that resulted in prolonged sadomasochistic entanglement with therapists.

Profound transference regressions that result in patients actively trying to incorporate their therapists into their lives as lovers or parents frequently signify the presence of a borderline personality disorder. When fully developed, such regressions may require separation of therapist and patient, with transfer of the patient to another therapist and, at times, to another mode of treatment.

The best means of dealing with severe adverse transference reactions is for therapists to seek consultation, either by seeing the consultant directly, having the patient visit the consultant, or seeing a consultant in conjunction with the patient. The latter course may help the consultant to spot behaviors or attributes of the therapist that contributed to the development of the adverse transference reaction. The process of consultation also paves the way for transferring patients. Several patients caught up in destructive alliances with therapists have had successful outcomes of therapy after transfer to therapists who originally served as consultants.

Countertransference

Each adverse transference reaction has its countertransference counterpart. Erotic transferences may be stimulated by therapists' unconscious wish to be sexually desired. Dependent transferences can be cultivated by therapists who wish to dominate or who need to be needed.

One important clue to countertransference is therapist behaviors toward one patient that differ from therapist behaviors toward other patients. Such behaviors can include too much or too little personal involvement or self-disclosure, inordinate activity or passivity, being overjudgmental, or failing to set limits. Another clue to countertransference is stereotyped behavior toward one patient or to patients with similar diagnoses or dynamics.

Many of therapists' emotional reactions to patients are reasonable responses; such is usually the case in dealing with borderline patients. Weiner (1982a) has suggested a diagnostic sign of borderline personality disorder: a mixture of intense, chaotic emotions in the therapist that mirror the emotions of the borderline patient. Failure to heed the borderline sign can lead to a countertransference-based stalemate in which therapists masochistically submit to patients' emotional storms instead of pressing patients to control themselves.

Failure to fear an overtly dangerous person is an important countertransference reaction that can stimulate dangerous persons to violence as a means to force acknowledgement of them as potent persons.

Transference Gratification

Transference gratification is therapists' attempts to fulfill directly patients' infantile wishes or alleviate patients' infantile fears. Treatment by transference gratification is based on the premise that damage done to patients early in their lives can be corrected by experiences with the therapist in the here-and-now; this is what Alexander and French (1946) called the corrective emotional experience. For example, therapists may attempt to be totally available to patients as a means to create an experience of reliable nurturing. Or, they may assure patients that they will never abandon them, or that they will see that patients do not harm themselves or others.

It seems unlikely that psychotherapists can literally undo traumas suffered by their patients, whether the traumas were the product of actual events or patients' fantasies. It seems more likely that psychotherapists can alter the attitudes and perceptions produced by these traumas (Goulding & Goulding, 1978).

All persons have needs that may be residuals of early childhood conflicts and fixations, but they are so universal that they must be accepted as givens. Those are needs for therapists' genuine interest, their acceptance of the patient as a person, and their willingness to direct the therapeutic process and to set limits within the therapeutic relationship (Strupp, 1977).

Therapists' fear of all transference gratification stems from Freud's (1912/1958) cautions that departure from a strictly neutral, interpretive stance blocks therapeutic access to patients' unconscious minds and can lead to therapists joining with patients in sexual and other forms of acting out (Jones, 1957). Put more broadly, therapists can diminish patients' prospects for change if they become too deeply entangled in providing personal gratification to them.

There are, however, indications for major transference gratification, generally in treating severely ego-impaired persons unable to deal with the stresses of reality, their id drives, or their superegos. One transference gratification that therapists may provide for these people is acknowledging them as ill and providing them protection from reality in the form of hospitalization, or temporary relief from responsibilities for others or for self-care. Another is protection from their id drives through reducing interpersonal interactions that might stimulate sexual or aggressive impulses. Protection from superego, whether too harsh or too lax, comes from institutional rules and restraints. The tendency toward splitting that occurs in the psychologically primitive or regressed person is managed by using a treatment team that allows the staff to be split into those who gratify and those who frustrate. As the person with severe ego impairment begins to recover, supports are gradually withdrawn and the patients' own ego takes over the functions formerly assumed by the hospital staff.

Lesser forms of this type of gratification occur in outpatient work when a patient with good ego strength is temporarily overwhelmed. If a man is unexpectedly served divorce papers, his therapist can urge him to consult a lawyer to find out what his rights are; the difficulties that led up to the wife's action can be dealt with after the patient has a better grip on his present real situation.

At times, patients request advice or guidance. Some of these requests are really demands for transference gratification as in the case of the patient who asks her therapist if he likes her or if they can hold hands. Others are legitimate requests for professional expertise; whether the patient's child or spouse should be professionally evaluated, or when medical evaluation of a symptom such as fatigue should be undertaken.

Deciding what is a request for transference gratification and whether or not to gratify the patient is based on the clinician's evaluation of the realities of the patient's life, the clinician's dynamic formulation, and his or her clinical judgment (Weiner, 1983a).

In general, the greater the patient's ego impairment, the greater will be the need for transference gratification in the sense of therapists being caring, protective persons who are willing to substitute their judgment for that of their patients. The exception to this general rule is with patients who press for sexual involvement with their therapists. This is to be avoided with all patients for the obvious reason that when mutual sexual gratification begins, all other forms of constructive activity halt, and the focus of therapy changes from helping the patient grow to satisfying the patient's (or the therapist's) sexual drive (Weiner, 1982b).

The level at which therapy is conducted also dictates whether transference gratification will promote or hinder therapy, as discussed in Chapters 10 and 11 on repressive and ego-supportive therapies, respectively. In no situation is the therapist's disinterest in the patient as a person or lack of professional concern a positive influence.

WORKING THROUGH IMPASSES

Impasses that result from simple technical error are relatively easy to resolve, once the technical error is detected. Other impasses are extremely difficult to resolve because they stem from the enmeshed needs and defenses of both therapist and patient.

Once the therapist (or patient) notes that nothing positive is happening or that the patient's condition is gradually worsening, the question of an impasse should be raised. While it is to be expected that the evocative treatment of characterologic difficulties will ordinarily raise those patients' level of psychological discomfort, therapists must also maintain awareness of their patients' life situations so that their patients are not pushed to face themselves at the price of adequate coping. On the other hand, while therapists generally seek to raise their patients' level of comfort with themselves, patients are not helped to become so self-satisfied that they totally relinquish their objectivity and their responsibility for themselves.

The steps in impasse resolution are suspecting an impasse, detecting an impasse, defining the nature of the impasse, formulating a provisional plan for resolution, and modifying that plan as needed. Therapists' tools in defining the nature of the impasse and formulating a plan for resolution are:

1. *Reassessment of the patient's environmental supports and deficits and the means by which they can be increased or diminished.* If increased sexual interest or display of sexuality by the patient would alienate sources of support, means must be found to provide that support while helping patients to gain more comfort with their sexuality and to help them find means of expressing sexuality that do not threaten family support. A woman who lives in a sexually repressive family can work toward enjoying sexual relations with her husband without giving others the impression that she is overtly interested in sex.

2. *Reassessment of the patient's interactional style, coping skills, defense mechanisms, and biological vulnerability to mental illness.* Schizoid persons do not become extroverts, in spite of their wish to do so. Therapists must realize that personality change does not usually involve major change in defensive or coping styles. Schizoid patients become less shy. Obsessive patients become more flexible. Hysteric patients become less self-centered and have less need for self-display, but fundamental character styles do not change.

Failure to appreciate biological vulnerability to mental illness can result in therapists overtaxing susceptible individuals and precipitating episodes of mental illness. They may fail to appreciate that biological cushioning by antipsychotic or antidepressant medication is needed by many patients who wish to understand themselves and to change psychologically, but whose defense mechanisms are brittle and likely to crumble instead of bend. A history of manic-depressive illness (Klerman, 1978) or schizophrenia (Kety, 1978) in a first-degree relative may point to such vulnerability and indicate a need for psychotropic medication and a shift in level of psychotherapy from evocative or ego-supportive to repressive.

3. *Reassessment of physical status for nonpsychiatric disorders that produce symptoms of emotional disorders.* The list of these disorders is quite long. It is sufficient here to say that many physical disorders can produce symptoms that are ordinarily attributed to emotional causes, including generalized anxiety, panic attacks, and depression. Although many persons would rather think of themselves as having a

physical disorder than an emotional disorder, certain psychologically minded persons readily attribute a primary emotional etiology to their difficulties because their symptoms worsen during times of emotional stress. Unfortunately, many symptomatic disorders, whether or not they are primarily emotional, worsen during times of emotional stress.

4. Reassessment of patients' ability to cooperate. Patients who appear to be stalemated because they will not come to appointments regularly or because they will not confide in the therapist need to be evaluated for their ability to meet the requirements of the prescribed therapy. The same is true of an anorexia nervosa patient whose weight is steadily declining. The latter's ability to verbalize and to rationalize may conceal the immaturity of the patient's ego or the degree that the patient is driven by the weight phobia. In some instances, an arbitrary maximum weight loss such as 20 percent of the patient's original body weight must be set as a cutoff point beyond which hospitalization is required.

5. Reassessment of the therapist's ability to deal with the patient under the present circumstance in the therapist's or the patient's life. Therapists need to consider their major life conflicts and the quality of their object relations. The patient's marital problems may be too similar to those of the therapist. In that instance, the therapist may overidentify with the patient or the patient's spouse. Therapists in conflict with their adolescent children may find themselves overly critical of adolescents whom they are treating.

During times of great personal vulnerability, such as illness, divorce, or bereavement, therapists may find it difficult to deal with certain patients. The obviously ill therapist may draw forth protective responses from patients who wish to avoid taxing the therapist. Highly regressed patients may be unable to deal with their terror of potential abandonment at these times. Therapists who have been subject to recent or unresolved object loss may be unable to avoid turning relationships with certain persons toward whom they feel positively into quasisocial relationships.

Finally, the therapist must ask if the patient is struggling to surmount a life hurdle with which the therapist has been unsuccessful; for instance, the separation process that accompanies the transition from adolescence to early adulthood, or the transition from competition to generativity, or the transition from early to middle adulthood (Levinson, 1978).

6. Reassessment of the need for a contract or reevaluation of an existing contract with persons who play important roles in the life of the identified patient. It may become important during the patient's treatment to involve others, be they professionals, members of the patient's family, or friends of the patient, who were not originally involved in the treatment plan. These extra individuals may be required to provide elementary needs such as food and shelter, a supportive environment, or an environment that opposes acting out by the patient.

Persons who were involved in the initial treatment contract may need to change the extent or the nature of their roles vis-à-vis the patient. Increased support and structure may be necessary if patients temporarily become overwhelmed by feelings or environmental demands; decreased support and structure will be needed as patients become better able to cope.

It may be necessary for the family as a whole or individual family members to be treated. This is especially important when major role changes must be accomplished – disentangling parents from oedipal attachments to their adolescent children, or changing a crippling attitude of one spouse toward another.

7. Reassessment of patients' progress in relation to the difficulties they and their therapists originally agreed upon as the focus of treatment. For this type of reassessment, it is important that there be a written record of the original agreement – time distorts the memory of therapists and patients alike. It may be that the patient's original symptom has abated and that the stalemate in therapy has to do with a different set of problems. A patient who has become less fearful of crowds may now be facing the more difficult problem of establishing and maintaining intimate relationships. If there is no evidence of a transference-countertransference block in a therapeutic endeavor for which a motivated patient has adequate ego strength and environmental support, a different therapeutic approach may be called for. A phobic symptom that has not yielded to an evocative therapy may respond better to a repressive mode using behavioral measures and antianxiety drugs. Even when repressive techniques are employed, they may need to be applied multimodally. Desensitization, relaxation training, and assertiveness training may well need to be combined to produce a positive affect (Gatchel, 1984).

8. Reassessing the patient–therapist relationship. The stumbling block for many patients is the transference-countertransference relationship. The question from patients' point of view is whether or not they experience the therapist as critical, suggesting an alliance of the therapist with the punitive aspect of the patient's superego, or whether the patients experience the therapist as totally on their side against the world – suggesting an alliance of the therapist with patients' id drives or with pathologic ego defenses.

From the therapist's side, excessive comfort or discomfort (including boredom) are important signs of countertransference. Boredom, which is often the therapist's way to avoid dealing with anger toward the patient, can be dealt with by the therapist seeking out and supporting positive aspects of the patient and avoiding dealing directly with the frustrating aspects of the patient until gains have been made in either the personal relationship between therapist and patient or in the patient's therapy.

9. Obtaining adequate support for the therapist through consultation, supervision, or personal therapy. Therapists feel stigmatized by their own need for consultation, supervision, or personal therapy, just as lay persons do. There is an element of narcissistic injury in admitting to oneself or a respected peer that treatment of certain patients is especially difficult, and that because of personal prejudices or attitudes those patients' treatment is compromised. Therapists can avoid building narcissistic walls about their therapeutic endeavors by having regular informal case discussions with peers, devoted to sharing concerns and technical problems. Such sharing helps therapists to maintain reasonable perspectives on themselves.

The author has presented many examples of impasse resolution (Weiner, 1974; Weiner, 1982a; Weiner, 1983b) with inpatients, outpatients, individual therapy patients, and group therapy patients. In no case did a single insight-producing intervention by a therapist produce a remarkable change in the patient. Ordinarily, a change in the therapist's attitude or technical approach enabled therapist and patient to work more constructively. At times when a therapist's nontherapeutic attitude toward a patient was unalterable, transfer of the patient to another therapist using the same technique worked well. At other times, the second therapist needed to employ a different technique, as shown in the following vignette.

Mr. W., a 27-year-old man, sought continued treatment after his therapist at another outpatient facility was transferred and could no longer work with him. The patient stated that he had learned much about himself during his year of therapy, but that the experience had not enabled him to function better.

Mr. W. was told that if he were willing to accept a time-limited therapy (one session per week for 10 weeks) he could be treated by a senior therapist as part of a demonstration for therapists-in-training. He readily agreed and appeared enthusiastically for his first session the following week.

At his first treatment session, Mr. W. said that his primary difficulties were inability to follow through in efforts to maintain a professional dance career and to establish a mutually satisfactory relationship with his girl friend. He felt as if he were drifting, that he was not actively guiding his own life.

Evaluation by his new therapist revealed no evidence of mental illness or symptoms of anxiety or depression severe enough to require medication. The patient had good verbal skills, was of at least bright normal intelligence, and was psychologically minded, but gave much evidence that he tended to rationalize his general passivity and his periodic impulsiveness instead of using his self-awareness to mobilize himself or to set limits for himself. His presentation was flamboyant and histrionic. He dramatized and gestured extravagantly.

He barely sustained himself financially through working as a waiter between his few acting/dancing jobs. He looked down on being a waiter and saw his *real* career as on the stage. The patient, who had been exclusively homosexual in his late teens and early twenties, had developed a heterosexual preference before entering therapy and had essentially abandoned sexual relations with men. Unfortunately, the woman whom he was pressing for a deep relationship did not want an exclusive intimate relationship at that point in her life.

Mr. W.'s first treatment had focused on exploring and resolving childhood traumas and conflicts. It was the patient's understanding that dealing with those traumas and resolving those conflicts would enable him to deal more effectively in his daily living, but that had not been the case. His new therapist thought that a repressive approach would be better for this man, given the short time allotted to treatment and his tendency to use insight in the service of rationalization. Accordingly, the therapist suggested that they pay attention to the patient managing certain aspects of his daily living more constructively. In particular, the therapist stated that Mr. W. needed to assume more responsibility for himself. For example, the patient needed to sell his car. He couldn't afford to get it in working order and he needed to pay off several hundred dollars in fines for various violations. He also needed to improve his physical condition if he truly intended to return to dancing. Furthermore, he needed to take his job as a waiter more seriously because it was his primary means of earning a livelihood. The patient reported that he was a good waiter and made a good income when he stopped deriding himself and put forth sufficient effort.

The patient was intrigued by this new plan of action and was pleased at the therapist's praise when he took constructive steps. He began attempts to sell his car and also stopped taking taxis to work. He couldn't afford them, and could easily walk or hitch a ride. He soon realized that he did not want the strict physical discipline needed to stay in dancing and began paying more attention to his job. As a result, he felt better about himself, met several women on the job, began dating them, and relinquished the woman who really didn't want him. The therapist encouraged him to see being a waiter as a worthwhile and financially renumerative occupation.

At the end of 10 sessions, the patient was offered the opportunity to continue his therapy in a trainee-led group, but the patient refused, saying that he felt much more in charge of his own life and wanted to try being responsible for himself.

In this case, the impasse was alleviated by changing from an evocative to a repressive approach. Despite the patient's seeming aptitude for an evocative treatment, he did better in a treatment with a concrete focus that did not promote rationalization and that valued action over introspection.

SUMMARY

Impasse resolution is facilitated by dealing with impasses as interactional processes instead of fixed aspects of therapists or patients.

Both contractual and process impasses result from the interaction of factors that alter therapists' understanding of and reactions to patients and factors that affect patients' understanding and reactions to their therapists.

If therapists regard impasses as dynamic systems in tension instead of labeling patients as uncooperative or untreatable, and if they can shift their therapeutic approach according to the needs of their patients and within a coherent frame of reference, many treatment stalemates can be resolved successfully.

CHAPTER 16

Termination

When termination occurs, patients have the opportunity to face issues such as their reactions to separation from important persons, to the transience of object relations, and to life as a series of transitions. The termination process can be dealt with in many ways: as permanent or temporary, as a vacation or a graduation from treatment, or as a transition from a professional relationship to a social relationship with the therapist (Easson, 1971).

Many patients are reluctant to leave their therapists and try to avoid termination. Others try to avoid the termination process by abruptly dropping out of therapy. Therapists, of course, have the same difficulties and may cling to their patients or deal with their patients so as to avoid the impact of losing an important personal relationship.

The formation of new friendships outside of therapy attenuates the impact of termination. While it might be argued that making new friends helps avoid facing separation from the therapist and dealing with the process of leave-taking, the value of friendship probably outweighs the value of dealing with separation from the therapist because, as Yalom (1980) suggests, living is in great measure a denial of loss and death.

In this chapter, we will deal with termination as part of the overall therapeutic experience; termination is the aspect of therapy that is the most significant for persons who need to learn how to deal with leave-taking and with loss, and for those who were unable to adequately assimilate positive introjects in their earlier lives.

INDICATIONS FOR TERMINATION OF TREATMENT

Psychotherapy may be terminated because it has been partly or fully successful, because the termination process is the crux of therapy, or because the patient's mental state is becoming worse. Termination may also be indicated when therapists are unable to tolerate certain patients, when an unresolvable impasse has developed, or when patients' diminished motivation makes further therapy unproductive.

Success

Most therapists use their observations and patients' subjective reports as indicators of progress. Recently, tests such as the Beck Depression Inventory (Beck, Rush, Shaw, & Emery, 1979) and the Hamilton Rating Scale for Depression (Hamilton, 1960, 1967) have been used to ascertain response in treating depression, but few therapists use objective measures of their patients' progress.

Success is gauged in relation to the goals established at the initiation or during the process of therapy, and in terms of patients' former level of maladjustment or discomfort and their overall life situation. Some treatments aim only at preventing recurrent decompensations; some work toward changing a limited segment of a patient's psychological and interpersonal life, while others attempt more global change. Some patients' defenses are reinforced; others are encouraged to relax their defenses and explore themselves. In certain cases, success involves increased discomfort. Persons who formerly discharged emotional tension by impulsive action learn to bear the discomfort of emotional tension.

Success may involve assuming responsibility for one's actions instead of using neurotic symptoms to avoid new situations or personal responsibility. Thus, a woman who, on a neurotic basis, had experienced a series of extramarital liaisons became aware of how and why she attracted men. With this knowledge, she then faced conscious choices as to whether she would continue that behavior or would invest more of herself in her work and her relationship with her husband. She eventually compromised by having a nonsexual intimate relationship with another man while becoming more involved with her work and more accepting of her husband.

Another woman whose sexuality was inhibited came eventually to appreciate and enjoy her sexuality, but then had to assume the responsibility for determining when and with whom.

Criteria for success are different for repressive, ego-supportive, and evocative therapies.

Repressive therapy. From the therapist's point of view, termination is indicated when patients have accomplished the educational task prescribed, such as ex-psychotics recognizing that they have an emotional illness, or abusive parents adopting healthier means of controlling their children and managing their own aggression. When adequate repression or suppression has been stimulated and sufficient defenses have been mobilized against the eruption of primary process or raw, unsublimated impulses, patients are usually better able to deal with certain concrete tasks. Ex-psychotics may return to their jobs and child abusers may establish reasonable limits for their children, and both thereby experience greater self-esteem. Termination from a repressive therapy may consist of a transition from formal therapy to a mutually supportive semisocial self-help group.

Ego-supportive therapy. The therapist seeks evidence of more effective interpersonal interaction in the therapeutic relationship, with the development of appropriate dependency and autonomy in the place of overdependent clinging or pseudo-independence. Ego defenses are modified and superego demands are eased. There is greater cooperation and mutuality in patients' day-to-day relationships. Patients' self-esteem is enhanced as a result of their improved interpersonal relationships and their taking responsibility for themselves instead of blaming others or being unable to turn to others for help at times of need.

Evocative therapy. Therapists' evaluation of patients for termination from an evocative therapy is more complicated because these patients show less disturbed behavior, there are fewer disturbances in relationships to serve as markers, and patients' complaints may have been largely subjective. Usually, however, the resolution of transference distortions manifesting between patient and therapist allows some objectification of the patient's progress.

Psychodynamically, patients use fewer neurotic and immature defense mechanisms (Vaillant, 1977) and become more willing and able to face and assume responsibility for parts of themselves that were previously disowned, and to take action in ways that were formerly blocked.

Termination as the Crux of Therapy

Many persons have not faced the task of psychological separation from the significant persons in their lives, and therefore have not been able to introject and identify adequately with them and have not developed the skills to establish new relationships.

Many patients whose overall level of function and self-awareness have improved do not wish to take the next step of taking in what has been learned and leaving the person from whom they have learned it. Based on Freud's (1923/1961) observation that relinquishment fosters identification, one means to encourage the process of introjection and identification with the positive aspects of the therapist is through termination.

The process is introduced to patients as being part of growing up. As shown in the next example concerning Mrs. A. T. (see also Chapter 7), it becomes necessary at some point to give up those we love and value and those on whom we depended earlier in life and to make new attachments, or to make use of what we have learned as part of ourselves.

Mrs. A. T.'s former therapist of 13 years had told her that it would be useful for her to stay in therapy permanently to ease the strain of living and to thereby avoid aggravating her rheumatoid arthritis. Her former therapist, a psychological substitute for parents whom she had experienced as inadequate and uncaring, encouraged her to feel that all emotional issues could be understood and resolved.

Her new therapist, whom she began seeing when she moved to a new city, had a different point of view. He encouraged her dependence on peers and on her own judgment, and pointed out that her own taking charge of her arthritis treatment had kept her from becoming crippled. They discussed her idealization of her former therapist as a perfect parent, and concluded that not even a perfect parent can or should shield a child from the hardships of life; that part of good parenting is allowing a child to develop her own resources and to function as an adult in her own family.

Having worked on accepting herself as an adult in an unpredictable, uncertain world, she also worked toward termination of therapy by spacing sessions out to one every other week.

Deterioration or Regression

Some patients are harmed by their psychotherapy (Lambert, Bergin, & Collins, 1977). When a person's psychological condition is worsening, active consideration must be given to terminating psychotherapy and ascertaining what type of treatment, if any, is better. Worsening does not refer to the occasional acting out that occurs in response to an overly vigorous intervention or a failure of the therapist to intervene. It is a steady deterioration of job performance and interpersonal relationships, and the appearance of more primitive psychological defenses and coping mechanisms. The reader is referred to Chapter 15 for a full discussion of managing therapeutic impasses.

TYPES OF TERMINATION

The types of termination are proposed termination, enforced termination, circumstantial termination, and inappropriate or premature termination.

Proposed

Therapists' proposal of termination can indicate that patients have accomplished the tasks set forth in their contract. It gives patients a chance to evaluate their progress and compare it with the therapists' view. It may also raise other issues that patients have postponed dealing with. A proposal of termination can be initiated by therapists stating that patients have accomplished what they set out to do and by raising the issue of whether they have thought about possible termination. If further issues do not arise over a period of time, the therapist initiates the leave-taking process. Proposal of termination to Mrs. A. T. helped foster greater self-dependence and greater peer dependence.

Enforced

An enforced termination is a unilateral decision by the therapist that continuing in therapy is against the patient's best interest, and is employed with patients who are worsening in therapy or who are incompatible with their therapists. The following is an example of an enforced termination.

Mrs. B. was a woman of limited ego strength who lapsed briefly into psychosis when stressed. During the course of her therapy, she developed a highly erotized transference reaction to her therapist that blocked further progress and resulted in regressed clinging to him. Her deadlock was finally resolved by first transferring the individual portion of her combined individual and group therapy to another therapist. After she became firmly established with the second therapist, her first therapist terminated treatment in spite of her insistence that she would really stop clinging to him if he would only give her a chance. He held his ground and refused to communicate with her after their formal termination (except for a brief conversation in which he said that the transfer was made because he cared for her, not because he wished to desert her), and she was finally able to attach constructively to her new therapist.

Enforced termination is also fitting for persons who substitute therapy for social lives of their own. Those persons may be referred to social clubs or other organizations whose chief purpose is socialization.

Circumstantial

Circumstantial terminations from therapy are quite common. Patients become physically ill, transfer in the course of their employment, or return home from college at the end of a semester.

Circumstantial termination is common where periodic turnover of professional personnel makes it impossible for some patients to continue, or when only short-term therapy can be offered. Terminations are also important as part of a therapist's training experience. They help therapists deal with the mechanisms and emotional impact of leave-taking.

Because circumstantial terminations are based on external circumstances rather than the needs of patients, much anger may be aroused in patients who feel short-changed. Therapists, who are identified with their patients' plight, may feel much guilt. However, the most reasonable and useful attitude for therapists is that they have given what has been possible under the circumstances, and that everyone and everything has its limits. Patients are then encouraged to use the process of leave-taking to strengthen themselves by learning to face that aspect of reality.

Arrangements need to be made for continuing the therapy of patients who require it (Glenn, 1971), but many patients will elect a period of no treatment, knowing they can obtain further help if they feel the need.

Psychotherapy with college students can be geared to circumstantial terminations and be scheduled only during the school year. Indeed, much of the literature on short-term therapy concerns the treatment of college students (Gustafson, 1984). In training situations, therapy may also be time-limited if transfer to another therapist is not possible at the end of therapists' period of service or at their graduation.

Premature

As noted earlier, many terminations are premature in the sense that patients have not yet attained the benefits from therapy that would be expected if treatment had continued.

Occasionally, patients fail to return to sessions without giving notice. More commonly, there are warnings of an impending premature termination. Increasing dread of sessions is a frequent sign, as is unwillingness of patients to disclose themselves in therapy. Overdisclosure is also an indicator of a potential premature termination. Patients who reveal their sex lives or moral misconduct in great detail during a first session are likely to drop out because of the angry or rejecting response anticipated from the therapist or from actually stimulating the therapist's anger.

When patients unaccountably fail to appear for one or more sessions, it is the therapist's responsibility to establish contact and determine what is going on. An undisclosing patient's reluctance to be open can be gently dealt with, and the overexposing patient may need to be questioned about the tendency to disclose all and the effect those disclosures have had on people in the past.

Premature terminations in early treatment are probably due to a poor fit between patient and therapist. Premature terminations at later points may have many precipitating factors, usually related to mismanagement of the patient–therapist relationship.

Seasonal premature terminations are common. They occur shortly before, during, or after the therapist's vacation. They are partly related to feelings of being deserted by a parent and are partly an identification with the aggressor – becoming one who leaves instead of one who is left. Seasonal terminations may also be influenced by the time of year. Therapists usually take their vacation during the summer, the time at which work and school pressures often diminish.

Intrapsychic factors play an important role in premature termination. Patients often fear that they will lose control of their sexual or aggressive impulses. Patients may also fear their own self-punishing tendencies in interpersonal relationships, or project the disapproving aspects of their superego onto the therapist. Or, the therapy may recreate a painful interpersonal situation.

Therapists can forestall many terminations by selecting patients carefully and by building a pretermination delay into the therapeutic contract. They can also be alert to hints of potential flight from treatment, including missed appointments, tardiness for sessions, and failure to pay the bill. Patients may in those ways stimulate the therapist's anger and then rationalize their leaving as a reaction to the therapist's anger or disapproval.

In repressive therapies, therapists may insist that it is best for patients to remain for the period of their therapeutic contract and encourage them to stay.

Ego-supportive or evocative therapists encourage the expression of feelings about the proposed termination. They begin by asking the patient's idea as to the therapist's reaction to the suggestion of termination. Therapists can follow by discussing the impact of leaving therapy on the patients themselves, and the personal significance for the therapist of the patient's leaving. In evocative therapy, the emphasis is on feelings and associations of patients to the idea of leaving therapy, and patients' experiences of having been left. In both ego-supportive and evocative therapies, patients who are considering leaving can be asked to respond to the therapist's reactions, thus underscoring the fact that their contemplated act has interpersonal and intrapsychic consequences.

Proposing a cooling off period can provide the time necessary for the therapist and patient to deal fully with the reasons for, and consequences of, an early termination.

Many patients are unwilling to discuss financial difficulties in therapy, thus preventing consideration of alternative action or even a temporary adjustment in fee until the time of crisis has passed. Thus, the therapist needs to be actively in touch with the patient's real situation, as well as the psychological issues.

Premature termination due to a therapist leaving can be a positive or negative experience depending on the therapist's management of his or her departure. A departing therapist can undermine the patient's ability to function with another therapist through excessive transference gratification or failure to deal with the patient's anger or sense of desertion. In the case of excessive gratification, patients regress and demand similar gratification from the new therapist. When patients' anger over their loss is not dealt with, this is often acted out against the new therapist, who is literally driven away. Patients may also flee rather than face desertion again.

METHODS OF TERMINATION

It is possible to wean patients from therapy by decreasing the length and frequency of sessions, but the two principal methods of termination are vacation from therapy and outright termination. Vacation from therapy is useful under several circumstances. At times, a patient's job or finances will not allow continuation in therapy. Patients in financial straits for whom the therapist feels it unwise to reduce or waive the fee may also be placed on vacation status with the stipulation that they may reenter therapy as soon after they reapply as the therapist can accept them.

Vacation from therapy is also a useful means of terminating persons who do not tolerate well the idea of permanently losing the therapist. For those persons, leaving the therapist is made equivalent to taking a job away from home, but being able to return if it does not work out well.

There is no single diagnostic category of persons who cannot accept outright termination. The common denominator may be inadequate ability to introject or identify, or the inability to face symbolic death or permanent separation. Patients who require termination by vacation from therapy usually indicate their need for that type of termination by expressed fear of permanent separation or severe regression when faced with the prospect of permanent separation from the therapist.

The following example illustrates a situation in which vacation from therapy was deemed more useful than dealing with termination issues.

When Mr. Z. was first seen by the therapist, he was a 13-year-old seventh grader. He was a small, quiet boy who reluctantly revealed his fear of undressing before physical education classes and his fear of eating in the school cafeteria with other children. His mother told the therapist that he had been school phobic intermittently since first grade, expressing fear that harm might come to her, and easing his fear by performing compulsive rituals that involved touching the door jambs a certain number of times. His mother said that his school phobia had improved after psychological treatment with another therapist a year previously, but it reexacerbated when he started seventh grade. Further history revealed that although of normal birth weight and the product of a normal delivery, he had been listless and swollen at birth, and had blood in the superficial tissues of his eyes. Afterward, however, he developed normally. When the patient was about two years of age, his father developed an emotional illness that became chronic and was diagnosed as schizophrenia. His father, in addition, self-medicated with alcohol and later became totally disabled.

The therapist gave Mr. Z. an indefinite excuse from physical education and an excuse from eating lunch at school. That, together with a small dose of antihistamine at bedtime, greatly alleviated his anxiety. Because of his reticence, Mr. Z.'s visits were quickly reduced from weekly to biweekly to monthly, and, after a year, visits were discontinued.

When he was 15, Mr. Z. urged his mother to allow him to be circumcised, but became very anxious a few days before surgery. At that time, he returned to see the therapist. He said that he no longer needed his rituals to leave the house in the morning and that he had lost his former concern that his mother might die. The therapist nevertheless suggested postponing surgery until the patient was a bit more mature. At age 16, Mr. Z. underwent circumcision, and afterward had very little problem undressing in front of others. When he was a senior in high school, his school avoidance problem arose again briefly. When he was 19 and at the end of his senior year, he returned to see his therapist because he was sexually impotent with his girlfriend. The therapist dealt with the issue very concretely and made suggestions as to how they might get more physically comfortable with each other.

Two years later, at age 21, Mr. Z. returned briefly as a college student to talk about his fear of interpersonal relations, which he related to the fact that he perspired profusely from under his arms. The next series of visits occurred when he was 22, had started a relationship with another girl, and was disconcerted that he was again unable to attain an erection. Sessions with him on a weekly to biweekly basis over the next six months consisted of discussing his relationship with his girlfriend and techniques by which he might get comfortable enough to have an erection. He finally succeeded in having an erection and penetrating her, and they began having intercourse regularly. Throughout the sessions concerning his sexual difficulties were interlaced discussions of his concerns about living away from home and attending college. Mr. Z. had always been a poor student, and his work in college was average to poor. The therapist encouraged him to concentrate on finding a job instead of floundering in college. Eventually, Mr. Z. moved into an apartment on his own and secured a job working with his hands, with which he was quite satisfied. At that time, the therapist suggested a vacation from therapy, which Mr. Z. found quite acceptable.

In this patient, the evidence of possible brain damage at birth, of possible biological predisposition to mental illness, and lifelong separation anxiety indicated a repressive approach with the promise of an ongoing relationship, thus suppressing the patient's concerns about desertion and fragmentation instead of trying to deal with them and work them through, a process that might have endangered Mr. Z.'s fragile ego.

PROCESS OF TERMINATION

The process of termination begins with the therapist considering termination of a patient or a patient considering leaving therapy. The process, once the decision is made, is dealt with in different ways depending on the type of treatment.

The process of termination includes dealing with grief and separation from an emotionally significant person, and frequently reactivates responses to other important separations, such as leaving home or the death or parents or siblings. The separation process is often accompanied by transient regression into former symptoms and patterns of defense and/or relationships.

In a repressive therapy, leave-taking may be highly ritualized and may follow the acquisition of certain designated skills. On the other hand, leave-taking may be treated as a matter of course. Grief is sidestepped. Because intense feelings have been minimized, they require no working through. The final session is used to reiterate what the patients have learned and to reinforce the positive feelings between therapist and patient.

When patients in ego-supportive or evocative therapy decide to terminate, the therapist searches for evidence of resistance, especially a transference resistance. For example, patients may be attempting to determine their value to the therapist. If a patient's proposal of termination does not involve resistance, the therapist can then deal with his or her own resistance, if any, to separating from the patient. If therapists propose termination, they first explore their own motivation for wanting to terminate a particular patient's treatment and later help the patient work through concerns about separation.

Even when the decision to terminate therapy is mutual, understanding why is still useful. The therapist may be bored or angry with the patient. The patient, sensing the therapist's boredom or anger, may be trying to avoid it.

Mrs. A. S., who was in the final stage of her individual therapy, was told by her therapist that he would be leaving the city for a year. The patient's response was partly a sense of desertion, partly a realization that she could be on her own, and partly a positive view of the therapist leaving.

The therapist's disclosure to Mrs. A. S. that he was leaving came six months before his intended departure. Four months before his departure, she suggested they reduce to every other week, saying that she was doing well enough on her own. Later, however, it developed that part of her wanting to decrease the frequency of sessions was a sense that the therapist was losing interest in her and was a means to avoid dealing with her anger with the therapist. Once her anger was expressed, she decided that she was cutting off her nose to spite her face and continued on a once-a-week basis until the therapist left. She had meanwhile asked the therapist to recommend another therapist whom she might see should she need to continue therapy.

In ego-supportive and evocative therapies, the first step after agreeing to terminate is to allow patients to express their feelings. The next step is to set a date for termination. Leave-taking from an ego-supportive therapy may require a few weeks to a few months. Leaving therapy is treated as a positive step forward, and the ambivalence of the patient is minimized.

There are additional steps in leaving an evocative therapy that may take longer. Patients are encouraged to experience and express their reactions to the anticipated loss, to express feelings that develop during the separation process, and to deal with reactivated feelings from other losses. Ambivalence on the part of departing patients usually runs high, and mild regressions often occur. A process of mutual decathexis begins, and new or improved relationships outside therapy often develop as further evidence of readiness to depart.

HINDRANCES TO TERMINATION

From the patient's point of view, termination may symbolize abandonment or loss of hope by the therapist that the patient can progress further. It may also imply loss of symbolic parental nurturance or of a life-style of authority-dependence. Resistance to termination can be a form of hostile clinging. Important unresolved transferences can often be brought into the open by the therapist's proposal of termination.

Hindrances to termination from the therapist's point of view include the convenience of working with the same patients, avoiding the issue of loss, the difficulty of finding and integrating new patients, countertransference, and the value of the patient as a person to the therapist.

EFFECTS OF TERMINATION ON THE THERAPIST

While patients' graduation can be a source of pride for therapists, they also lose an important relationship and suffer the narcissistic injury of realizing that the graduating patients can do without them. There is the further injury that patients may leave without fulfilling all of their therapist's wishes for them.

Viewed positively, termination encourages accepting the cycle of birth and death and prepares patients for the numerous separations they will endure in the course of their lives.

INTERMINABLE VERSUS BRIEF THERAPY

A case can be made for lifelong psychotherapy as a necessary augmentation of impaired ego functioning when there are inadequate environmental supports. It can also be argued that lending permanent support discourages seeking support in ordinary social relationships. If permanent support is necessary, it probably requires only brief, infrequent visits and not weekly sessions.

Because it has been recognized that therapy often lasts as long as it is allowed to last (Stieper & Wiener, 1959), there has been a recent emphasis on short-term therapy (Rush, 1982; Gustafson, 1984). Short-term treatment with discrete goals may be one means of avoiding growth-thwarting dependency on therapy, and may be useful as a specific means of dealing with various types of loss.

PROLONGED ABSENCE OF THE THERAPIST

Occasionally, therapists must be absent from their practices for prolonged periods of time. Sometimes, as in the case of accident or illness, the absence is unexpected. At other times, as in the case of an extensive planned trip or a sabbatical, the absence of the therapist can be anticipated and planned for.

The author has had experiences with both types of absence. The former type occurred when an illness resulted in the author's hospitalization for a month and absence from his practice for six weeks (Weiner, 1976b). At the time the therapist's illness was first diagnosed, patients were told he would be on leave from the office indefinitely, but that he was returning. Patients who felt the need to continue in therapy without interruption were offered the names of several therapists. Patients were told that the therapist was in the hospital in another city and was expected to recover and resume full practice. Those patients who took the trouble to get in touch with the therapist were told the nature of the therapist's illness (heart attack) and were told when he was expected to be released from the hospital and when he would be likely to resume practice.

The author's absence from practice was, of course, complicated by patients' feelings over him having been ill. Two of the patients whom he had seen formerly did not return, both presumably because of their concern about his vulnerability. For others who did return, their reactions were a mixture of anger over having been deserted, and sympathy for the therapist's plight. Most patients appreciated having been given concrete information as to what had happened to the therapist and how long it would be before his return.

In the second instance, the author was awarded a one year special study assignment in another city. He began preparing his patients approximately six months before his scheduled departure, and arranged coverage for prescription refills, for stand-in therapy, and worked toward termination of those persons who could be terminated. Patients' anger and feelings of abandonment were dealt with, as were patients' congratulations on the special assignment. In all instances, the author viewed patients' productions in the weeks and months immediately following his announcement as products of their reactions to loss, and used it as a means to explore (when feasible) patients' reactions to loss and abandonment. The author also followed his own advice not to overgratify patients whom he was terminating, but in two instances felt that the best treatment was continued therapy by telephone instead of transferring those patients to other therapists. In both cases, the patients had been in long-term treatment. They were persons with whom trust had developed only gradually, and for whom the benefits of face-to-face therapy were seen as less desirable than the benefits of continuing in an attenuated fashion with the author.

TRANSFERRING PATIENTS

Transferring patients poses special problems (Scher, 1970). Patients are most frequently transferred in teaching settings in which the transferring therapists often feel guilty about learning from their patients and then abandoning them (Sederer, 1975). In these situations, departing therapists are very likely to overgratify patients by providing advice, suggestions, or excessive concern about the patient's environmental or psychological problems. When transferred patients are first seen by their new therapists, they idealize their former therapists, who have succeeded in deflecting their anger over being deserted, and tend to denigrate the new therapists, whom they find unable to live up to the level of their former therapists.

It therefore behooves departing therapists, unless working with very fragile patients, to deal at some level with the patients' sense of being deserted, abandoned, and left to an uncertain fate. In a repressive therapy, it is probably best accomplished by reassurance that the next therapist is competent. In an ego-supportive therapy, patients can be encouraged to discuss feelings about losing the therapist as a person, and in an evocative therapy, fantasies are allowed to emerge.

On the other hand, new therapists have the job of gently deidealizing the former therapist so that a therapeutic alliance can be developed. The disillusionment of patients about their former therapists need not take place all at once, but can be accomplished over time, insuring that the anger expressed toward the former therapist does not emerge in such a way as to promote acting out or to stimulate an overt depression.

As noted in Chapter 7, Mrs. A. T. had idealized her former therapist. She credited him with enabling her to have a positive sexual relationship with her husband and for helping to keep her rheumatoid arthritis in check.

Her new therapist said nothing negative about Mrs. A. T.'s former therapist, but expressed very different feelings about the nature and duration of her therapy. Eventually, Mrs. A. T. commented that her former therapist was a talkative, authoritarian person who at times talked more than she and often substituted his judgment for hers. Finally, she became angry over his benevolent tyranny, recognized that it was the product of her wish to be cared for as a child, and developed a view of her former therapy as very positive, but not completely growth-promoting.

Therapists who are working with transferred patients should have some preliminary information about the previous goals for that patient's treatment, the level at which the therapy operated, the former therapist's style, and the frequency of therapeutic sessions. If transferring therapists wish to lower a patient's anxiety about a new therapist, it is useful for the new therapist to make an appearance and to be actually introduced by the departing therapist. If a departing therapist wishes to allow the development of anxiety and fear-formation on the part of the patient (as in transfer to an evocative therapy), the transfer may be accomplished with little information given about the new therapist.

WHAT DOES TERMINATION REALLY MEAN?

Termination means that at a certain point in time, the therapist or patient determines that the benefits of continuing in therapy are minimal or outweighed by the time, expense, or other negative aspects of treatment. It does not mean that patients are permanently cured of life's problems, or that they will be able to handle all future problems with equanimity. It usually means that psychotherapy is no longer indicated or necessary to enable patients to deal with life's problems, and that patients can now make good use of inner resources, friends, or other forms of sustenance.

In the process of termination, therapists make it clear that departing patients are only human, that life is complex, and that turning to others for help in solving life's problems can indicate strength as well as weakness. The door is left open.

AFTER TERMINATION

Most patients, after terminating a successful therapy, readily relinquish their therapists. They remember their therapists fondly, reflect on particularly apt statements, use advice given them by their therapists, or ask themselves, when in a tight spot, how their former therapists would have encouraged them to handle it.

Most therapists, after bringing therapy to a successful conclusion, are also able to relinquish their patients as people; recalling particularly poignant sessions, important breakthroughs, and their overall satisfaction with their patients' progress.

Most patients do not care to take the risk of becoming disillusioned about their former therapists. They wish their ex-therapists to maintain the superhuman, or at least positive attributes with which they have been endowed during the course of therapy. This continued wish to idealize therapists probably reflects the universal wish for a good parent who is always accepting and available. Getting to know the therapist would destroy the myth.

Some therapists and patients wish to continue their relationship as friends (Easson, 1971). While there is no absolute contraindication to friendship between therapists and ex-patients, both need to be certain that they are not acting out of a wish to avoid important issues, such as separation, or a colluding to act out forbidden impulses. Both need to be aware that friendship precludes further psychotherapeutic interaction. The affection and approval needed from the new friend by the therapist eliminates the therapist's leverage. The therapist can advise the ex-patient friend whom to see for further therapy, but cannot be the therapeutic agent.

SUMMARY

The termination process involves many elements. It is both a leave-taking and a new beginning. It is both a time of loss and one of facing issues related to individuation (Mahler, 1979). Patients and therapists review what they have accomplished, anticipate future problems insofar as they are able to do so, and part company. They know their work is incomplete, because maturation is a never-ending process and because so many of life's problems cannot be anticipated or prepared for. To the extent that they can profitably do so, patients are encouraged to mourn. They are also urged to accept their therapists' framing of the leave-taking as an opportunity for continuing their growth and using their newly-acquired resources. Finally, patients are encouraged to return to therapy, should they feel the need.

Appendix

At present, there are few biological markers for emotional disorders, and few objective means for following the treatment of emotional disorders.

In order to quantify severity of illness and to follow the course of treatment, a number of rating scales have been developed over the past 25 years. The following five rating scales have been selected as the most useful and most easily learned scales of the many instruments available. They have the advantage over clinical observation that they are valid and replicable. It is not hard to foresee that at some point in the future, such tests may be needed to partially justify the initiation or continuance of treatment, much as clinical laboratory data are used to justify the administration of antibiotics.

The Mini-Mental State Examination (Folstein, Folstein, & McHugh, 1975) is used to detect organic impairment of brain function. Administered by the clinician, it is a short screening instrument that detects gross impairment. It lacks the sensitivity of more detailed neuropsychologic tests, but is useful in alerting clinicians to the probability of organic brain disorder and the need for further investigation.

The Brief Psychiatric Rating Scale (BPRS) (Overall & Gorham, 1962) is most useful in following the treatment of persons who are severely ill. It is conventionally rated using a severity of 4 points to indicate a psychotic level of function. A rating of 7 points indicates extremely severe pathology. Scoring the BPRS requires a period of training in these and other conventions. Provided they are adequately trained, the BPRS can be used by technician-level personnel.

The Hamilton Rating Scale for Depression (Hamilton, 1967) may be used as a diagnostic aid or as a measure of treatment progress. It is useful for inpatients and outpatients, and may be scored by trained technicians.

The newest scale is the Geriatric Depression Scale (Yesavage, Brink, Rose, Lum, Huang, Adey, & Leirer, 1983). This scale is designed to reduce the influence of signs and symptoms that are specifically affected by aging and by the presence of physical illness, such as sleep disturbance and weight and appetite loss. It concentrates on the emotional and ideational components of depression.

These tests add a long-needed element of objectivity to clinicians' evaluations. Eventually, these tests may be replaced by biological tests. Until that time, they enable therapists to more effectively assess severity of illness and response to treatment.

THE MINI-MENTAL STATE EXAMINATION

	Score	*Points*

Orientation

1. What is the   Year? — 1
                 Season? — 1
                 Date? — 1
                 Day? — 1
                 Month? — 1

2. Where are we? State? — 1
                 County? — 1
                 Town or city? — 1
                 Hospital? — 1
                 Floor? — 1

Registration

3. Name three objects, taking one second to say each. Then ask the patient all three after you have said them. Give one point for each correct answer. Repeat the answers until the patient learns all three. — 3

Attention and Calculation

4. Serial sevens. Given one point for each correct answer. Stop after five answers. *Alternative*: Spell WORLD backwards. — 5

Recall

5. Ask for names of three objects learned in Question 3. Give one point for each correct answer. — 3

Language

6. Point to a pencil and a watch. Have the patient name them as you point. — 2

7. Have the patient repeat "No ifs, ands, or buts." — 1

8. Have the patient follow a three-stage command: "Take the paper in your right hand. Fold the paper in half. Put the paper on the floor." — 3

9. Have the patient read and obey the following: "CLOSE YOUR EYES." (Write it in large letters.) — 1

10. Have the patient write a sentence of his or her own choice. (The sentence should contain a subject and an object and should make sense. Ignore spelling errors when scoring.) — 1

11. Enlarge the design printed below to 1 to 5 cm per side and have the patient copy it. (Give one point if all sides and angles are preserved and if the intersecting sides form a quadrangle.) — 1

                                                      = Total 30

A score of 23 or less suggests cognitive impairment in a person with eighth grade education or better.

From Folstein, M. F., Folstein, S. E., & McHugh, P. R. (1975). "Mini-mental state." A practical method of grading the cognitive state of patients for the clinician. *Journal of Psychiatric Research, 12,* 189–198. By permission.

BRIEF PSYCHIATRIC RATING SCALE

	Not Present	Mild	Moderate	Severe	Not Ratable
1. SOMATIC CONCERN: Degree of concern over present bodily health. Rate the degree to which physical health is perceived as a problem by the patient, whether complaints have a realistic basis or not.	1	OCCAS. 2 3	EXAG. 4 5	PREOCC. 6 7	0
2. ANXIETY-ANXIETY STATEMENTS: Worry, fear, or overconcern for present or future. Rate solely on the basis of verbal report of patient's own subjective experiences. Do not infer anxiety from neurotic defense mechanisms.	1	WORRIED 2 3	FEARFUL 4 5	PANICKED 6 7	0
3. EMOTIONAL WITHDRAWAL: Deficiency in relating to others; seclusiveness. Rate only the degree to which the patient gives the impression of failing to be in emotional contact with other people.	1	DOESN'T INITIATE 2 3	WITHDRAWS FROM 4 5	REPELS CONTACT 6 7	0
4. CONCEPTUAL DISORGANIZATION/DISORGANIZATION IN SPEECH: Degree to which the thought processes are confused, disconnected, or disorganized. Rate on the basis of integration of the verbal products of the patient; do not rate on the basis of the patient's subjective impression of his own level of functioning.	1	VAGUE 2 3	UNCLEAR 4 5	INCOHERENT TALK 6 7	0
5. GUILT FEELING/GUILT STATEMENTS: Overconcern or remorse for past behavior. Rate on the basis of the patient's subjective experiences of guilt as evidenced by verbal report with appropriate affect; do not infer guilt feelings from depression, anxiety, or neurotic defenses.	1	OVERCONCERN 2 3	PREOCCUPIED 4 5	DELUSIONS OF GUILT 6 7	0

BRIEF PSYCHIATRIC RATING SCALE (*continued*)

	Not Present	Mild	Moderate	Severe	Not Ratable
6. TENSION/TENSION BEHAVIOR: Physical and motor manifestations of tension, "nervousness," and heightened activation level. Tension should be rated solely on the basis of physical signs and motor behavior and not on the basis of subjective experiences of tension reported by the patient.	1	SEEMS TENSE 2 3	RESTLESS 4 5	AGITATED 6 7	0
7. MANNERISMS AND POSTURING: Unusual and unnatural motor behavior which causes certain mental patients to stand out in a crowd of normal people. Rate only abnormality of movements; do not rate simple heightened motor activity.	1	OCCAS. 2 3	FREQUENT 4 5	PERVASIVE 6 7	0
8. GRANDIOSITY/GRANDIOSE STATEMENTS: Exaggerated self-opinion, conviction of unusual ability or powers. Rate only on the basis of patient's statements about himself or self in relation to others, not on the basis of his demeanor.	1	EXPANSIVE 2 3	SPECIAL ABILITIES 4 5	DELUSIONAL STATE 6 7	0
9. DEPRESSIVE MOOD: Despondency in mood, sadness. Rate only degree of despondency; do not rate on the basis of inferences concerning depression based upon general retardation and somatic complaints.	1	SAD 2 3	DESPONDENT 4 5	DESPAIRING 6 7	0
10. HOSTILITY—STATEMENTS AND BEHAVIOR: Animosity, contempt, threats, belligerence, disdain for other people. Rate solely on the basis of reported feelings and of actions of the patient toward others; do not infer hostility from neurotic defenses, anxiety, or somatic complaints.	1	ANNOYED 2 3	HOSTILE 4 5	RAGING 6 7	0

(*continued*)

BRIEF PSYCHIATRIC RATING SCALE (continued)

	Not Present	Mild	Moderate	Severe	Not Ratable
11. SUSPICIOUSNESS: Belief (delusional or otherwise) that others have now, or have had in the past, malicious or discriminatory intent toward the patient. On the basis of verbal report and behavior, rate only those suspicions currently held, whether they concern past or present circumstances.	1	SEEMS GUARDED 2 3	SAYS DOESN'T TRUST 4 5	PARANOID DELUSIONS 6 7	0
12. HALLUCINATORY BEHAVIOR/HALLUCINATION STATEMENTS: Perceptions without normal external stimulus correspondence. Rate only those experiences which are reported to have occurred during the rating period and which are described as distinctly different from the thought and imagery process of normal people.	1	OCCAS. WITH INSIGHT 2 3	OFTEN AND NO INSIGHT 4 5	PERVASIVE 6 7	0
13. MOTOR RETARDATION/BEHAVIOR: Reduction in energy level, evidenced in slowed movements and speech, reduced body tone, decreased number of movements. Rate on the basis of observed behavior of the patient only; do not rate on the basis of patient's subjective impression of own energy level.	1	SLOWED 2 3	RETARDED 4 5	CATATONIC 6 7	0
14. UNCOOPERATIVENESS: Evidences of resistance, unfriendliness, resentment, and lack of readiness to cooperate with ward procedures and with others.	1	RESENTS 2 3	RESISTS 4 5	REFUSES 6 7	0
15. UNUSUAL THOUGHT CONTENT: Unusual, odd, strange, or bizarre thought content. Rate here the degree of unusualness, not the degree of disorganization of thought processes.	1	ODD 2 3	BIZARRE 4 5	IMPOSSIBLE 6 7	0

294

BRIEF PSYCHIATRIC RATING SCALE (continued)

	Not Present	Mild	Moderate	Severe	Not Ratable
16. BLUNTED AFFECT: Reduced emotional tone, apparent lack of normal feeling or involvement.	1	LOWERED FEELING 2 3	FLAT 4 5	MECHANICAL 6 7	0
17. EXCITEMENT: Heightened emotional tone, increased reactivity, agitation, impulsivity.	1	INCREASED EMOTION 2 3	INTENSE 4 5	OFF THE WALL 6 7	0
18. DISORIENTATION: Confusion or lack of proper association for person, place, or time.	1	MUDDLED 2 3	CONFUSED 4 5	DISORIENTED 6 7	0
19. LOSS OF FUNCTIONING*: Rate general level of functioning.	1	MILD LOSS 2 3	MODERATE LOSS 4 5	SEVERE LOSS 6 7	0

Reprinted with permission of authors and publisher from Overall, J. E., & Gorham, D. R. (1962). The brief psychiatric rating scale. *Psychological Reports, 10,* 799–812 (Modified, 1966).
*Item 19 is a global scale that is not added in with the other items. Items 1 to 18 are added together to give the total score.

HAMILTON PSYCHIATRIC RATING SCALE FOR DEPRESSION

For each item, select the one "answer" that best characterizes the patient and check the corresponding numbered box.

---

1. DEPRESSED MOOD (Sadness, hopeless, helpless, worthless)

   0=Absent
   1=These feeling states indicated only
      on questioning
   2=These feeling states spontaneously
      reported verbally

0	1	2	3	4

   3=Communicates feeling states nonverbally—i.e., through facial expression, posture, voice, and tendency to weep
   4=Patient reports VIRTUALLY ONLY these feeling states in his spontaneous verbal and nonverbal communication

2. FEELINGS OF GUILT

   0=Absent
   1=Self-reproach, feels he has let
      people down
   2=Ideas of guilt or rumination over
      past errors or sinful deeds

0	1	2	3	4

   3=Present illness is a punishment. Delusions of guilt.
   4=Hears accusatory or denunciatory voices and/or experiences threatening visual hallucinations

3. SUICIDE

   0=Absent
   1=Feels life is not worth living
   2=Wishes he were dead or any thoughts
      of possible death to self

0	1	2	3	4

   3=Suicide ideas or gesture
   4=Attempts at suicide (any serious attempt rates 4)

4. INSOMNIA EARLY

   0=No difficulty falling asleep
   1=Complains of occasional difficulty
      falling asleep—i.e., more than
      ½ hour

0	1	2

   2=Complains of nightly difficulty
      falling asleep

5. INSOMNIA MIDDLE

0=No difficulty
1=Patient complains of being restless
and disturbed during the night
2=Waking during the night—any
getting out of bed rates 2 (except
for purposes of voiding)

0	1	2

6. INSOMNIA LATE

0=No difficulty
1=Waking in early hours of the
morning but goes back to sleep
2=Unable to fall asleep again if he
gets out of bed

0	1	2

7. WORK AND ACTIVITIES

0=No difficulty
1=Thoughts and feelings of incapacity,
fatigue or weakness related to
activities; work or hobbies

0	1	2	3	4

2=Loss of interest in activity—hobbies or work—either directly reported by patient, or
indirect in listlessness, indecision, and vacillation (feels he has to push self to work
or activities)
3=Decrease in actual time spent in activities or decrease in productivity. In hospital,
rate 3 if patient does not spend at least three hours a day in activities (hospital job
or hobbies) exclusive of ward chores.
4=Stopped working because of present illness. In hospital, rate 4 if patient engages in
no activities except ward chores, or if patient fails to perform ward chores un-
assisted.

8. RETARDATION (Slowness of thought and speech; impaired ability to concentrate; decreased motor activity)

0=Normal speech and thought
1=Slight retardation at interview
2=Obvious retardation at interview
3=Interview difficult
4=Complete stupor

0	1	2	3	4

(*continued*)

9. AGITATION

0=None
1="Playing with" hands, hair, etc.
2=Hand-wringing, nail-biting, hair-
pulling, biting of lips

0	1	2

10. ANXIETY PSYCHIC

Physiological concomitants of anxiety, such as:
Gastrointestinal—dry mouth, wind, indigestion, diarrhea, cramps, belching
Cardiovascular—palpitations, headaches
Respiratory—hyperventilation, sighing
Urinary frequency
Sweating

0=Absent
1=Mild
2=Moderate
3=Severe
4=Incapacitating

0	1	2	3	4

12. SOMATIC SYMPTOMS—GASTROINTESTINAL

0=None
1=Loss of appetite, but eating
without staff encouragement.
Heavy feelings in abdomen.
2=Difficulty eating without staff urging. Requests or requires laxatives or medication
for bowels or medication for GI symptoms.

0	1	2

13. SOMATIC SYMPTOMS—GENERAL

0=None
1=Heaviness in limbs, back of
head. Backaches, headaches,
muscle aches. Loss of energy
and fatigability.
2=Any clear-cut symptom rates 2

0	1	2

14. GENITAL SYMPTOMS

Symptoms such as: loss of libido, menstrual disturbances

0=Absent
1=Mild
2=Severe

0	1	2

15. HYPOCHONDRIASIS

0=Not present
1=Self-absorption (bodily)
2=Preoccupation with health
3=Frequent complaints, requests
   for help, etc.
4=Hypochondriacal delusions

0	1	2	3	4

16. LOSS OF WEIGHT—Rate either A or B

A. When rating by history:

0=No weight loss
1=Probable weight loss associated
   with present illness
2=Definite (according to patient)
   weight loss
3=Not assessed

0	1	2	3

B. On weekly ratings by ward psychiatrist, when actual weight changes are measured:

0=Less than 1 lb. weight loss in
   week
1=Greater than 1 lb. weight loss in
   week
2=Greater than 2 lb. weight loss in week
3=Not assessed

0	1	2	3

17. INSIGHT

0=Acknowledges being depressed and ill
1=Acknowledges illness but attributes
   cause to bad food, climate, over-
   work, virus, need for rest, etc.
2=Denies being ill at all

0	1	2

18. DIURNAL VARIATION

A. Note whether symptoms are worse in morning or evening. If NO diurnal variation, mark "None."

0=No variation
1=Worse in A.M.
2=Worse in P.M.

0	1	2

(*continued*)

B. When present, mark the severity of the variation. Mark "None" if NO variation.

0=None
1=Mild
2=Severe

0	1	2

19. DEPERSONALIZATION AND DEREALIZATION
Such as: feelings of unreality, nihilistic ideas

0=Absent
1=Mild
2=Moderate
3=Severe
4=Incapacitating

0	1	2	3	4

20. PARANOID SYMPTOMS

0=None
1=Suspicious
2=Ideas of reference
3=Delusions of reference and persecution

0	1	2	3

21. OBSESSIONAL AND COMPULSIVE SYMPTOMS

0=Absent
1=Mild
2=Severe

0	1	2

Reprinted with permission of author from Hamilton, M. (1967). Development of a rating scale for primary depressive illness. *British Journal of Social and Clinical Psychology, 6,* 278–296.
This scale is used for rating the severity of depression. A score of less than 11 suggests that no depression is present.

THE GERIATRIC DEPRESSION SCALE

Choose the best answer for how you felt over the past week.

1. Are you basically satisfied with your life?	Yes/No
2. Have you dropped many of your activities and interests?	Yes/No
3. Do you feel that your life is empty?	Yes/No
4. Do you often get bored?	Yes/No
5. Are you hopeful about the future?	Yes/No
6. Are you bothered by thoughts you can't get out of your head?	Yes/No
7. Are you in good spirits most of the time?	Yes/No
8. Are you afraid that something bad is going to happen to you?	Yes/No
9. Do you feel happy most of the time?	Yes/No
10. Do you often feel helpless?	Yes/No
11. Do you often get restless and fidgety?	Yes/No
12. Do you prefer to stay at home, rather than going out and doing new things?	Yes/No
13. Do you frequently worry about the future?	Yes/No
14. Do you feel you have more problems with memory than most?	Yes/No
15. Do you think it is wonderful to be alive now?	Yes/No
16. Do you often feel downhearted and blue?	Yes/No
17. Do you feel pretty worthless the way you are now?	Yes/No
18. Do you worry a lot about the past?	Yes/No
19. Do you find life very exciting?	Yes/No
20. Is it hard for you to get started on new projects?	Yes/No
21. Do you feel full of energy?	Yes/No
22. Do you feel that your situation is hopeless?	Yes/No
23. Do you think that more people are better off than you are?	Yes/No
24. Do you frequently get upset over little things?	Yes/No
25. Do you frequently feel like crying?	Yes/No
26. Do you have trouble concentrating?	Yes/No
27. Do you enjoy getting up in the morning?	Yes/No
28. Do you prefer to avoid social gatherings?	Yes/No
29. Is it easy for you to make decisions?	Yes/No
30. Is your mind as clear as it used to be?	Yes/No

From Yesavage, J. A., Brink, T.L., Rose, T. L., Lum, O., Huang, V., Adey, M., & Leirer, V. O. (1983). Development and validation of a geriatric depression screening scale: A preliminary report. *Journal of Psychiatric Research, 17*, 37–49. By permission.
A score of 14 points or more suggests the presence of depression, which needs to be confirmed by clinical evaluation. The underlined items are scored positively for depression.

References

Adams, S., & Orgel, M. (1975). *Through the mental health maze: A consumer's guide to finding a psychiatrist, including a sample consumer/therapist contract.* Washington, D.C.: Public Citizens Research Group.

Adler, G. (1975). Hospital treatment of borderline patients. *American Journal of Psychiatry, 130,* 32–36.

Adler, G. (1979). The myth of the alliance with borderline patients. *American Journal of Psychiatry, 136,* 642–645.

Alexander, F. (1950). *Psychosomatic medicine.* New York: W. W. Norton.

Alexander, F., & French, T. M. (1946). *Psychoanalytic therapy: Principles and application.* New York: Ronald Press.

Altman, N. (1975). Hypochondriasis. In J. J. Strain & S. Grossman (Eds.), *Psychological care of the medically ill* (pp. 76–92). New York: Appleton-Century-Crofts.

Altshul, V. A. (1977). The so-called boring patient. *American Journal of Psychotherapy, 31,* 533–545.

American Psychiatric Association (1980). *Diagnostic and statistical manual of mental disorders* (3d. ed.). Washington, D. C.: American Psychiatric Association.

Ansbacher, H., & Ansbacher, R. (1956). *The individual psychology of Alfred Adler.* New York: Basic Books.

Appelbaum, S. (1978). How strictly confidential? *International Journal of Psychoanalysis and Psychotherapy, 7,* 220–222.

Arieti, S. (1974). An overview of schizophrenia from a predominantly psychological approach. *American Journal of Psychiatry, 131,* 241–244.

Arieti, S. (1977). Psychotherapy of severe depression. *American Journal of Psychiatry, 134,* 864–868.

Arlow, J., & Brenner, C. (1964). *Psychoanalytic concepts and the structural theory.* New York: International Universities Press.

Armstrong, S. H., & Weiner, M. F. (1981). Noncompliance with post-transplant immunosuppression. *International Journal of Psychiatry in Medicine, 11,* 85–95.

Aruffo, R. N. (1984). Comments on the therapeutic aspects of the psychoanalytic process. Presented at Department of Psychiatry Grand Rounds, The University of Texas Health Science Center at Dallas, May 25.

Ayllon, T., & Skirban, W. (1973). Accountability in psychotherapy: A test case. *Journal of Behavior Therapy and Experimental Psychiatry, 4,* 19–29.

Baker, S. L., Jr. (1980). Traumatic war disorders. In H. I. Kaplan, A. M. Freedman, &

B. J. Sadock (Eds.), *Comprehensive textbook of psychiatry* (Vol. 3) (pp. 1829-1842). Baltimore: Williams & Wilkins.

Balint, M. (1968). *The basic fault.* London: Tavistock.

Bandura, A. (1971). Psychotherapy based on modeling principles. In A. E. Bergin & S. L. Garfield (Eds.), *Handbook of psychotherapy and behavior change* (pp. 653-708). New York: John Wiley & Sons.

Bandura, A. (1974). A behavior theory and the models of man. *American Psychologist, 29,* 859-869.

Barnhouse, R. T. (1978). Sex between patient and therapist. *Journal of the American Academy of Psychoanalysis, 6,* 533-546.

Beavers, W. R., Lewis, J. M., Gossett, J. T., & Phillips, V. A. (1975). Crucial variables in healthy family systems. *Dallas Medical Journal, 61,* 313-316.

Beck, A. T. (1976). *Cognitive therapy and the emotional disorders.* New York: International Universities Press.

Beck, A. T., Rush, A. J., Shaw, B. F., & Emery, G. (1979). *Cognitive therapy of depression.* New York: Guilford.

Beck, A. T., Ward, C. H., Mendelson, M., Mock, J., & Erbaugh, J. (1961). An inventory for measuring depression. *Archives of General Psychiatry, 4,* 561-571.

Beecher, H. K. (1946). Pain in man wounded in battle. *Annals of Surgery, 123,* 96-105.

Beitman, B. D. (1983). Categories of countertransference. *Journal of Operational Psychiatry, 14,* 82-90.

Bennett, A. E. (1973). Psychiatric management of geriatric depressive disorders. *Diseases of the Nervous System, 34,* 222-225.

Benson, D. F. (1979). *Aphasia, alexia, and agraphia.* New York: Churchill Livingstone.

Berger, M. M. (1958). Nonverbal communication in group psychotherapy. *International Journal of Group Psychotherapy, 2,* 161-179.

Berger, M. M. (Ed.). (1970). *Videotape techniques in psychiatric training and treatment.* New York: Brunner/Mazel.

Bermak, G. E. (1977). Do psychiatrists have special emotional problems? *American Journal of Psychoanalysis, 37,* 141-146.

Berne, E. (1961). *Transactional analysis in psychotherapy.* New York: Grove Press.

Berne, E. (1964). *Games people play.* New York: Grove Press.

Berne, E. (1966). *Principles of group treatment.* New York: Oxford University Press.

Berzins, J. I. (1977). Therapist-patient matching. In A. S. Gurman & A. M. Razin (Eds.), *Effective psychotherapy: A handbook of research* (pp. 222-251). New York: Pergamon Press.

Black, R. G. (1975). The chronic pain syndrome. *Surgical Clinics of North America, 55,* 999-1011.

Blos, P. (1962). *On adolescence.* New York: Free Press.

Bowers, M. B., Jr., Steidl, J., Rabinovitch, D., et al. (1980). Psychotic illness in mid-life. In W. H. Norman & T. J. Scaramella (Eds.), *Mid-Life: Developmental and clinical issues* (pp. 73-83). New York: Brunner/Mazel.

Boyer, L. (1977). The treatment of a borderline patient. *Psychoanalytic Quarterly, 46,* 386-424.

Brenner, C. (1973). *An elementary textbook of psychoanalysis* (rev. ed.). New York: International Universities Press.

Brenner, C. (1982). *The mind in conflict.* New York: International Universities Press.

Breuer, J., & Freud, S. (1957). [*Studies on hysteria.*] New York: Basic Books. (Originally published, 1895.)

Brownfain, J. (1971). The A.P.A. professional liability insurance program. *American Psychologist, 26,* 648-652.

Buckley, P., Karasu, T. B., & Charles, E. (1979). Common mistakes in psychotherapy. *American Journal of Psychiatry, 136,* 1578-1580.

Busse, E. W., & Blazer, D. G. (1980). Disorders related to biological functioning. In E. W. Busse & D. G. Blazer (Eds.), *Handbook of geriatric psychiatry* (pp. 390–414). New York: Van Nostrand Reinhold.

Butler, R. N. (1975). Psychiatry and the elderly: An overview. *American Journal of Psychiatry, 132,* 893–900.

Cancro, R. (1983). Individual psychotherapy in the treatment of chronic schizophrenic patients. *American Journal of Psychotherapy, 37,* 493–501.

Cassell, E. J. (1979). Reactions to physical illness and hospitalization. In G. Usdin & J. M. Lewis (Eds.), *Psychiatry in general medical practice* (pp. 103–131). New York: McGraw-Hill.

Chesler, P. (1971). *Women and madness.* New York: Doubleday.

Chessick, R. D. (1968). The "crucial dilemma" of the therapist in the psychotherapy of borderline patients. *American Journal of Psychotherapy, 22,* 655–666.

Chessick, R. D. (1971). *Why psychotherapists fail.* New York: Science House.

Chrzanowski, G. (1977). Problem patients or troublemakers? Dynamic and therapeutic considerations. *American Journal of Psychotherapy, 31,* 516–524.

Cohen, M. B., Baker, G., Cohen, R. A., Fromm-Reichmann, F., & Weigert, E. (1954). An intensive study of twelve cases of manic-depressive psychosis. *Psychiatry, 17,* 103–137.

Cohen, R. J. (1979). *Malpractice: A guide for mental health professionals.* New York: Free Press.

Crasilneck, H. B., & Hall, J. A. (1975). *Clinical hypnosis.* New York: Grune & Stratton.

Dahlberg, C. C. (1970). Sexual contact between patient and therapist. *Journal of Contemporary Psychoanalysis, 6,* 107–124.

Davanloo, H. (1977). *Basic principles and techniques of short-term dynamic psychotherapy.* New York: Spectrum Publications.

Dewald, P. A. (1983). Elements of change and cure in psychoanalysis. *Archives of General Psychiatry, 40,* 89–95.

Dodds, E. R. (1971). *The Greeks and the irrational.* Berkeley: University of California Press.

Dubey, J. (1974). Confidentiality as an absolute requirement of the therapist: Technical necessities for absolute privilege in psychotherapy. *American Journal of Psychiatry, 131,* 1093–1096.

Dunbar, F. (1948). *Psychosomatic diagnosis.* New York: Hoeber.

Easson, W. M. (1971). Patient and therapist after termination of psychotherapy. *American Journal of Psychotherapy, 25,* 635–642.

Edelwich, J. L. (1980). *Burn-out: Stages of disillusionment in the helping professions.* New York: Human Sciences Press.

Elkind, D. (1980). Developmental structuralism of Jean Piaget. In H. I. Kaplan, A. M. Freedman, & B. J. Sadock (Eds.), *Comprehensive textbook of psychiatry* (3d. ed., Vol. 1) (pp. 371–378). Baltimore: Williams & Wilkins.

Ellis, A., & Grieger, R. (1977). *The handbook of rational-emotive therapy.* New York: Springer.

Engel, G. L. (1959). Psychogenic pain and the pain-prone patient. *American Journal of Medicine, 26,* 899–918.

Engel, G. L. (1972). A life setting conducive to illness: The giving-up–given-up complex. In L. H. Schwartz and J. L. Schwartz (Eds.), *The psychodynamics of patient care* (pp. 376–387). Englewood Cliffs, NJ: Prentice-Hall.

Erikson, E. H. (1959). *Identity and the life cycle.* New York: W. W. Norton.

Erikson, E. H. (1963). *Childhood and society* (2d. ed.). New York: W. W. Norton.

Fenichel, O. (1945). *The psychoanalytic theory of neurosis.* New York: W. W. Norton.

Fenichel, O. (1953). *The collected papers of Otto Fenichel.* New York: W. W. Norton.

Folstein, M. F., Folstein, S. E., & McHugh, P. R. (1975). "Mini-mental state." A practical method for grading the cognitive state of patients for the clinician. *Journal of Psychiatric Research, 12,* 189–198.

Foulkes, S. H. (1968). Interpretation in group analysis. *International Journal of Group Psychotherapy, 18,* 432–445.

Frank, J. D. (1974). Psychotherapy: The restoration of morale. *American Journal of Psychiatry, 131,* 271–274.

Frankl, V. (1959). *Man's search for meaning: An introduction to logotherapy.* Boston: Beacon Press.

Freedman, A. M. (1980). Confidentiality. In H. I. Kaplan, A. M. Freedman, & B. J. Sadock (Eds.), *Comprehensive textbook of psychiatry* (3d ed., Vol. 3) (pp. 3231–3235). Baltimore: Williams & Wilkins.

French, T. M. (1958). *The integration of behavior* (Vol. 3). *The reintegrative process in a psychoanalytic treatment.* Chicago: University of Chicago Press.

Freud, A. (1946). *The ego and the mechanisms of defense.* New York: International Universities Press.

Freud, S. (1953). [On psychotherapy.] In J. Strachey (Ed. and trans.), *The standard edition of the complete psychological works of Sigmund Freud* (Vol. 7) (pp. 257–268). London: Hogarth Press. (Originally published, 1904.)

Freud, S. (1955). [Beyond the pleasure principle.] In J. Strachey (Ed. and trans.), *The standard edition of the complete psychological works of Sigmund Freud* (Vol. 18) (pp. 3–44). London: Hogarth Press. (Originally published, 1920.)

Freud, S. (1955). [Group psychology and the analysis of the ego.] In J. Strachey (Ed. and trans.), *The standard edition of the complete psychological works of Sigmund Freud* (Vol. 18), (pp. 67–134). London: Hogarth Press. (Originally published, 1921.)

Freud, S. (1957). [Mourning and melancholia.] In J. Strachey (Ed. and trans.), *The standard edition of the complete psychological works of Sigmund Freud* (Vol. 14) (pp. 237–260). London: Hogarth Press. (Originally published, 1917.)

Freud, S. (1958). [Recommendations for physicians on the psychoanalytic method of treatment.] In J. Strachey (Ed. and trans.), *The standard edition of the complete psychological works of Sigmund Freud* (Vol. 12) (pp. 109–121). London: Hogarth Press. (Originally published, 1912).

Freud, S. (1958). [Remembering, repeating, and working through.] In J. Strachey (Ed. and trans.), *The standard edition of the complete psychological works of Sigmund Freud* (Vol. 12) (pp. 145–156). London: Hogarth Press. (Originally published, 1914.)

Freud, S. (1960). *The interpretation of dreams.* New York: Basic Books. (Originally published, 1900.)

Freud, S. (1960) [Three essays on the theory of sexuality.] In J. Strachey (Ed. and trans.), *The standard edition of the complete psychological works of Sigmund Freud* (Vol. 8) (pp. 125–243). London: Hogarth Press. (Originally published, 1905.)

Freud, S. (1961). [The ego and the id.] In J. Strachey (Ed. and trans.), *The standard edition of the complete psychological works of Sigmund Freud* (Vol. 19) (pp. 3–68). London: Hogarth Press. (Originally published, 1923.)

Freud, S. (1964). [New introductory lectures on psycho-analysis.] In J. Strachey (Ed. and trans.), *The standard edition of the complete psychological works of Sigmund Freud* (Vol. 23) (pp. 3–196). London: Hogarth Press. (Originally published, 1932.)

Freud, S. (1964). [An outline of psychoanalysis.] In J. Strachey (Ed. and trans.), *The standard edition of the complete psychological works of Sigmund Freud* (Vol. 23) (pp. 141–208). London: Hogarth Press. (Originally published, 1940.)

Friedman, H. J. (1975). Psychotherapy of borderline patients: The influence of theory on technique. *American Journal of Psychiatry, 132,* 1048–1051.

Friedman, M., & Rosenman, R. H. (1974). *Type A behavior and your heart.* New York: Alfred A. Knopf.

Garfield, S. L. (1971). Research in client variables in psychotherapy. In A. E. Bergin & S. L. Garfield (Eds.), *Handbook of psychotherapy and behavior change* (pp. 271–298). New York: John Wiley & Sons.

Garfield, S. L., & Wolpin, M. (1963). Expectations regarding psychotherapy. *Journal of Nervous and Mental Disorders, 137*, 358-362.

Gatchel, R. J. (1984). Behavioral treatment techniques in medical settings. In F. G. Guggenheim & M. F. Weiner (Eds.), *The manual of psychiatric consultation and emergency care* (pp. 363-372). New York: Jason Aronson.

Gladfelter, J. H. (1970). Videotape supervision of co-therapists. In M. M. Berger (Ed.), *Videotape techniques in psychiatric training and treatment.* New York: Brunner/Mazel.

Glenn, M. L. (1971). Separation anxiety: When the therapist leaves the patient. *American Journal of Psychotherapy, 25*, 437-446.

Glick, I. D., & Kessler, D. R. (1980). *Marital and family therapy.* New York: Grune & Stratton.

Goldfarb, A. I., & Turner, H. (1953). Psychotherapy of aged persons II. Utilization and effectiveness of "brief" therapy. *American Journal of Psychiatry, 109*, 916-921.

Goldfried, M., & Davidson, G. (1976). *Clinical behavior therapy.* New York: Grune & Stratton.

Goulding, R., & Goulding, M. M. (1978). *The power is in the patient: A TA/Gestalt approach to psychotherapy.* San Francisco: T. A. Press.

Granet, R. B., & Kalman, T. P. (1982). Anniversary reactions in therapists. *American Journal of Psychiatry, 139*, 1599-1600.

Green, A. (1977). The borderline concept. In P. Hartocollis (Ed.), *Borderline personality disorder: The concept, the syndrome, the patient* (pp. 15-44). New York: International Universities Press.

Greenson, R. R. (1954). The struggle against identification. *Journal of the American Psychoanalytic Association, 2*, 200-217.

Greenson, R. R. (1967). *The technique and practice of psychoanalysis.* New York: International Universities Press.

Groesbeck, C. J., & Taylor, B. (1977). The psychiatrist as wounded physician. *American Journal of Psychoanalysis, 37*, 131-139.

Guggenheim, F. G., & Weiner, M. F. (Eds.) (1984). *Manual of psychiatric consultation and emergency care.* New York: Jason Aronson.

Gunderson, J. G. (1973). Controversies about the psychotherapy of schizophrenia. *American Journal of Psychiatry, 130*, 677-681.

Gunderson, J. G. (1977). Characteristics of borderlines. In P. Hartocollis (Ed.), *Borderline personality disorder: The concept, the syndrome, the patient* (pp. 173-192). New York: International Universities Press.

Gunderson, J. G. (1978). Patient-therapist matching: A research evaluation. *American Journal of Psychiatry, 135*, 1193-1197.

Gustafson, J. P. (1984). An integration of brief dynamic psychotherapy. *American Journal of Psychiatry, 141*, 935-943.

Haley, J. (1971). Communication and therapy: Blocking metaphors. *American Journal of Psychotherapy, 25*, 214-227.

Hamilton, M. (1960). A rating scale for depression. *Journal of Neurology, Neurosurgery and Psychiatry, 23*, 56-62.

Hamilton, M. (1967). Development of a rating scale for primary depressive illness. *British Journal of Social and Clinical Psychology, 6*, 278-296.

Hartmann, E. L. (1980). Sleep. In H. I. Kaplan, A. M. Freedman, & B. J. Sadock (Eds.), *Comprehensive textbook of psychiatry* (3d ed., Vol. 1) (pp. 165-177). Baltimore: Williams & Wilkins.

Hendler, N. (1984). The chronic pain patient. In F. G. Guggenheim & M. F. Weiner (Eds.), *The manual of psychiatric consultation and emergency care* (pp. 233-242). New York: Jason Aronson.

Hiatt, H. (1971). Dynamic psychotherapy with the aging patient. *American Journal of Psychotherapy, 25*, 591-600.

Hofer, M. A. (1975). The principles of autonomic function in the life of man and animals. In S. Arieti (Ed.), *American handbook of psychiatry* (rev. ed., Vol. 4) (pp. 528–552). New York: Basic Books.

Horowitz, M. J. (1983). *Image formation and psychotherapy*. New York: Jason Aronson.

Johansen, K. H. (1979). A theoretical basis for the management of the hospitalized borderline patient. *Current Concepts in Psychiatry, 5,* 8–16.

Jones, E. (1957). *Life and work of Sigmund Freud* (Vol. 3). New York: Basic Books.

Jung, C. G. (1964). *Man and his symbols*. New York: Doubleday.

Karasu, T. B. (1977). Psychotherapies: An overview. *American Journal of Psychiatry, 134,* 851–863.

Karasu, T. B. (1979). Psychotherapy of the medically ill. *American Journal of Psychiatry, 136,* 1–11.

Keleman, S. (1971). *Sexuality, self, and survival*. San Francisco: Jossey-Bass.

Kernberg, O. (1968). The treatment of patients with borderline personality organization. *International Journal of Psychoanalysis, 49,* 600–619.

Kernberg, O. F. (1975). *Borderline conditions and pathological narcissism*. New York: Jason Aronson.

Kernberg, O. F. (1980). *Internal world and external reality*. New York: Jason Aronson.

Kernberg, O. F., Burnstein, E., Coyne, L., et al. (1972). Psychotherapy and psychoanalysis: Final report of the Menninger Foundation psychotherapy research project. *Bulletin of the Menninger Clinic, 36,* 1–275.

Kety, S. S. (1978). Genetic and biochemical aspects of schizophrenia. In A. M. Nicholi (Ed.), *The Harvard guide to modern psychiatry* (pp. 93–102). Cambridge, MA: Belknap Press.

Kibel, H. D. (1980). The importance of a comprehensive clinical diagnosis for group psychotherapy of borderline and narcissistic patients. *International Journal of Group Psychotherapy, 30,* 427–440.

Klerman, G. (1978). Affective disorder. In A. M. Nicholi (Ed.), *The Harvard guide to modern psychiatry* (pp. 253–280). Cambridge, MA: Belknap Press.

Kohut, H. (1971). *The analysis of the self*. New York: International Universities Press.

Kohut, H. (1977). *The restoration of the self*. New York: International Universities Press.

Korn, E. K., & Johnson, K. (1983). *Visualization: The uses of imagery in the health professions*. Homewood, IL: Dow-Jones Irwin.

Kris, E. (1952). *Psychoanalytic explorations in art*. New York: International Universities Press.

Krystal, H. (1978). Trauma and affects. *Psychoanalytic Study of the Child, 33,* 81–116.

Kubler-Ross, E. (1969). *On death and dying*. New York: Macmillan.

Lager, E., & Zwerling, I. (1983). *Psychotherapy in the community: A psychoanalytically based guide to the treatment of the adult*. St. Louis: Warren H. Green.

Lambert, M. J., Bergin, A. E., & Collins, J. L. (1977). Therapist-induced deterioration in psychotherapy. In A. S. Gurman & A. M. Razin (Eds.), *Effective psychotherapy: A handbook of research* (pp. 452–481). New York: Pergamon.

Langs, R. J. (1973). *The technique of psychoanalytic psychotherapy* (Vol. 1). New York: Jason Aronson.

Leuner, H. (1969). Guided affective imagery (GAI): A method of intensive psychotherapy. *American Journal of Psychotherapy, 23,* 4–22.

Levinson, D. J. (1978). *The seasons of a man's life*. New York: Alfred A. Knopf.

Levitz, I. S., & Stunkard, A. J. (1974). A therapeutic coalition for obesity: Behavior modification and patient self-help. *American Journal of Psychiatry, 131,* 423–428.

Lewis, J. M., Beavers, W. R., Gossett, J. T., & Phillips, V. A. (1976). *No single thread: Psychological health in family systems*. New York: Brunner/Mazel.

Lieberman, M. A., Yalom, I. D., & Miles, M. D. (1973). *Encounter groups: First facts*. New York: Basic Books.

Liebman, R., Minuchin, S., & Baker, L. (1974). An integrated program for anorexia nervosa. *American Journal of Psychiatry, 131,* 432–436.

Liff, Z. (1970). Impasse: Interpersonal, intergroup, and interactional. *Group Process, 3,* 7-30.

Lindemann, E. (1944). Symptomatology and management of acute grief. *American Journal of Psychiatry, 101,* 141-148.

Little, M. (1951). Counter-transference and the patient's response to it. *International Journal of Psychoanalysis, 32,* 32-40.

Low, A. (1952). *Mental health through will training.* Boston: Christopher Publishing House.

Luborsky, L., McLellan, T., Woody, G. E., O'Brien, C. P., & Auerbach, A. (1985). Therapist success and its determinants. *Archives of General Psychiatry, 42,* 602-611.

Mahler, M. S. (1979). *The selected papers of Margaret S. Mahler, M. D.* (Vol. 2). New York: Jason Aronson.

Malan, D. H. (1976). *The frontier of brief psychotherapy.* New York: Plenum.

Malan, D. H., Balfour, F. H. G., Hood, V. G., & Shooter, A. M. N. (1976). Group psychotherapy, a long-term followup study. *Archives of General Psychiatry, 33,* 1303-1315.

Mann, J. (1973). *Time-limited psychotherapy.* Cambridge, MA: Harvard University Press.

Martin, P. A. (1976). *A marital therapy manual.* New York: Brunner/Mazel.

Masserman, J. H. (1959). The biodynamic approaches. In S. Arieti (Ed.), *American handbook of psychiatry* (Vol. 2) (pp. 1680-1696). New York: Basic Books.

Masserman, J. H. (1980). Biodynamics. In H. I. Kaplan, A. M. Freedman, & B. J. Sadock (Eds.), *Comprehensive textbook of psychiatry* (3d ed., Vol. 1) (pp. 782-789). Baltimore: Williams & Wilkins.

Masterson, J. F. (1976). *Psychotherapy of the borderline adult.* New York: Brunner/Mazel.

McCarley, T. (1975). The psychotherapist's search for self-renewal. *American Journal of Psychiatry, 132,* 221-226.

McCarty, G. J. (1975). The leader using audiovisual methods. In Z. Liff (Ed.), *The leader in the group* (pp. 187-202). New York: Jason Aronson.

Miller, W. R., Rossellini, R. A., & Seligman, M. E. P. (1977). Learned helplessness and depression. In J. D. Moser & M. E. P. Seligman (Eds.), *Psychopathology: Experimental models* (pp. 104-130). San Francisco: Jossey-Bass.

Mirsky, I. A. (1958). Physiologic, psychologic, and social determinants in the etiology of peptic ulcer. *American Journal of Digestive Diseases, 3,* 285-314.

Mitchell, K. M., Bozarth, J. D., & Kraufft, C. C. (1977). A reappraisal of the therapeutic effectiveness of accurate empathy, nonpossessive warmth, and genuineness. In A. S. Gurman & A. M. Razin (Eds.), *Effective psychotherapy: A handbook of research* (pp. 482-502). New York: Pergamon.

Mogul, K. (1979). Women in midlife: Decision, rewards, and conflicts related to work and careers. *American Journal of Psychiatry, 136,* 1139-1143.

Mosher, L. R., & Keith, S. J. (1979). Research on the psychosocial treatment of schizophrenia. *American Journal of Psychiatry, 136,* 623-631.

Muncie, W. (1959). The psychological approach. In S. Arieti (Ed.), *American handbook of psychiatry* (Vol. 2) (pp. 1317-1332). New York: Basic Books.

Muncie, W. (1956). Treatment in psychobiologic psychiatry: Its present status. In F. Fromm-Reichmann & J. L. Moreno (Eds.), *Progress in psychotherapy* (pp. 119-126). New York: Grune & Stratton.

Murphy, G. E., Simons, A. D., Wetzel, R. D., & Lastman, P. J. (1984). Cognitive therapy and pharmacotherapy. *Archives of General Psychiatry, 41,* 33-44.

Myers, J. K., & Auld, I. R. (1955). Some variables related to outcome of psychotherapy. *Journal of Clinical Psychology, 11,* 51-54.

Nadelson, C., Notman, M., & Feldman, J. (1974). The pregnant therapist. *American Journal of Psychiatry, 131,* 1107-1111.

Nadelson, T. (1977). Borderline rage and the therapist's response. *American Journal of Psychiatry, 134,* 748-751.

Nichols, M. P., & Zax, M. (1977). *Catharsis in psychotherapy.* New York: Gardner Press.

Notman, M. T. (1980). Changing roles for women at mid-life. In W. H. Norman & T. J.

Scaramella (Eds.), *Mid-Life: Developmental and clinical issues* (pp. 85-109). New York: Brunner/Mazel.

Oberman, E., Wood, M., & Clifton, A. (1969). Reaching the externalizers – a three phase approach. *American Journal of Psychiatry, 125*, 1404-1411.

Overall, B., & Aronson, H. (1962). Expectations of psychotherapy in lower socioeconomic class patients. *American Journal of Orthopsychiatry, 32*, 271-272.

Overall, J. E., & Gorham, D. R. (1962). The Brief Psychiatric Rating Scale. *Psychological Reports, 10*, 799-812.

Pattison, E. M., & Kaufman, E. (1979). Alcohol and drug dependence. In G. Usdin & J. M. Lewis (Eds.), *Psychiatry in general medical practice* (pp. 305-336). New York: McGraw-Hill.

Pavlov, I. P. (1941). *Conditional reflexes and psychiatry.* New York: International Publishers.

Perls, F. S. (1969). *Gestalt therapy verbatim.* Lafayette, CA: Real People Press.

Petrich, J., & Holmes, T. H. (1977). Life change and onset of illness. *Medical Clinics of North America, 61*, 825-838.

Piaget, J. (1954). *The Construction of reality in the child.* New York: Basic Books.

Pierce, R. A., Nichols, M. P., & DuBrin, J. R. (1983). *Emotional expression in psychotherapy.* New York: Gardner Press.

Polster, E., & Polster, M. (1973). *Gestalt therapy integrated.* New York: Brunner/Mazel.

Pope, B. (1977). Research in therapeutic style. In A. S. Gurman & A. M. Razin (Eds.), *Effective psychotherapy: A handbook of research* (pp. 356-394). New York: Pergamon.

Pope, K. S., Simpson, N. H., & Weiner, M. F. Z. (1978). Malpractice in outpatient psychotherapy. *American Journal of Psychotherapy, 32*, 593-601.

Puryear, D. A. (1979). *Helping people in crisis.* San Francisco: Jossey-Bass.

Rabkin, J. G. (1977). Therapists' attitudes toward mental illness and health. In A. S. Gurman & A. M. Razin (Eds.), *Effective psychotherapy: A handbook of research* (pp. 162-188). New York: Pergamon.

Reisberg, B. (1983). Clinical presentation, diagnosis, and symptomatology of age-associated cognitive decline and Alzheimer's disease. In B. Reisberg (Ed.), *Alzheimer's disease: The standard reference* (pp. 173-187). New York: Free Press.

Reiser, M. F. (1975). Changing theoretical concepts in psychosomatic medicine. In S. Arieti (Ed.), *American handbook of psychiatry* (2d ed., Vol. 4) (pp. 477-500). New York: Basic Books.

Rich, C. L., & Pitts, F. N. (1980). Suicide by psychiatrists: A study of medical specialists among 18,730 consecutive physician deaths during a five year period, 1967-72. *Journal of Clinical Psychiatry, 41*, 261-263.

Robertiello, R. C. (1975). Iatrogenic psychiatric illness. *Journal of Contemporary Psychotherapy, 7*, 3-8.

Roberts, J. L., Kimsey, L. R., Logan, D. L., & Shaw, G. (1970). How aged in nursing homes view death and dying. *Geriatrics, 25*, 115-119.

Rogers, C. R. (1951). *Client-centered therapy.* Boston: Houghton Mifflin.

Rogers, C. R. (1957). The necessary and sufficient conditions of therapeutic personality change. *Journal of Consulting Psychology, 21*, 95-103.

Rogers, C. R. (1961). *On becoming a person.* Boston: Houghton Mifflin.

Rogers, C. R., Gendlin, E. T., Kiesler, D., & Truax, C. B. (1967). *The therapeutic relationship and its impact: A study of psychotherapy with schizophrenics.* Madison: University of Wisconsin Press.

Rossi, E. L. (Ed.). (1980). *The collected papers of Milton H. Erickson on hypnosis* (Vol. 4). New York: Irvington.

Roth, B. E. (1980). Understanding the development of a homogeneous, identity-impaired group through countertransference phenomena. *International Journal of Group Psychotherapy, 30*, 405-426.

Roy v. Hartogs. (1975). 366 NYS 2d 297 (Civ. Ct. N.Y. County).

Rush, A. J. (Ed.). (1982). *Short-term psychotherapies for depression.* New York: Guilford.
Rutherford, R. B., Jr. (1975). Establishing behavioral contracts with delinquent adolescents. *Federal Probation, 39,* 29–32.
Sachar, E. H. (1975). The current status of psychosomatic medicine. In J. J. Strain & J. Grossman (Eds.), *Psychological care of the medically ill.* (pp. 54–63). New York: Appleton-Century-Crofts.
Sadock, V. A. (1980). Sexual autonomy, endocrinology, and physiology. In H. I. Kaplan, A. M. Freedman, & B. J. Sadock (Eds.), *Comprehensive textbook of psychiatry* (3d ed., Vol. 2) (pp. 1667–1686). Baltimore: Williams & Wilkins.
Saretsky, T. (1977). The resolution of impasses in borderline states. *Contemporary Psychoanalysis, 13,* 519–532.
Saretsky, T. (1980). The analyst's narcissistic vulnerability: Its effect on the treatment situation. *Contemporary Psychoanalysis, 16,* 82–89.
Sattler, J. M. (1977). The effects of client–therapist racial similarity. In A. S. Gurman & A. M. Razin (Eds.), *Effective psychotherapy: A handbook of research* (pp. 252–290). New York: Pergamon.
Saul, L. (1958). *Technique and practice of psychoanalysis.* New York: J. B. Lippincott.
Schectman, F., De La Torre, J., & Garza, A. C. (1979). Diagnosis separate from psychotherapy: Pros and cons. *American Journal of Psychotherapy, 23,* 291–302.
Scheidlinger, S. (1980). The concept of regression in group psychotherapy. In S. Scheidlinger (Ed.), *Psychoanalytic group dynamics: Basic readings.* New York: International Universities Press.
Scher, M. (1970). The process of changing therapists. *American Journal of Psychotherapy, 25,* 278–286.
Scher, M., Benedek, E., Candy, A., Carey, K., Mules, J., & Sachs, B. (1976). Psychiatrist-wife-mother: Some aspects of role integration. *American Journal of Psychiatry, 133,* 830–834.
Schimel, J. L. (1980). Some thoughts on the use of wit and humor in the treatment of adolescents. *New Directions for Mental Health Services, 5,* 15–23.
Schorr, J. I. (1974). *Psychotherapy through imagery.* New York: International Medical Book Corporation.
Schutz, W. (1967). *Joy.* New York: Grove Press.
Sederer, L. (1975). Psychotherapy patient transfer: Secondhand rose. *American Journal of Psychiatry, 132,* 1057–1061.
Shapiro, D. (1971). The analyst's own analysis. *American Journal of Psychoanalysis, 24,* 5–42.
Shuman, D. W., & Weiner, M. F. (1982). The privilege study: An empirical examination of the psychotherapist–patient privilege. *University of North Carolina Law Review, 60,* 893–942.
Sifneos, P. E. (1975). Problems of psychotherapy in patients with alexithymic characteristics and physical disease. *Psychotherapy and Psychosomatics, 26,* 65–70.
Sifneos, P. E. (1979). *Short-term dynamic psychotherapy.* New York: Plenum.
Silverman, J. S., Silverman, J. A., & Eardley, D. A. (1984). Do maladaptive attitudes cause depression? *Archives of General Psychiatry, 41,* 28–32.
Simons, R. D., Morris, J. L., Frank, H. A., Green, L. L., & Malin, R. M. (1979). Pain medication contracts in problem patients. *Psychosomatics, 20,* 118–127.
Singer, B. A., & Luborsky, L. (1977). Countertransference: The status of clinical versus quantitative research. In A. S. Gurman & A. M. Razin (Eds.), *Effective psychotherapy: A handbook of research* (pp. 433–451). New York: Pergamon.
Singer, J. L. (1974). *Imagery and daydream methods in psychotherapy and behavior modification.* New York: Academic Press.
Singer, J. L., & Pope, K. S. (1978). The use of imagery and fantasy techniques in psychotherapy. In J. L. Singer & K. S. Pope (Eds.), *The power of the human imagination* (pp. 3–34). New York: Plenum.

Slipp, S. (1982). Introduction, in S. Slipp (Ed.), *Curative factors in dynamic psychotherapy* (pp. 1-20). New York: McGraw-Hill.

Stampfl, T. G., & Levis, D. J. (1967). Essentials of implosive therapy: A learning theory based on psychodynamic behavioral therapy. *Journal of Abnormal Psychology, 72*, 496-503.

Sternbach, R. A. (1974). *Pain patients: Traits and treatment.* New York: Academic Press.

Sternlicht, M. (1965). Psychotherapeutic techniques useful with the mentally retarded: A review and critique. *Psychiatric Quarterly, 39*, 84-90.

Stevens, J. O. (1975). *Legacy from Fritz.* Palo Alto, CA: Science and Behavior Books.

Stieper, D. R., & Wiener, D. N. (1959). The problem of interminability in outpatient psychotherapy. *Journal of Consulting Psychology, 23*, 237-242.

Stoller, R. J. (1968). *Sex and gender.* New York: Science House.

Stone, L. (1961). *The psychoanalytic situation.* New York: International Universities Press.

Strupp, H. H. (1969). Toward a specification of teaching and learning in psychotherapy. *Archives of General Psychiatry, 21*, 203-212.

Strupp, H. H. (1977). A reformulation of the therapist's contribution. In A. S. Gurman & A. M. Razin (Eds.), *Effective psychotherapy: A handbook of research* (pp. 1-22). New York: Pergamon.

Strupp, H. H. (1980). Success and failure in time-limited psychotherapy. *Archives of General Psychiatry, 37*, 595-603.

Sullivan, H. S. (1956). Clinical studies in psychiatry. In H. S. Perry, M. L. Gawel, & M. Gibbon (Eds.), *The collected works of Harry Stack Sullivan* (pp. 3-361). New York: W. W. Norton.

Tarachow, S. (1963). *An introduction to psychotherapy.* New York: International Universities Press.

Tolpin, M. (1983). Corrective emotional experiences: A self-psychological reevaluation. In A. Goldberg (Ed.), *The future of psychoanalysis* (pp. 363-379). New York: International Universities Press.

Tuttman, S. (1982). Repression: A curative factor or impediment in psychodynamic psychotherapy. In S. Slipp (Ed.), *Curative factors in dynamic psychotherapy* (pp. 177-198). New York: McGraw-Hill.

Ulanov, A. B. (1979). Followup treatment in cases of patient/therapist sex. *Journal of the American Academy of Psychoanalysis, 7*, 101-110.

Vaillant, G. E. (1977). *Adaptation to life.* Boston: Little, Brown.

Vaillant, G. E. (1978). Natural history of male psychological health IV. What kinds of men do not get psychosomatic illness. *Psychosomatic Medicine, 40*, 420-431.

Vaillant, G. E. (1981). Dangers of psychotherapy in the treatment of alcoholism. In M. H. Bean & E. Zinberg (Eds.), *Dynamic approaches to the understanding and treatment of alcoholism* (pp. 36-54). New York: Free Press.

Wallace, E. R., IV (1983). *Dynamic psychiatry in theory and practice.* Philadelphia: Lea & Febiger.

Wayne, G. J. (1953). Modified psychoanalytic therapy in senescence. *Psychoanalytic Review, 40*, 99-116.

Wechsler, D. S. (1975). *The Wechsler Adult Intelligence Scale.* New York: The Psychological Corporation.

Weeks, G. R., & L'Abate, L. (1982). *Paradoxical psychotherapy: Theory and practice with individuals, couples, and families.* New York: Brunner/Mazel.

Weiner, M. F. (1970). Levels of intervention in group psychotherapy. *Group Process, 3*, 67-81.

Weiner, M. F. (1973). Termination of group psychotherapy. *Group Process, 5*, 85-96.

Weiner, M. F. (1974). The psychotherapeutic impasse. *Diseases of the Nervous System, 35*, 259-261.

Weiner, M. F. (1975). "Individual" versus conjoint therapy. *Diseases of the Nervous System, 36*, 546-549.

Weiner, M. F. (1976a). Convalescence: The forgotten phase of illness. *Diabetes Educator, 2*, 15–17.

Weiner, M. F. (1976b). Don't waste a crisis – your patient's or your own. *Medical Economics*, March 8, pp. 227–236.

Weiner, M. F. (1977). Catharsis in psychotherapy – a review. *Group Process, 7*, 173–184.

Weiner, M. F. (1980). Healthy and pathological love. In K. S. Pope, et al., *On love and loving* (pp. 114–132). San Francisco: Jossey-Bass.

Weiner, M. F. (1981). Contracts in psychotherapy. *Journal of Psychiatric Treatment and Evaluation, 3*, 131–135.

Weiner, M. F. (1982a). Identification in psychotherapy. *American Journal of Psychotherapy, 36*, 109–116.

Weiner, M. F. (1982b). *The psychotherapeutic impasse*. New York: Free Press.

Weiner, M. F. (1983a). *Therapist disclosure* (2d. ed.). Baltimore: University Park Press.

Weiner, M. F. (1983b). Assessment and resolution of impasse in group psychotherapy. *International Journal of Group Psychotherapy, 33*, 317–336.

Weiner, M. F. (1984a). *Techniques of group psychotherapy*. Washington, D.C.: American Psychiatric Press.

Weiner, M. F. (1984b). Outcome of psychoanalytically oriented group psychotherapy. *Group, 8*, 3–12.

Weiner, M. F. (1985). Theories of personality and psychopathology: Other schools. In H. I. Kaplan & B. J. Sadock (Eds.), *Comprehensive textbook of psychiatry* (Vol. 4) (pp. 451–458). Baltimore: Williams & Wilkins.

Weiner, M. F., & Caldwell, T. (1981). Stresses and coping in ICU nursing. II. Nurse support groups on intensive care units. *General Hospital Psychiatry, 3*, 129–134.

Weiner, M. F., & Caldwell, T. (1983). The process and impact of an ICU nurse support group. *International Journal of Psychiatry in Medicine, 13*, 47–55.

Weiner, M. F., & Crowder, J. D. (in press). Psychotherapy and cognitive style. *American Journal of Psychotherapy*.

Weiner, M. F., & King, J. S. (1977). Self-disclosure by the therapist to the adolescent patient. In P. Giovacchini & S. Feldstein (Eds.), *Adolescent psychiatry* (Vol. 5) (pp. 449–459). New York: Jason Aronson.

Weiner, M. F., & Lovitt, R. (1984). An examination of patients' understanding of information from health care professionals. *Hospital and Community Psychiatry, 35*, 619–620.

Weiner, M. F., & Shuman, D. W. (1983). The privilege study. *Archives of General Psychiatry, 40*, 1027–1030.

Weiner, M. F., & Shuman, D. W. (1984). What patients don't tell their therapists. *Integrative Psychiatry, 2*, 28–31.

Weiner, M. L. (1975). *The cognitive unconscious: A Piagetian approach to psychotherapy.* Davis, CA: International Psychological Press.

Whitehorn, J. C., & Betz, B. (1954). A study of psychotherapeutic relationships between physicians and schizophrenic patients. *American Journal of Psychiatry, 111*, 321–331.

Whitman, R. M. (1973). Dreams about the group: An approach to the problem of group psychology. *International Journal of Group Psychotherapy, 23*, 408–420.

Wilkins, W. (1977). Expectancies in applied settings. In A. S. Gurman & A. M. Razin (Eds.), *Effective psychotherapy: A handbook of research* (pp. 325–355). New York: Pergamon.

Wilmer, H. A. (1982). What do you say when a patient tells you a dream. *Texas Medicine, 78*, 46–48.

Winnicott, D. W. (1965). *The maturational process and the facilitating environment*. New York: International Universities Press.

Wolf, E. S. (1982). Self-theory and intimacy. In M. Fisher & G. Stricker (Eds.), *Intimacy* (pp. 65–78). New York: Plenum.

Wolf, E. S. (1983). Concluding statement. In A. Goldberg (Ed.), *The future of psychoanalysis* (pp. 495–505). New York: International Universities Press.

Wolpe, J. (1969). *The practice of behavior therapy.* New York: Pergamon.

Wong, N. (1980). Combined group and individual treatment of borderline and narcissistic patients: Heterogeneous versus homogeneous groups. *International Journal of Group Psychotherapy, 30,* 389–404.

Wyatt *v.* Stickney (1971). 325 F Supp. 781 (M.D. Ala.).

Yablonsky, Z. (1976). *Psychodrama.* New York: Basic Books.

Yalom, I. D. (1970). *The theory and practice of group psychotherapy.* New York: Basic Books.

Yalom, I. D. (1975). *The theory and the practice of group psychotherapy* (2d ed.). New York: Basic Books.

Yalom, I. D. (1980). *Existential psychotherapy.* New York: Basic Books.

Yalom, I. D. (1983). *Inpatient group psychotherapy.* New York: Basic Books.

Yesavage, J. A., Brink, T. L., Rose, T. L., Lum, O., Huang, V., Adey, M., & Leirer, V. O. (1983). Development and validation of a geriatric depression screening scale: A preliminary report. *Journal of Psychiatric Research, 17,* 37–49.

Zborowski, M. (1969). *People in pain.* San Francisco: Jossey-Bass.

Zetzel, E. (1971). A developmental approach to the borderline patient. *American Journal of Psychiatry, 127,* 867–871.

Zipkin *v.* Freeman (1968). 436 S.W. 2d (Mo.).

Zitrin, C. M., Klein, D. F., & Woerner, M. G. (1978). Behavior therapy, supportive psychotherapy, imipramine, and phobias. *Archives of General Psychiatry, 35,* 307–316.

Index

315